交通行业高职高专规划教材

Gangkou Lihuo Yingyu
港口理货英语

主编 赵鲁克

内 容 提 要

本书从港口与船舶、货物、货物积载、货物装卸、理货业务、集装箱理货业务等六个大项目着手，用英文较系统地介绍了港口理货业务以及相关知识。每一项目下均辅有相关情景对话，以提高读者专业交流能力。

本书可作为高职院校专业教材，也可供港口装卸及理货人员及相关专业人员参考使用。

图书在版编目(CIP)数据

港口理货英语／赵鲁克主编. —北京：人民交通出版社股份有限公司，2015.1
交通行业高职高专规划教材
ISBN 978-7-114-12050-3

Ⅰ.①港… Ⅱ.①赵… Ⅲ.①货物运输−港口管理−英语−高等职业教育−教材 Ⅳ.①H31

中国版本图书馆 CIP 数据核字(2015)第 027197 号

交通行业高职高专规划教材

书　　　名：	港口理货英语
著 作 者：	赵鲁克
责 任 编 辑：	赵瑞琴
出 版 发 行：	人民交通出版社股份有限公司
地　　　址：	(100011)北京市朝阳区安定门外外馆斜街 3 号
网　　　址：	http://www.ccpcl.com.cn
销 售 电 话：	(010)59757973
总 经 销：	人民交通出版社股份有限公司发行部
经　　　销：	各地新华书店
印　　　刷：	北京市密东印刷有限公司
开　　　本：	787×1092　1/16
印　　　张：	13
字　　　数：	300 千
版　　　次：	2015 年 3 月　第 1 版
印　　　次：	2023 年 8 月　第 3 次印刷
书　　　号：	ISBN 978-7-114-12050-3
定　　　价：	34.00 元

(有印刷、装订质量问题的图书由本公司负责调换)

交通行业高职高专规划教材编委会

主　　　任　宋士福

副 主 任　杨巨广

委　　　员　（以姓氏笔画为序）
　　　　　　仇桂玲　刘水国　刘俊泉　刘祥柏　苏本知
　　　　　　张来祥　周灌中

编写组成员　（以姓氏笔画为序）
　　　　　　王　峰　井延波　孙莉莉　李风雷　李永刚
　　　　　　李君楠　吴广河　吴　文　佟黎明　张　阳
　　　　　　范素英　郑　渊　赵鲁克　郝　红　徐先弘
　　　　　　徐奎照　郭梅忠　谭　政

前　　言

随着我国国民经济的持续增长和对外贸易的发展,国内各港口呈现空前发展之势,港口对外业务激增。为了适应这一形势,我们编写了这本《港口理货英语》教材,以培养这方面的专门人才。本书用英文介绍了与港口装卸和理货业务相关的基础知识,以六个大项目为统领分别论述了港口、船舶、货物、货物装卸、装卸机械、积载、垫舱及隔票、理货业务、相关理货单证、计数、分票、理残和溢短、理货程序和集装箱理货等内容。特别重点介绍了集装箱业务及理货方面的内容,以适应当前运输业务的发展方向。为了理论和实际相结合,各子项目还结合专业内容,编写了相关情景对话,以便学员结合工作实践进行专业口语训练。

本书在编写过程中得到了刘祥伯教授和李凤雷老师的大力支持,在此表示感谢。鉴于编者的理论及实践经验的局限性,以及日新月异的科技进步所带来的业务创新和操作技术的提高,本教材内容的不足之处,敬请读者反馈,以便今后修订和完善。

编者
2015 年 1 月

目 录

Project 1　Port and Ship ·· 1
　Program 1　Port ·· 1
　Program 2　Ship ·· 6
　Program 3　General Structure of Cargo Vessel ··· 10
　Program 4　Ship's Cargo-handling Eguipment ·· 14
　Program 5　Shipboard Organization ·· 18
Project 2　Cargo ·· 23
　Program 1　Types of Cargo ·· 23
　Program 2　Transport Packing of Cargo ·· 27
　Program 3　Cargo Marks ··· 31
Project 3　Stowage of Cargo ·· 35
　Program 1　Generality of Stowage of Cargo ·· 36
　Program 2　Stowage Factor ··· 39
　Program 3　Stowage Plan ·· 43
　Program 4　Segregation ··· 47
　Program 5　Separation ··· 51
　Program 6　Dunnage ·· 54
Project 4　Cargo Handling ·· 59
　Program 1　Loading and Unloading ·· 59
　Program 2　Handling of General Cargo ··· 63
　Program 3　Handling of Dry Bulk Cargo ··· 67
　Program 4　Handling of Dangerous Cargo ··· 71
Project 5　Cargo-tallying Service ·· 75
　Program 1　Ocean Shipping Tally ·· 76
　Program 2　Papers of Tally ··· 79
　Program 3　Tallying Cargo ·· 83
　Program 4　Mark-Assorting ·· 87

	Program 5	Mixed-up of Cargo	90
	Program 6	Counting	94
	Program 7	Short-landed and Over-landed Cargo	98
	Program 8	Dealing with the Over-landed and Short-landed Cargo	101
	Program 9	Checking the Damage	105
	Program 10	Sweepings	108

Project 6 Container-tallying Service ... 112

    Program 1　Containerization ... 113

    Program 2　Laying-out of Goods Inside Containers ... 117

    Program 3　Interchange of Container Load Goods ... 121

    Program 4　Container-handling Technology ... 124

    Program 5　Documents of Container Load Goods ... 128

    Program 6　Basis for Tallying Containers ... 132

    Program 7　Container Damage-checking Technology ... 136

    Program 8　Container Tallying Procedure and Methods ... 139

Appendix 1　Sentences for Cargo Tallying ... 143

Appendix 2　Sentences for Stevedoring ... 190

Appendix 3　Tally Papers and Ocean Shipping Documentations ... 194

Appendix 4　Main Parts of a Ship ... 196

参考文献 ... 198

Project 1　Port and Ship

Project Description

The port and ship are places where cargo is handled. And a good knowledge of the port and ship will provide a foundation for the persons who engaged in the operation of cargo handling and the service of cargo tallying which supports and guarantees the cargo-handling conducting properly and efficiently with least claims.

Knowledge Objective

1　The role of port and the functions port plays in its development of generations.
2　Types of ship.
3　General structure of cargo ships and their cargo handling equipments.
4　shipboard organization.

Ability Objective

1　Have the ability to know what generation a port is undergoing by its current operation.
2　Have the ability to promote oneself and follow closely to the trend of port development.
3　Capable of knowing the type of ship's general structure and its gears based on its usage.
4　Have the ability of identifying the position of person according to the work he conducts.

Tasks

1　Have a comprehensive realization of port by visiting a port.
2　Go on board a ship to know about the structure and gears of different ships and the organization of a ship.
3　Look up the information about the trend of development of port and ship, and the current situation of them.

Program 1　Port

The port plays a role as hub of the waterway transportation and inland transportation in the network on which cargo is assembled and distributed, and forms a link to connect the vessels and other transport instruments, and provides services such as the berthing of vessels, handling of cargo, storage, barging and other relevant businesses, etc.

Up to now, the development of ports has experienced three generations already with respect of port status in the national economy and functions it plays.

The first generation of ports existed before the year of 1950. Their chief functions laid on the transshipment of marine shipment, temporary storage of cargo, receiving and delivery of cargo, which plays a role as hub of transportation.

The second generation of ports spanned the years from 1950s through 1980s. Addition to the functions of the first-generation port, the activities of industry and commerce which bring added-value to the cargo were involved, which made port become a centre of cargo handling and additional services.

The third generation of ports appeared in the late of 1980s and has lasted up to present. During this period, the interdependent of economic bodies is becoming essential, and the integration of global economy is thriving. Therefore, ports have upgraded their functions and further strengthened the relations with the city and customers, and provided additional comprehensive services beyond the boundary of ports, such as information collection and processing for transportation and trading, goods distribution, etc. which makes the port develop into the logistics centre of trade.

The basic operational facilities of port include wharf, pontoon, pier, passenger station, handling machinery, vessel, warehouse, pile-yard, etc.

Nowadays, the operation of port is the business of private or municipal firms. Very few ports are operated directly by the state. In China, almost all of large ports have been restructured with shareholding system, and port operation is carried out by group corporation.

Notes

1 The port plays a role as hub of the waterway transportation and inland transportation in the network on which cargo is assembled and distributed, and forms a link to connect the vessels and other transport instruments, and provides services such as the berthing of vessels, handling of cargo, storage, barging and other relevant business, etc.

港口是运输网络中水陆运输的枢纽,是货物的集散地以及船舶与其他运输工具的衔接点;它可提供船舶靠泊、货物装卸、储存、驳运以及其他相关业务。

2 Up to now, the development of ports has experienced three generations already with respect of port status in the national economy and functions it plays.

按港口在国民经济的地位和所起的作用,到目前为止可把港口发展划分为三代。

3 The first generation of ports existed before the year of 1950. Their chief functions laid on the transshipment of marine shipment, temporary storage of cargo, receiving and delivery of cargo, which plays a role as hub of transportation.

第一代港口是指1950年以前的港口,其功能为海运货物的转运、临时存储以及货物的收发等,那时的港口是运输枢纽中心。

4 The second generation of ports spanned the years from 1950s through 1980s. In addition to

the functions of the first-generation port, the activities of industry and commerce which bring added-value to the cargo were involved, which made port become a centre of cargo handling and additional services.

第二代港口是指20世纪50年代至80年代的港口,其功能除具有第一代港口的功能外,又增加了使货物增值的工业、商业功能,港口成为装卸和服务的中心。

5 During this period, the interdependent of economic bodies is becoming essential, and the integration of global economy is thriving. Therefore, port has upgraded its functions and further strengthened the relations with the city and customers it inhabits, and provides additional comprehensive services beyond its original boundary, such as information collection and processing for transportation and trading, goods distribution, etc. which makes the port develop into the logistics centre of trade.

在这一时期,各经济实体相互依赖依存愈发重要,全球经济一体化日益蓬勃发展,因而港口进一步提高其功能,更加强了与所在城市和客户的联系,使港口的服务超出了原来港口的界限,增添了诸如运输、贸易的信息服务,货物配送综合服务,使港口成为贸易的物流中心。

Vocabulary

vessel [ˈvesl]	n. 船
assemble [əˈsembl]	v. 集合, 聚集, 装配
instrument [ˈinstrumənt]	n. 工具, 手段, 器械
marine [məˈriːn]	adj. 海运的, 航海的
stowage [ˈstəuidʒ]	n. 堆装物
interdependent [ˌintə(ː)diˈpendənt]	adj. 相互依赖的, 互助的
essential [iˈsenʃəl]	adj. 本质的, 实质的, 基本的
integration [ˌintiˈgreiʃən]	n. 综合
upgrade [ˈʌpgreid]	v. 升级, 上升
strengthen [ˈstreŋθən]	v. 加强, 巩固
comprehensive [ˌkɔmpriˈhensiv]	adj. 全面的, 广泛的
boundary [ˈbaundəri]	n. 边界, 分界线
process [prəˈses]	v. 加工, 处理
logistics [ləˈdʒistiks]	n. 物流
municipal [mju(ː)ˈnisipəl]	adj. 地方性的
shareholding [ˈʃeəˌhəuldiŋ]	n. 股权
thrive [θraiv]	v. 兴旺, 繁荣

Exercises

1 Answer the following questions according to the text you have read.

(1) What are the functions of the port according to the text?

(2) How many generations has the port experienced?

(3) When did the third generation of the port appear?

(4) What are the main differences among the three generations of ports?

(5) What are the main facilities involved in a port?

2　Select the best answer.

(1) The port is considered to be a place _____.

　　a) which provides services such as the berthing of vessels, handling of cargo, storage, barging and other relevant businesses, etc

　　b) where a hub is formed engaged in cargo collection and distribution in waterway transportation and inland transportation

　　c) which forms a link to connect the vessels and other transport instruments

　　d) all above

(2) Up to now, ports have gone through _____.

　　a) two generations

　　b) three generations

　　c) four generations

　　d) one generation

(3) During the first generation of ports, the port became _____.

　　a) a center of cargo handling and additional services

　　b) a hub of transportation

　　c) logistics centre of trade

　　d) financial trade center

(4) In which generation does the port see the thriving of global economy integration?

　　a) the second generation

　　b) the first generation

　　c) the generation appeared before 1950'

　　d) the third generation

(5) Nowadays, ports are playing more and more important role in the national economy, and most ports are operated _____.

　　a) by the group corporation

　　b) by the private entity

　　c) by the state

　　d) by the Communications Dept of State

3　Put into Chinese.

(1) The port plays a role as a hub of the waterway transportation and inland transportation on which cargo is assembled and distributed, and forms a link to connect the vessels and other transport instruments.

(2) Their chief functions laid on the transshipment of marine shipment, cargo temporary stow-

age, receiving and delivering.

(3) In China, most ports are given more autonomy in their operations.

(4) Large volume of cargo imported and exported in a country goes through the port.

(5) Every year, a substantial amount of money is invested into the building and maintenance of the infrastructure of ports.

4 Put into English.

(1) 港口在一国的国民经济中起的作用越来越大。

(2) 大部分进出口货物须通过港口进行装卸。

(3) 港口可提供诸如船舶靠泊、货物装卸、储存、转运等服务。

(4) 港口在发展的第三阶段已成为物流中心。

(5) 海洋运输业的兴旺促进了港口的发展。

Dialogue

A: Hi, glad to see you!

B: Hi, me too.

A: Have you been to our port before?

B: Yes, twice. It has been more than 10 years since I visited here the last time when our ship called at your port.

A: What's your impression?

B: It is great indeed. The first time I came it was not so clean, but now it looks like a big garden, and at that time, the road around was not so wide, we got a traffic jam and it almost took us one hour to reach the quayside.

A: It was really too bad! But now you can see that we have widened the road, and other infrastructures of the port have been also reconstructed and upgraded.

B: You say it. The change of the port almost makes me at a loss, I can't find where I familiar with the first time here.

A: Aha, the place you stand here is a new-built terminal for handling ore with a capacity of 200,000 tons, which is one of the biggest ore terminals among our nation's.

B: Really? I should like have realized it. Yes, I can see the huge pile of ore stored in the open yard, however, you can hardly see any ore fine floating amidst the air.

A: Yes, there is a water spraying system to prevent ore pollution. We have taken measures to improve productivity and meanwhile to protect environment.

B: We should learn from you. By the way, may I know the cargo volume handled annually at your port?

A: The cargo throughput last year reached 165 million tons, an increase of 25 million tons or 10% over the corresponding period of 2006.

B: Marvelous!

Program 2 Ship

The type of cargo vessels is determined by the goods carried.General speaking, cargo vessels can be divided into two basic types.One type carries dry cargo, and the other carries liquid cargo.Multi-deck vessels are a traditional type of dry cargo ships, the hold of which is divided horizontally by one or two tweendecks.Break general cargoes are carried by these ships.Dry bulk cargo is carried in bulk carriers which do not have tweendecks.Liquid carriers are specially built to carry bulk liquid cargo such as petroleum products.

In the past, the most used cargo ships were general cargo freighters which can carry any and all cargoes to and from any of the world's major ports.With the development of maritime transportation, a number of cargo ships which are designed for carrying particular commodity, or group of commodities, have appeared one after another.Container vessels are designed to deal with break bulk cargoes in standard unit permitting quick loading and unloading with special machinery and equipment, which have developed rapidly in recent years and most of break bulk cargo is shipped by the container vessel.Colliers are designed to carry coal, timber carrier to carry kinds of timber.Similarly, liquid chemical tanker, liquefied gas carrier, LASH (lighter-aboard-ship), O.B.O (ore/bulk/oil) ships, refrigerate vessels and roll-on/roll-off vessels etc.have been commonly seen.

Also, the ship can be classified with respect of the operational mode of business and the types of sailing schedule.

We call, based on the trade route and means of freight forward, those of cargo ships which operate on fixed routes, running fixed itinerary of ports of call, and operate on a regular sailing schedule "liners", and those which do not operate on a fixed sailing schedule, but only trade in all parts of the world in search of cargo "tramp". The ship engaged in "liner" service belongs to general cargo ship, and the "tramp" ship mainly deal with the dry bulk cargo or liquid bulk cargo.A very large proportion of the world's trade is carried in tramp vessels.Tramp vessels are engaged under a document called a charter party, on a time or voyage basis.

Notes

1 The type of cargo vessels is determined by the goods carried.General speaking, cargo vessels can be divided into two basic types.One type carries dry cargo, and the other carries liquid cargo.Multi-deck vessels are a traditional type of dry cargo ships, the hold of which is divided horizontally by one or two tweendecks.

船舶类型是根据所载运的货物进行划分的,基本上划分为两种:一种是干货船,另一种是液体货船。传统干货船具有多个甲板,其货舱在水平位置上被一个或两个二层甲板所分割。

2 In the past, the most used cargo ships were general cargo freighters which can carry any

and all cargoes to and from any of the world's major ports. With the development of maritime transportation, a number of cargo ships which are designed for carrying particular commodity, or group of commodities, have appeared one after another.

在过去,大多数货船为杂货船,在世界各主要港口进行各种货物的运输。随着海运业的发展,许多专门用来运输某一种或某一类货物的专用船舶接连出现。

3 We call, based on the trade route and means of freight forward, those of cargo ships which operate on fixed routes, serving a group of ports and operate on fixed sailing schedule "liners", and those which do not operate on a fixed sailing schedule, but only trade in all ports of the world in search of cargo "tramp". A very large proportion of the world's trade is carried in tramp vessels. Tramp vessels are engaged under a document called a charter party, on a time or voyage basis.

根据航线和揽货方式,我们将那些有固定航线和一定停靠港并有固定航期的货船称作"班轮",而将那些没有确定航期并在世界各地港口进行揽货运输的货船称作"不定期货船"。世界贸易中很大一部分货物是通过不定期货船运输的。不定期货船运输是按照租船合同以租运时间或租运航次进行运营的。

Vocabulary

liquid [ˈlikwid]	n. 液体,流体
horizontally [ˌhɔriˈzɔntli]	adv. 地平地,水平地
tweendeck [ˈtwiːnˌdek]	n. 双层甲板
bulk [bʌlk]	n. 散装
petroleum [piˈtrəuliəm]	n. 石油
commodity [kəˈmɔditi]	n. 日用品,商品
timber [ˈtimbə]	n. 木材,木料
collier [ˈkɔliə]	n. 运煤船
liquefy [ˈlikwifai]	v. (使)溶解,(使)液化
refrigerate [riˈfridʒəreit]	v. 使冷却,使变冷
route [ruːt]	n. 路线,通道
schedule [ˈʃedjuːl; ˈskedʒjul]	n. 时间表,进度表
charter [ˈtʃɑːtə]	v. 租,包(车,船等)

Exercises

1 Answer the following questions according to the text.
(1) How many basic types can cargo vessels be divided into? What are they?
(2) What kind of vessels are used to transport petroleum products?
(3) What are the container vessels designed for?
(4) What kind of vessels is called tramp?
(5) How does the liner operate?

2 Select the best answer.

(1) General speaking, the type of cargo vessels is determined _____.

    a) by the goods carried on board

    b) by the ownership

    c) by the structure of the vessel

    d) by the ports the vessel calls

(2) Vessels which are of one or two tweendecks are suitable to carry _____.

    a) bulk cargo

    b) general cargo

    c) liquid cargo

    d) containers

(3) Container vessels belong to _____.

    a) multi-deck vessels

    b) break bulk cargo freighters

    c) bulk cargo vessels

    d) roll on/ roll off vessels

(4) Iron ore is preferably carried by _____.

    a) the bulk cargo ship

    b) the general cargo ship

    c) the container vessel

    d) the tanker

(5) A liner is one type of vessels that _____.

    a) operates on a schedule determined by the market

    b) mainly carries bulk cargo

    c) has multi-decks

    d) has no fixed rout

3 Put into Chinese.

(1) Multi-deck vessels are a traditional type of dry cargo ships, the hold of which is divided horizontally by one or two tweendecks.

(2) A number of cargo ships which are designed for carrying particular commodity, or group of commodities, have appeared one after another.

(3) We call, based on the trade route run and means of freight forward, those of cargo ships which operate on fixed routes, serving a group of ports and operate on fixed sailing schedule "liners".

(4) The tramp ship is dry cargo vessel operating a worldwide services with no fixed schedule and fixed ports of call.

(5) Container vessels are designed to deal with break bulk cargoes in standard unit permitting quick loading and unloading with special machinery and equipment.

Project 1　Port and Ship

4　Put into English.

(1)这是一艘散货船,载有3000吨煤炭运往新加坡。

(2)这艘杂货船的净载重量是8000吨。

(3)这是一艘现代化的集装箱船载有5250个标准集装箱(TEU)。

(4)我们使用滚装船来装运出口的小轿车。

(5)从事班轮运输的船舶有固定的航期、固定的航线和固定的挂靠港。

Dialogue

A：Welcome on board the MV Haisheng.

B：Thank you.It is a really a very big general cargo ship.

A：Yes.But it is also designed to carry many containers.

B：I see.What is its length and breadth?

A：Her LOA is 300 m and breadth 40 m.

B：So she must be able to carry a lot of cargo.

A：Yes,that's true.She has a DWTC of more than 50,000 tons.

B：How many containers is she designed to carry?

A：Around 250 TEU.

B：What's her full speed at sea?

A：It can reach 20 knots.

B：The bridge is situated at the stern with the engine below.

A：That's right.And nowadays many large vessels are constructed like this.

B：How many decks are there altogether?

A：There are 5 decks.

B：On which deck is the bridge?

A：It's on fifth deck.

B：I see.Where is the galley,then?

A：You will find the galley on the first deck.

B：Is the ratings' messroom also on the first deck?

A：No.it is on the second deck,next to the hospital.

B：Then what's next to the galley on the first deck?

A：A laundry.OK,the steward will show you how to use the washing machines.

B：Are there any cabins on the second deck?

A：No,there aren't any.But there are ones on the third deck.

B：What is there on the third deck?

A：Well,one cabin for the Pilot and one for the Chief Officer.Between them is the officers' messroom.

B：And the Master's room must be at the fourth deck,I think.

A：Yes.It is between the radio room and the Chief Engineer's cabin.The radio room is left to the Master's.

B: Thank you for your introduction.

A: My pleasure. You will get more familiar with the vessel soon, I believe.

B: I hope so.

Notes

1. LOA: length of overall 的缩写,指船体总长度。
2. DWTC: deadweight tonnage of cargo 的缩写,指货物载重吨位。
3. TEU: twenty-four equivalent unit 的缩写,指24英尺集装箱换算单位(简称标准箱)。
4. rating's messroom 普通船员餐厅。

Program 3 General Structure of Cargo Vessel

A ship consists of three parts: the main hull, the superstructure and various kinds of equipments. The hull is the actual shell of the ship. It is made of frames covered with plating. The hull is divided up into a number of watertight compartments by decks and bulkheads. Bulkheads are upright steel walls going across the ship. The hull contains the engine room, cargo space and a number of tanks. In dry cargo ships the cargo space is divided into holds while in liquid cargo ships into tanks.

The deck extending from bow to the stern is called the main deck, on top of which there are three "island": forecastle, bridge, and poop—superstructure as is so called. The fore part of a ship is called the bow and the rear part the stern.

The right side of the ship is professionally called the starboard side and the other side port side. The beam is the greatest width of the ship. Near the bridge is the funnel. Smoke and gases pass through the funnel from the engine which is fitted near the bottom of the ship. The engine drives the propeller at the stern of the ship. The draught is the depth of the ship's bottom or keel below the water surface.

At the fore and aft ends of the hull are fore peak tanks and the aft peak tanks which are mainly used for ballast.

Single deck vessels have one deck. The most suitable cargoes for single deck vessels are heavy cargoes carried in bulk, such as coal, grain and iron ore.

The tweendeck type of vessel has other decks below the main deck, and all run the full length of the vessel. These additional decks below the main deck are known as the tweendecks. Vessels in the liner trades often have more than one tweendeck, and they are known as the upper and lower tweendecks. A vessel with tweendecks is very suitable for general cargo, as not only is the cargo space divided into separated tiers, but also the tweendeck prevents too much weight from bearing on the cargo at the bottom of the hold.

Equipments usually include the engines, ancillary devices serving the electric installations, pipe system, deck equipments (anchor, quarter, berthing, and lifting etc.), life security apparatus, communication and pilot devices, and livelihood accommodations.

Notes

1 The hull is divided up into a number of watertight compartments by decks and bulkheads.
船壳被甲板和舱壁分成多个水密舱室。

2 The tweendeck type of vessel has other decks below the main deck, and all run the full length of the vessel. These additional decks below the main deck are known as the tweendecks. Vessels in the liner trades often have more than one tweendeck, and they are known as the upper and lower tweendecks.
多重甲板类型船舶在主甲板下有其他甲板,其与船舶长度等长,被称作中间甲板(二层甲板)。从事班轮运输的船舶带有两个二层甲板分别称为上二层甲板和下二层甲板。

3 A vessel with tweendecks is very suitable for general cargo, as not only is the cargo space divided into separated tiers, but also the tweendeck prevents too much weight from bearing on the cargo at the bottom of the hold.
带中间甲板的船只非常适合装杂货,因为中间甲板不仅使载货舱容被分成隔开的几层,而且使货船底部的货物免受过大的重量。

4 Equipments usually include the engines, ancillary devices serving the electric installations, pipe system, deck equipments (anchor, quarter, berthing, and lifting etc.), life security apparatus, communication and pilot devices, and livelihood accommodations.
船舶设备通常包括轮机、电气辅助装置、管道系统、甲板上设备(锚、舵、靠泊设备、起吊设备等)救生装置,通信导航装置,和生活设施。

Vocabulary

superstructure	[ˈsjuːpəˌstrʌktʃə]	n. 上部构造,上层建筑
hull	[hʌl]	n. 外壳,船体
shell	[ʃel]	n. 壳,外形
frame	[freim]	n. 结构,框架
plating	[ˈpleitiŋ]	n. 电镀,被覆金属
watertight	[ˈwɔːtətait]	adj. 不漏水的,水密的
compartment	[kəmˈpɑːtmənt]	n. 间隔间,车厢
deck	[dek]	n. 甲板
bulkhead	[ˈbʌlkhed]	n. 隔壁,防水壁
stern	[stəːn]	n. 船尾
forecastle	[ˈfəuksl]	n. 前甲板,船头的船楼,前甲板下面的水手舱
poop	[puːp]	n. 船尾,船尾楼

bow [bau]	n. 船首
rear [riə]	n. 后面,后方,背后
starboard [ˈstɑːbəd,-bɔːd]	n. 右舷
beam [biːm]	n. 梁
funnel [ˈfʌnəl]	n. 漏斗,烟囱
propeller [prəˈpelə]	n. 推进者,推进物
draught [drɑːft]	n. 拖,拉
aft [ɑːft]	adv. 在船尾
ballast [ˈbæləst]	n. 压舱物,沙囊
anchor [ˈæŋkə]	n. 锚
berthing [bəːθiŋ]	n. 停泊地
apparatus [ˌæpəˈreitəs]	n. 器械,设备,仪器
livelihood [ˈlaivlihud]	n. 生计,谋生

Exercises

1 Answer the following questions according to the text you have read.

（1）What does a ship consist of?

（2）What are bulkheads according to the text?

（3）What is the difference between the cargo space in dry cargo ship and that in liquid cargo ship?

（4）What are on the main deck?

（5）What are the two sides of a ship respectively called?

2 Choose the best answer.

（1） According to the hull design and construction, cargo vessels can be classified into _____.

　　a) the single deck vessel and the "three-island" vessel

　　b) the "three-island" vessel and the tweendeck type of vessel

　　c) the single deck vessel and the main deck vessel

　　d) the single deck vessel and the tweendeck type of vessel

（2）Timber can be stowed _____.

　　a) only on deck　　　　　　　　b) only in holds

　　c) in forecastle, bridge and poop　　d) both on deck and in holds

（3）The tweendeck type of vessel has _____ below the main deck.

　　a) no deck　　　　　　　　　　b) another deck

　　c) two decks　　　　　　　　　d) additional decks

（4）The additional decks below the main deck are called _____.

　　a) tweendecks　　　　　　　　b) upper tweendecks

　　c) lower holds　　　　　　　　d) lower tweendecks

(5) If a heavy cargo is distributed to separated tiers throughout the ship, _____.

　　a) the weight pressure in the lower hold is reduced.

　　b) the ship gets greater stability

　　c) damage to cargo is reduce a lot

　　d) cargo is well protected

3　Mark the following statements true (T) or false (F).

(1) The hull is made of frames covered with plating.

(2) The superstructure is on top of the main deck.

(3) The right side of a ship is called the starboard side.

(4) The funnel is far away from the bridge.

(5) Fore peak tanks and aft peak tanks are usually used for ballast.

4　Put into Chinese.

(1) The hull is divided up into a number of watertight compartments by decks and bulkheads.

(2) In dry cargo ships the cargo space is divided into holds while in liquid cargo ships into tanks.

(3) The right side of the ship facing the bow is called the starboard side and other side is the port side.

(4) At the fore and aft ends of the hull are fore peak tanks and the aft peak tanks which are mainly used for ballast.

(5) Equipments usually include the engines, ancillary devices serving the electric installations, pipe system, deck equipments (anchor, quarter, berthing, and lifting etc.), life security apparatus, communication and pilot devices, and livelihood accommodations.

5　Put into English.

(1) 同类型船舶的结构大体相同。

(2) 船首楼、桥楼和船尾楼是船舶的上层建筑。

(3) 船舱是用来装货的水密空间。

(4) 前尖舱和后尖舱的主要作用是通过压舱水来调整船舶平衡的。

(5) 这是一艘多甲板船,有两个二层甲板,即,一个下二层甲板,一个上二层甲板。

Dialogue

A：OK, here we are. This is the very bridge.

B：How nice it is!

A：That's the place where the officers steer the ship and keep watches.

B：I see. Ah, it's radar, isn't it?

A：Yes. Do you know when we turn on the radar?

B：When it is dark or foggy, or when the traffic is heavy.

A：That's right. Here is the steering wheel.

B：Oh, it's not like a traditional wheel.

A: It's a modern one.Sometime it could be a joystick.

B: I think it's the maritime communication center on board.

A: Right.Our ship is equipped with a very modern satellite system.

B: Terrific.Can I have a look at the operator's manual?

A: Sure.Here we are.Have you ever use a VHF set?

B: Yes,I got trained on the subject at my school,about a year ago.

A: So you know how to operate it?

B: I think so.Push the button to speak and release it to listen.

A: Good.Come over here.This is the GPS.Do you know what it is used for?

B: It gives our correct position by coordinating fixes by satellite.

A: Right.And this is the telegraph.The engines can be controlled through the telegraphs in the engine control room.

B: Look,there are so many meters here.What are they?

A: They are various recorders for the navigation of ship.

B: OK.Have you got ARPA on board?

A: Sure,there it is.This system makes navigation easier.

B: And GMDSS?

A: Yes,already,I'll show you later.

B: What about ECDIS?

A: It's newly installed.There it is.

B: I think there's a lot I need to learn.

Notes

1　GPS：Global Positioning System 的缩写，指全球定位系统。

2　ARPA：Automatic Radar Plotting Aid 的缩写，指自动雷达标绘仪。

3　GMDSS：Global Maritime Distress and Safety System 的缩写，指全球海上遇险与安全系统。

4　ECDIS：Electronic Chart Display and Information System 的缩写，指电子海图显示与信息系统。

Program 4　Ship's Cargo-handling Equipment

As trade and traffic grows,the technical concern with cargo handling equipment and facilities on ships and in ports will naturally continue and will be closely related to the types of ships.Given below are the main divisions of ship's equipment.

First,there are the conventional system of derrick and winches.There are two kinds of these: the regular lift with capacities of two to ten tons,with which some cargo,for example,in pallet with-

in ten tons can be handled; and the jumbo boom (heavy derrick) that are capable of handling up to 100 tons. With the jumbo boom, heavy lifts such as boiler, truck, etc. can be lifted for loading or unloading.

The winch is of course the machine providing power to hoist or lower the fall. They can be driven either by steam or by electricity.

Derricks and winches are often used in the "union purchase" arrangement. Here one derrick is positioned over the hold, the other over the pier, and the lifting wires are connected to the same hook. If the ship is loading, the derrick over the pier lifts the cargo while the other derrick pulls it horizontally over to the hatch and lowers it into the hold; for loading, the procedure is reversed. While very efficient, this system has been largely replaced on newer ships by cranes. The latter are usually gantry cranes of great capacity and speed and are used on container and other specialized ships.

A third group includes cargo elevators used in container ships and barge carriers to transport the units into place. The fourth group consists of various types of conveyor belts, which are used in general cargo ships, specialized ships, and some self-unloading bulk carries. The next group, used on roll-on/roll-off ships, consists of ramps. These provided access to all decks on the ship from ports in the bow, sides, or stern.

A final division is liquid and slurry pump systems, used in tankers, bulkers, combination carriers.

Notes

1 As trade and traffic grows, the technical concern with cargo handling equipment and facilities on ships and in ports will naturally continue and will be closely related to the types of ships.

随着贸易和交通的发展,人们必然将关心船舶与港口装卸设备技术的发展,而它们与船型又有着密切的关系。

2 While very efficient, this system has been largely replaced on newer ships by cranes.

尽管这种方式效率很高,但在较新的船上大多已被起重机所取代。

3 The fourth group consists of various types of conveyor belts, which are used in general cargo ships, specialized ships, and some self-unloading bulk carries.

第四类是各种各样的皮带输送机,用于杂货船、专用船和一些自卸式散货船。

4 These provided access to all decks on the ship from ports in the bow, sides, or stern.

这些位于船首、船侧或船尾的跳板为从港区进入船上各层甲板提供了通路。

Vocabulary

traffic ['træfik]   n. 交通,运输
technical ['teknikəl]   adj. 工艺的,技术的
division [di'viʒən]   n. 分(开),分割;划分,区分

conventional [kən'venʃənl]		adj. 常规的，通常的，传统的
derrick ['derik]		n. 吊杆
winch [wintʃ]		n. 绞盘，绞车；曲柄
jumbo boom		重吊杆
boiler ['bɔilə]		n. 锅炉
hoist [hɔist]		n. 升高；举起；绞起
union purchase		双杆联吊
procedure [prə'si:dʒə]		n. 过程，步骤
elevator ['eliveitə]		n. 升降机，电梯
belt [belt]		n. 皮带
slurry pump		淤浆泵，料浆泵

Exercises

1　Answer the following questions according to the text you have read.

(1) What are the conventional system of equipment in a ship for handling cargo?

(2) As to the heavy lifts what kind of equipment is used to handle it?

(3) Talk about the working principle of "union purchase".

(4) Nowadays, what kind of equipment is applied for handling containers?

(5) What are the fourth group of equipment in a ship?

2　Choose the best answer.

(1) The development of cargo-handling equipment will be connected with _____.

　　a) the kinds of ships　　　　b) the structure of ships

　　c) the kinds of ports　　　　d) the facility of ports

(2) The conventional system consists of _____.

　　a) hold and pier　　　　　　b) derricks and winches

　　c) hook and lifting wires　　　d) union purchase

(3) In the "union purchase" arrangement, _____ if the ship is discharging.

　　a) the derrick over the pier lifts the cargo

　　b) the derrick over the hatch lifts the cargo

　　c) both the derricks lift the cargo together

　　d) no derricks lift the cargo

(4) The system of derricks and winches has been largely replaced on newer ships by cranes _____ it is very efficient.

　　a) when　　　　　　　　　b) because

　　c) unless　　　　　　　　　d) though

(5) Roll-on/roll-off ships are equipped with _____.

　　a) cargo elevators　　　　　b) conveyor belts

　　c) ramps　　　　　　　　　d) pump system

3 Put into Chinese.

Various forms of derrick rig are used in a cargo ship, the most common use if the single derrick being as a "single swing derrick". Adjacent derrick boom may be used in the system known as "union purchase". With the system, one derrick is kept over the hatch, the other over the side of the ship. The cargo runners are shackled together and the cargo is lifted from the hatch and swung out board without any further movement of the derrick.

4 Put into English.

(1)吊杆和起货机时船舶上常见的货物装卸设备。

(2)吊杆的负荷量通常不超过10吨。

(3)重吊杆可用于重量不超过100吨的重件的起吊。

(4)各种类型的皮带机常见于散货船上。

(5)滚装船上的跳板为车辆进入船舶甲板提供通路。

Dialogue

A: Now let's go to the forecastle and have a look.

B: Is the forecastle the deck area at the front of ship?

A: Yes, that's it. Here we are. This is the capstan.

B: What is it used for?

A: Like the windlass, it is used for heaving ropes and the chain cable for anchors.

B: And this is the winch for winding cable, isn't it?

A: Yes, it is for handling cargo. And these are bitts or bollards.

B: What for?

A: They are used to securing ropes or cables when mooring a ship.

B: What's the stick at the front of the ship?

A: That's jackstaff, for displaying a flag.

B: What flag?

A: The company's ensign when the vessel is in harbor. Now shall we go to the poop?

B: Great! Well, sir, I just find it much easier to learn things here than at school.

A: That's for sure. Oh! That's the poop. Have you heard of the fairlead?

B: Yes. There it is. Isn't used to guide the cables or ropes?

A: You're right. And we also use it to keep the cables or ropes in position in mooring and towing operation.

B: Is that so?

A: Yes. Look at the derrick. Do you find anything different about this derrick?

B: Mmm, It's much larger, like a crane.

A: Correct. We would rather call it a deck crane than a derrick. It greatly increase the cargo handling operation.

B: I have no doubt about it. What about the hatch covers, by the way? How are they opera-

ted?

A: Well, the opening and closing of the hatches is controlled by the highly automated hydraulic system.

B: That's terrific.

A: Do you see the radar scanner up there on the mast?

B: Yes, and I can see the signal flags, navigation lights, etc., all on the same mast. What's that large dish-shaped aerial behind the mast?

A: Oh, that's antenna for satellite communication. It has an automatic tracking system. OK, Shall we go to the bridge now?

B: Yes, I'm ready.

Notes

1 capstan 绞盘机; windlass 起锚器; jachstarff 旗杆; ensign 舰旗; fairlead 导缆孔; derrick 吊杆等均为船上甲板设备。

2 radar scanner 雷达扫描仪。

3 automatic tracking system 自动跟踪仪。

Program 5 Shipboard Organization

The crew is the staff who sails aboard a ship and are responsible for its operation, primarily while the vessel is at sea. It also has certain responsibilities while the ship is in port. For operating purposes, the crew of a cargo ship is divided into the deck department, engine department, and steward department (service department).

The head of shipboard organization is the captain, or master, of the ship who often works with the deck department. But he is in overall command of the ship. He is responsible for the safe navigation of his vessel, making out the best course of the voyage, and for the efficient loading, stowage, and discharging of cargo, preparing various documents for clearance and so on.

The deck department directly concerns with the cargo on board, and steers the ship. The chief officer or first mate takes charge of the deck department. He supervises the handling of cargo and is responsible for the upkeep of the ship and her equipment. He is assisted by two, three or more mates, depending on the size of the ship.

The engine department is in the charge of the chief engineer, who is responsible to the master both for the main propulsion machinery and for auxiliaries including electric plant, motors, pumps etc. He is also responsible for maintenance and repairs. He is assisted by a number of engineer officers, according to the size of the vessel. The ratings of the engine department include engine assistants, electricians, fitters, greasers and donkey men.

The steward department is under the control of the purser, who leads the cooks and stewards.

They prepare meals, do cleaning work and provide other service for the crew on board.

Ships may have special ratings in their crew, but the basic organization of cargo ships remains standard and is easily recognizable on any ship.

Notes

1 For operating purposes, the crew of a cargo ship is divided into the deck department, engine department, and steward department (service department).
按工作职能,船舶上的工作人员可分为甲板部、轮机部和管事部。

2 The deck department directly concerns with the cargo on board, and steers the ship. The chief officer or first mate takes charge of the deck department. He supervises the handling of cargo and is responsible for the upkeep of the ship and her equipment.
甲板部由大副负责直接看管船上的货物和船舶的驾驶。大副监管货物的装卸、负责船舶及其设备的维护。

3 Ships may have special ratings in their crew, but the basic organization of cargo ships remains standard and is easily recognizable on any ship.
船员中可能配有特殊编制人员,但货船的基本船员结构仍有一定的标准,而且可以在任何船上看到。

Vocabulary

crew [kruː]	n. 全体人员,船员
steward ['stjuəd]	n. (轮船,飞机等)乘务员,干事
steer [stiə]	v. 驾驶,掌舵
mate [meit]	n. 大副,助手
upkeep ['ʌpkiːp]	n. 保养,保养费
propulsion [prə'pʌlʃən]	n. 推进,推进力
auxiliary [ɔːɡ'ziljəri]	adj. 辅助,辅助力
pump [pʌmp]	n. 泵,抽水机
maintenance ['meintinəns]	n. 维护,保持
fitter ['fitə]	适当的,胜任的
greaser ['griːsə]	n. 加油器
purser ['pəːsə]	n. 事务长

Exercises

1 Answer the following questions according to the text you have read.
(1) What is the crew of a cargo ship divided into for operating purpose?
(2) Who is the head of the shipboard organization?
(3) What are the captain's duties?

(4) Who is in charge of the deck department?

(5) What are the engine department in charge of?

2　Choose the best answer.

(1) The crew of cargo ship are responsible for _____.

　　a) the operation while the vessel is at sea

　　b) the operation while the vessel is in port

　　c) the cargo carried

　　d) The operation while the vessel is both at sea and in port

(2) The captain takes in charge of _____.

　　a) the safe navigation of his vessel

　　b) the deck, engine and steward departments

　　c) the efficient loading, stowage and discharge of cargo

　　d) both the save navigation and the safe delivery of cargo

(3) The Chief Officer has the responsibility for _____.

　　a) supervising the handling of cargo

　　b) the upkeep of the ship and her equipment

　　c) supervising handling of cargo and the upkeep of the ship

　　d) supervising the handling of cargo and the upkeep of deck equipment

(4) _____ are in charge of the chief engineer.

　　a) The engine room

　　b) The main propulsion machinery and auxiliaries

　　c) The main propulsion machinery, maintenance and repair

　　d) The main propulsion machinery, auxiliaries, maintenance and repairs

(5) _____ are under control of the chief steward.

　　a) A carpenter, cooks and assistant stewards

　　b) A purser, cooks and assistant stewards

　　c) A radio operator, a purser and assistant stewards

　　d) Cooks, messmen and assistant stewards

3　Fill in each of the blanks in the following sentences with a suitable preposition or adverb.

(1) He is _____ overall command of the ship.

(2) He is responsible _____ the safe navigation of his vessel, making _____ the best course of the voyage, and for the efficient loading, stowage, and discharging of cargo, preparing various documents for clearance and so on.

(3) He is assisted _____ a number of engineers officers, according to the size of the vessel.

(4) The steward department is _____ the control of the purser, who leads the cooks and stewards.

(5) They prepare meals, do cleaning work and provide other service for the crew _____ board.

4 Put into Chinese.

(1) For operating purposes, the crew of a cargo ship is divided into the deck department, engine department, and steward department (service department).

(2) He is responsible for the safe navigation of his vessel, making out the best course of the voyage, and for the efficient loading, stowage, and discharging of cargo, preparing various documents for clearance and so on.

(3) The deck department directly concerns with the cargo onboard, and steers the ship.

(4) The engine department is in the charge of the chief engineer, who is responsible to the master both for the main propulsion machinery and for auxiliaries including electric plant, motors, pumps etc.

(5) Ships may have special ratings in their crew, but the basic organization of cargo ships remains standard and is easily recognizable on any ship.

5 Put into English.

(1) 甲板部、轮机部及管事部是船员编制的三个部门。

(2) 船长对安全航行和货物的安全交付负责。

(3) 管事部负责供应船员伙食。

(4) 电报员不属于船员编制的任何一个部门。

(5) 货物的装卸、积载及船舶的维修保养由大副负责。

Dialogue

A: Good afternoon, sir.

B: Good afternoon.

A: Now please say something in detail about the jobs and responsibilities for those working in the deck department, if you don't mind.

A: OK, let's start from the Captain. Well, the Captain is, as you know very well, the overall commander of all the three departments. He is responsible for the safety of navigation, the safety of the ship, the cargo and all those working on board.

A: He must very experienced navigator himself, I guess.

B: That goes without saying. Though he's the head of the whole vessel, he handles most of his work in the bridge.

A: What are the responsibility of the Chief Officer?

B: He is responsible to the master for the management of the deck department.

A: What does he chiefly do?

B: He looks after the cargo stowage, loading and discharging, and all the personnel on board. When at sea he does watch keeping on the bridge, together with the other mates. He is assisted by the Second and the Third Officer in his work.

A: What about the Second and the Third Officer, then?

B: The Second Officer is responsible to the master for keeping the ship on course and looking after all the equipment used for navigation.

A: And the Third Officer is in charge of the life-saving and fire-fighting equipment to make sure they are ready for use at any time.

B: You are right. It also the Third Officer's job to enter the telegraph orders into bell books when the vessel is under the command of the pilot or Captain.

A: I'm afraid I have little idea of what the bosun, the carpenter and other ratings on the deck department normally do?

B: Well, the bosun and the carpenter are directly responsible to the Chief Officer.

A: Yes? Namely…

B: The bosun is a man normally with a lot of knowledge and practical experience in seamanship. He is the leading hand on deck in charge of the sailor's work.

A: What about the carpenter? Does he do the kind of job as suggested by the name?

B: NO, little to do with wood work. He is usually a qualified shipwright. His regular job is to sound the tank and bilges for their depths, operate the windlass in anchoring operation, etc.

A: OK. Finally, the ratings. Tell me something about their jobs on board, please.

B: All right, in brief, they spend much time cleaning, painting and doing miscellaneous maintenance and repair work.

A: Thank you, thank you so much for telling me all this. Bye for the time being.

B: My pleasure. Bye.

Project 2　Cargo

Project Description

Cargo is goods or products transported. Traditionally, seaport terminals handle a wide range of maritime cargo, although the term is now extended to intermodal train, van or truck. A large variety of break bulk cargo (general cargo), bulk cargo, heavy lifts and so on is involved in a port's cargo-handling operation. In modern times, containers are used in most long-haul cargo transport.

Knowledge Objective

1　Types of cargo and their respective characteristics.
2　Transport packing of cargo and the function they play.
3　Cargo marks and its components.

Ability Objective

1　Have ability to identify the types of cargo.
2　Capable of choosing proper packing according to the characteristics of cargo.
3　Be able to handle dangerous cargos correctly based on their specific features.
4　Capable of identify the attributes of the cargo according to its marks.

Tasks

1　Attain the knowledge about the types of cargo by visiting a spot in wharf where cargo handling takes place or warehouses and pile ground where cargoes are stored.
2　Choose a proper packing when a certain kind of goods or product is given.
3　Make out shipping marks of cargo properly according to the informations given.

Program 1　Types of Cargo

The classification of cargo varies considerably based on different standards and practical application.

There are two basic types of cargo: bulk cargo and general cargo. Bulk cargo consists of a single commodity which is usually carried loose. It can be divided into liquid and dry bulk cargo. The former is carried in tankers, the example is crude oil. Dry bulk cargo, stowed in self-trimming

holds, is carried in bulk carriers. Iron-ore, coal, grain, fertilizer and sugar are commonly seen which fall into this type of cargo. They are loaded and unloaded automatically by many kinds of machinery. Although the cargo stows itself, it is important to maintain the ship's stability and to make sure that the cargo will not move during the voyage.

General cargo can be divided into containerized, non-containerized and reefer cargo. Non-containerized cargo is carried in multi-deck vessels. Varieties of packing are used for the goods for the purpose of protection or convenience of transportation and handling. As various kinds of cargoes are carried in one ship, proper segregation between them must be taken into consideration. Some cargoes such as tobacco and rubber have a strong odor and will taint delicate cargoes such as tea and rice. Other cargoes such as cement and fertilizers are dusty and will leave a residue behind them. Most attention must be paid to the dangerous cargoes which are of an inflammable, corrosive, poisonous and explosive nature. Heavy cargoes must not be stowed on top of fragile cargoes. Nowadays, various general cargoes are stuffed into containers of standard dimensions—containerization—so as to realize quick loading and unloading. Perishable cargoes such as meat, fruit, and dairy product are carried in ships with refrigerated holds.

Notes

1 Although the cargo stows itself, it is important to maintain the ship's stability and to make sure that the cargo will not move during the voyage.

虽然可以实现货物自动装船,但装船后不影响船舶的稳定性和航行期间货物不发生移动很重要。

2 As various kinds of cargoes are carried in one ship proper segregation between them must be taken into consideration.

由于各种各样的货物装在一艘船上,对于它们之间的正确隔离应当予以充分重视。

3 Most attention must be paid to the dangerous cargoes which are of an inflammable, corrosive, poisonous and explosive nature.

对于那些具有可燃性、腐蚀性、毒性和爆炸性的危险货物应当高度警惕。

Vocabulary

crude [kru:d]	adj. 天然的,未加工的,粗糙的
trim [trim]	adj. 整齐的,整洁的
	v. 整理,修整,装饰
fertilizer ['fə:ti‚laizə]	n. 肥料
automatically [‚ɔ:tə'mætɪkli]	adv. 自动地,机械地
stability [stə'biliti]	n. 稳定性
containerize [kən'teinəraiz]	v. 用集装箱装
reefer ['ri:fə(r)]	n. 冷藏车

Project 2　Cargo

segregation [ˌseɡriˈgeiʃən]	n. 隔离
rubber [ˈrʌbə]	n. 橡皮,橡胶
odor [ˈəudə]	n. 气味
taint [teint;tent]	v. 污染,感染
delicate [ˈdelikit]	adj. 精巧的,精致的
cement [siˈment]	n. 水泥
residue [ˈrezidjuː]	n. 残余,残渣,剩余物
inflammable [inˈflæməbl]	adj. 易燃的,易怒的
corrosive [kəˈrəusiv]	adj. 腐蚀的,腐蚀性的
poisonous [ˈpɔiznəs]	adj. 有毒的
explosive [iksˈpləusiv]	adj. 爆炸(性)的,爆发(性)的
perishable [ˈperiʃəbl]	adj. 易腐烂的
refrigerate [riˈfridʒəreit]	v. 使冷却,冷藏

Exercises

1　Answer the following questions according to the text you have read.

(1) What are the basic types of cargo?

(2) How many types can bulk cargo be divided into? What are they?

(3) What are various kinds of packing used for?

(4) Why should segregation be taken into consideration?

(5) How are the perishable cargoes carried nowadays?

2　Fill in each of the blanks in the following sentences with a suitable preposition or adverb.

(1) The classification of cargo varies considerably based _____ different standards and practical application.

(2) Bulk cargo consists _____ a single commodity which is usually carried loose.

(3) Iron-ore, coal, grain, fertilizer and sugar are commonly seen which fall _____ this type of cargo.

(4) As various kinds of cargoes are carried in one ship proper segregation between them must be taken _____ consideration.

(5) Heavy cargoes must not be stowed _____ top of fragile cargoes.

3　Choose the best answer.

(1) Basically, cargo can be classified into _____.
　　a) dry cargo and liquid cargo
　　b) general cargo and break bulk cargo
　　c) general cargo and special cargo
　　d) bulk cargo and general cargo

(2) Bulk cargo _____.

　　a）consists of more than one commodity

　　b）can be divided into dry bulk cargo and liquid bulk cargo

　　c）is usually packed

　　d）is usually discharged by machinery with hook

（3）General cargo _____．

　　a）is mostly packed

　　b）is carried in single-deck vessels

　　c）is divided into two kinds：containerized and non-containerized cargo

　　d）must be trimmed after loading

（4）Good separation must be made between _____．

　　a）general cargo and bulk cargo

　　b）heavy cargo and light cargo

　　c）rubber and sugar

　　d）steel bars and goat skin

（5）Containers are usually used for the content of _____．

　　a）general cargo

　　b）bulk cargo

　　c）liquid cargo

　　d）heavy lifts

4　Put into Chinese.

（1）The classification of cargo varies considerably based on different standards and practical application.

（2）Although the cargo stowed itself, it is important to maintain the ship's stability and to make sure that the cargo will not move during the voyage.

（3）General cargo can be divided into containerized, non-containerized and reefer cargo.

（4）Some cargoes such as tobacco and rubber have a strong odor and will taint delicate cargoes such as tea and rice.

（5）Perishable cargoes such as meat, fruit, and dairy product are carried in ships with refrigerated holds.

5　Put into English.

（1）杂货和散货属于两种不同种类的货物。

（2）散货可以分为干散货和液体散货。

（3）散货装船后通常要平舱以保证船舶平衡。

（4）可以将各种杂货装在集装箱内进行运输。

（5）易腐货物可以通过带有冷藏舱室的船舶运输。

Dialogue

　　A：Hello, Chief Tally, good morning.

B: Good morning, Chief-officer, what about the loading situation, all going well?

A: Frankly speaking, it is not so good.

B: Really? What's the problem?

A: In general, it is OK. But some damage has occurred to some export cargo. For example, some bagged and drummed cargo were not in good condition. Even though, I have told the foreman and the shipper not to load that cargo, yet, they still loaded them on board in the end. Of course, for the ship owner's sake, we are willing to load as much cargo as we can, the more cargo we load the more freight the owner can get. But as the chief officer, I must be responsible to the owner, I will put some remark on the mates receipt later anyway.

B: I see, Chief, it's clear. You're right. You can put some remark about the true condition of the cargo.

A: Thank you.

B: Well, Chief, how about the bulk cargo? Is it all right?

A: No, last night our night-duty officer found some bulk cargo in Hatch NO.2 was mixed with some impurities like small pieces of steelwire, some sticks or small pieces of string. My duty officer immediately told the foreman to ask the stevedores to pick them out. Unfortunately this was not done. I'm afraid that the quality of this cargo is not good, the consignee at the discharging port will possibly make a claim for the mixed cargo.

B: You are right, Chief, I quite understand. For these two problems, how about doing them like this: (1) Put some remarks about them on the mates receipt and shipping order to protect the owner's interest. (2) You'd better report the problems to your captain and shipping company. (3) Please keep somebody on duty during all the loading period to supervise the loading. Do you think it is a good idea, Chief?

A: Oh, yes, it is really a good idea. Thank you very much.

B: Not at all, Chief. Since you agree to do so, from now on, please go ahead with what we have discussed just now, and try to have a good ending of your work.

A: Yes, it sounds nice. Now I'm very happy and I'll attempt to reach an ideal result.

B: Right, that's the point. I believe you will. Now see you again.

A: OK, Chief-tally, great thanks for your advice. Bye-bye.

Program 2 Transport Packing of Cargo

The application of transport packing of cargo is an important link of the cargo moving chain for the shipping businesses, which keeps the cargo in good order and condition both for its quantity and quality. Goods are packed so that facilitate the transit, handling, delivery, custody and unitization.

The method of packing depends primarily on the nature of the goods themselves and the meth-

od of transit for the anticipated voyage. Packing is generally required to be strong and durable, economical, suitable, and practical.

There are numerous types of packing and a description of more important ones follows.

Baling is a form of packing consisting of a canvas cover often cross-looped by metal or rope binding. It is most suitable for paper, wool, cotton, carpets etc.

Bags, made of jute, cotton, plastic, or paper, are suitable for cement, fertilizer, sugar, flour, grains. Their prime disadvantage is that they are subject to damage by water, sweat, hooks or in the case of paper bags, breakage.

Cartons may be constructed of cardboard, strawboard or fiberboard. A wide range of consumer goods use this kind of inexpensive form of packing such as canned goods, medication, frozen meat, shoes, cigarettes, cotton pieces, tea etc. The principal disadvantage is its susceptibility to crushing and pilfering.

Crates are of wooden construction. Lightweight goods of large cubic capacity, such as light machinery, domestic appliances like refrigerator, cycles, and glasses.

Boxes, cases are also used extensively. Wooden in construction, they vary in size and capacity. Much machinery and other parts of expensive equipment, including cars and parts, are packed in this form.

Barrels, hogsheads and drums are used for the carriage of liquid or greasy cargoes. Examples are oils, paint, chemicals, wine etc. The main problem associate with this form of packing is the likelihood of leakage if the unit is not properly sealed and the possibility of the drums becoming rusty during transit.

Many goods have little or no form of packing and are carried loose. These include iron and steel plates, steel rails etc. Heavy lifts such as locomotive, road rollers, buses are also carried loose.

Notes

1 The application of transport packing of cargo is an important link of the cargo moving chain for the shipping businesses, which keeps the cargo in good order and condition both for its quantity and quality.

在航运业务中,货物的包装是货物运输过程的重要组成部分,以保证货物在数量和质量上处于完整和良好状态。

2 The method of packing depends primarily on the nature of the goods themselves and the method of transit for the anticipated voyage. Packing is generally required to be strong and durable, economical, suitable, and practical.

货物包装的方式主要取决于货物本身的性质和选择的运输方式。货物的包装应当坚固耐用和经济适用。

3 Bags, made of jute, cotton, plastic, or paper, are suitable for cement, fertilizer, sugar, flour, grains. Their prime disadvantage is that they are subject to damage by water, sweat, hooks or in the case of paper bags, breakage.

用麻、棉、塑料薄膜或纸制做的袋子适用于包装水泥、化肥、糖、面粉和谷物等。袋子包装的主要缺点是遇到水、汗湿、货钩容易损坏,纸袋易于破裂。

Vocabulary

facilitate [fəˈsiliteit]	vt. 使容易;使便利
transit [ˈtrænsit]	n. 运输,过境
custody [ˈkʌstədi]	n. 监督;监视;保护
unitization	单元化
anticipated [ænˈtisipeitid]	adj. 预期的;预料的;期待的
baling [ˈbeiliŋ]	n. 包装,打包
canvas [ˈkænvəs]	n. 粗帆布,帆布
jute [dʒuːt]	n. 黄麻
breakage [ˈbreikidʒ]	n. 破损
carton [ˈkɑːtən]	n. 纸盒;纸板箱
cardboard	纸板
strawboard	硬纸板
fiberboard	纤维板
medication [ˌmediˈkeiʃən]	n. 药物,药剂
susceptibility [səˌseptəˈbiliti]	n. 易感性,敏感性
pilfer [ˈpilfə]	vt. 偷窃
crate [kreit]	n. 条板箱
hogshead [ˈhɔgzhed]	n. 豪格海大桶
greasy [ˈgriːzi]	adj. 油污的
leakage [ˈliːkidʒ]	n. 泄露
locomotive [ˌləukəˈməutiv]	n. 火车头,机车

Exercises

1 Answer the following questions according to the text you have read.
(1) What are the main functions of packing?
(2) what are the requirements for the packing?
(3) What is the basis upon which the packing is selected properly?
(4) What kinds of goods are carried without packing? please list some of them.
(5) Is a packing need to be attractive or noticeable?

2 Choose the best answer.
(1) A good transport packing aims at _____.
    a) protecting the goods during transit
    b) being eye-catching to customers

c）promoting the sale of goods

d）to be a means of marketing

（2）Packing is needed for _____.

    a）egg iron   b）road roller

    c）iron ore   d）cigarettes

（3）cartons are suitable for _____.

    a）hardware   b）cigarettes

    c）steel bars   d）glasses

（4）cotton is usually packed _____.

    a）in the form of baling   b）in box

    c）in crate   d）in carton

（5）We usually use the barrel to pack _____.

    a）canned goods   b）oil

    c）wheat   d）fertilizer

3　Put into Chinese.

（1）I wonder if you could tell me something about the packing of cotton shirts.

（2）We use cardboard boxes for outer packing.

（3）In view of fragile nature of the goods, we place great importance on proper packing.

（4）We'll reinforce all those cardboard cartons with straps from outside.

（5）Your cartons are not thick and sturdy enough.

4　Put into English.

(1) 我觉得你们的包装需要进一步改进。

(2) 你们用这种包装来装这些仪器不合适。

(3) 要根据货物的特性来选择包装。

(4) 选择包装时我们也要考虑到经济性。

(5) 散装货一般不需要包装。

Dialogue

A：Now, we have come to talk about the way of packing for the apples, is that OK?

B：All right.

A：what is your idea?

B：This order shall be packed in cartons with polythene tops.

A：We'd like to have the commodity packed in the same way as those supplied last year.

B：But the purchase we've made this year was not packed that way. Not solely for the holiday, but for all seasons.

A：Have you got any samples here? I'd like to look at the outer pack.

B：Here you are.

A：Mm...I think it is good enough. And what about the outer packing?

B: In sea-worthy boxes, 50 packed to one box.

A: I suppose the boxes are about strapped as before?

B: You are right. We are always try to ensure that the boxes are safe in long-distance transport.

A: What is the size of the box?

B: We're using special boxes offered by the suppliers. They also undertake to pack the commodity according to the contract stipulations.

A: Do they have to send the apples to a special packer for packing?

B: No, they have a special workshop, offering packing services related to the customer's needs.

A: How convenient it is! Could you arrange for me a visit to the packing workshop sometime this week?

B: Sure, I'll notify you.

Program 3 Cargo Marks

As to the packed cargo, the cargo marks are the essential signs or labels which make the cargo to be identified and can facilitate transit, assorting, counting, and delivery of cargo. Meanwhile, the cargo marks, drawn by the shipper, indicate the weight, measurements, features and tips during handling of the cargo to be shipped so that ensure the integration of cargo and the safety of the carriers and stevedores.

Cargo marks can be classified into four categories, they are shipping marks, care marks, dangerous marks and original marks.

Shipping marks includes main mark and counter mark. Main mark, consisting of geometric figure and characters, is the basic mark which distinguishes between the cargo it presents and the other cargoes of the same consignment on board. It provides for the code or abbreviation of the consignee(shipper), contract number and order number, etc. Counter mark, the supplement of the main mark, indicates the destination port, lot number, package number, measurements and weight of the cargo etc.

The features of cargo is shown by care marks or indicative marks which makes people to be alert, by pattern and characters, during handling or custody of cargo such as THIS SIDE UP, KEEP DRY, HANDLE WITH CARE, AWAY FROM HEAT and USE NO HOOKS etc.

Dangerous mark points out the hazard nature and classification of the dangerous cargo with specially designated pattern and characters. The mark alerts people to take specially protective measures when they are meeting this kind of cargo.

Original mark is used for exported cargo which is particularly required in international trade. It is labeled in the packing of cargo with the name of the specific country making the cargo, and the certificate of origin may be provided if demanded.

Notes

1 As to the packed cargo, the cargo marks are the essential signs or labels which make the cargo to be identified and can facilitate transit, assorting, counting, and delivery of cargo.

对于包装的货物,货物标志是识别货物的重要标记或标识,有助于货物的运输、分理、计点、和交付。

2 Meanwhile, the cargo marks, drawn by the shipper, indicate the weight, measurements, features and tips during handling of the cargo to be shipped so that ensure the integration of cargo and the safety of the carriers and stevedores.

同时,由发货人所制作的货物标志注明货物的重量、尺寸、特性和装卸的注意事项以保证货物的完整性和运输工具及装卸人员的安全。

3 Dangerous mark points out the hazard nature and classification of the dangerous cargo with specially designated pattern and characters. The mark alerts people to take specially protective measures when they are meeting this kind of cargo.

危险货物标志用特别设计的图案和字母指出危险货物的危害性质和类别。该标志提醒人们遇到此类危险货物应采取的保护措施。

Vocabulary

assort	[əˈsɔːt]	vt. 把……分类
tip	[tip]	n. 顶,尖端
stevedore	[ˈstiːvidɔː]	n. 码头工人
geometric	[dʒiːəˈmetrɪk]	adj. 几何的
consignment	[kənˈsainmənt]	n. 托运物
abbreviation	[əˌbriːviˈeiʃən]	n. 简写,缩写
indicative	[inˈdikətiv]	adj. 指示的;表示的
hazard	[ˈhæzəd]	n. 危险(性),危险状态

Exercises

1 Answer the following questions according to the text you have read.

(1) what are the cargo marks?

(2) How the cargo marks are classified?

(3) What is the shipping marks?

(4) What are the main mark and its main elements?

(5) What are the care marks and its role?

2 Choose the best answer.

(1) Shipping marks are _____.

　　a) used to protect goods

  b）used to alert people of dangerous situation

  c）drawn by shipper

  d）are drawn by carrier

（2）Care marks are _____.

  a）used to identify goods

  b）used to make goods to be suitable for transport

  c）used to alert people to be careful during handling

  d）drawn by consignee

（3）The counter mark belongs to _____.

  a）shipping marks   b）care marks

  c）dangerous mark   d）original mark

（4）The feature of goods is reflected in _____.

  a）shipping marks   b）in main mark

  c）in care marks   d）in original mark

（5）The package number is indicated in _____.

  a）care marks   b）dangerous mark

  c）main mark   d）in shipping marks

3 Put into Chinese.

（1）Main mark is the basic mark which distinguishes between the cargo it presents and the other cargoes of the same consignment on board.

（2）Original mark is used for exported cargo which is particularly required in international trade.

（3）The features of cargo is shown by care marks or indicative marks which makes people to be alert during handling or custody of cargo.

（4）The stevedores must be familiar with the care marks during their handling of cargo.

（5）By knowing the shipping marks, people can distinguish one cargo from another.

4 Put into English.

（1）我们应当十分熟悉货物标志。

（2）主标志中包含有合同编号。

（3）通过运输标志我们可以知道货物的目的港。

（4）不同的运输标志表示不同票的货物。

（5）理货员根据装货单来核对货物。

Dialogue

A：Mr.Smith, there are some cases in the mast house. Are they all for this port?

B：I'm not sure. Please wait a minute. Let me go and ask the Chief Officer.

A：What did the Chief say about the cases?

B：They're not all for this port. Some are for Shanghai.

A: Terrible, the cargo there has been mixed up. Well, let's check the shipping marks.

B: How to check the shipping marks?

A: We usually check the shipping marks on the cases against those on the import manifests.

B: Mr.Zhao, there are plenty of letters and figures on the cases. Which part is the shipping marks?

A: Shipping marks are generally made up of the contract number, the destination port, the lot number and the case number.

B: Look here, the "Shanghai" must be the destination port. Then, we can tell the Shanghai cargo from those are for this port by this way.

A: Yes, you are right.

B: How about the words "Keep dry"? Are they shipping marks?

A: No. they are not shipping marks. We call them care marks. On the cases you can find different care marks such as "Handle with Care", "Don't Drop", "Keep Flat", "Use no Hooks" and "This Side Up".

Project 3 Stowage of Cargo

Project Description

Stowage of cargo is required to lay out the ship properly to prevent costly mistakes from occurring during loading process, which depends on whether the cargo plan is good or not. There several factors should be considered in making up a cargo plan including cargo distribution throughout the ship, stowage factor, cargo's safety segregation, separation and dunnage, ship's security and its stable navigation, etc. Both cargo and ship being kept away from damage is the major principle of cargo stowage.

Knowledge Objective

1 Have a good knowledge about the principle of cargo stowage.
2 The concept of the stowage factor and its calculation.
3 The knowledge of applying the tentative cargo plan and final stowage plan, and the difference between them.
4 Have a good understanding about the safety of both cargo and ship during the stowage of cargo which the segregation, separation and dunnage of cargo are involved.

Ability Objective

1 Have the ability to make a proper stowage of cargo in accordance with the principle of the stowage.
2 Capable of applying the stowage factor for the purpose of saving broken space during loading.
3 Be able to understand a tentative cargo plan and final stowage plan under the guidance of professionals.
4 Be able to know how to make proper segregation, separation and dunnage of cargo during loading based on the Shipping Order given.

Task

Assuming that a certain tons of various kinds of cargo, which are for successive destination ports, will be loaded on board a ship with five holds.
1 Make a sketch cargo plan in accordance with the principle of stowage.
2 Make proper segregation, separation and dunnage based on the characteristics of cargoes

protecting both cargo and ship from possibility of damage.

3　Make sure to maintain the ship seaworthy.

Program 1　Generality of Stowage of Cargo

There are several factors should be considered during the stowage of cargo. The first consideration must be given to safety. The cargo must be stowed in such a manner that the stability and the seaworthiness of the ship are secured. In practice, it is usual for the ship to be loaded a little deeper aft, to improve the vessel's movement through the water.

Then care should be given to the cargo to prevent it from damage or being injuriously affected. Cargo to be stowed can not contact with or near to the other cargoes which are of counteractive nature to it. For example, foodstuff, tea or cigarettes must not be stowed with rubber, otherwise, the former will be stained by the latter.

The disposition of the cargo is another concern during the stowing of the cargo. In order to ensure quick loading and unloading a general principle of stowing is required to be followed: Cargo for later or "deep" ports on the voyage has to be loaded first, and that for earlier ports loaded last. The lower holds should be first filled and then the tweendecks, and last the deck. In such arrangement, the cargo can be conveniently discharged at each port in rotation without "double handling".

And cargo must be evenly distributed vertically and longitudinally. If there is not an even distribution of cargo when the ship sails, with no compensation ballast, hogging or sagging may arise. Both hogging and sagging have an adverse effect on the hull, and impair the stability of the vessel.

It is advisable to arrange the cargo in such a way in terms of packing for keeping the cargo in good order and condition that the cargo with strong packing is to be stowed in the lower position and the weak upper; the light packages over the heavy ones; the large and hard in the midst of other, and the small and weak on head or stern of the ship.

The ship's deadweight and cubic capacity should be made best possible use. Generally 10 to 15 per cent of the total cubic capacity is allowed for broken stowage.

Notes

1　The cargo must be stowed in such a manner that the stability and the seaworthiness of the ship are secured. In practice, it is usual for the ship to be loaded a little deeper aft, to improve the vessel's movement through the water.

货物的积载应当保证船舶的稳定性和适航性。通常，货物的积载应使船舶稍微后倾以有利于船舶的航行。

2　The disposition of the cargo is another concern during the stowing of the cargo. In order to ensure quick loading and unloading a general principle of stowing is required to be followed: Cargo for later or "deep" ports on the voyage has to be loaded first, and that for earlier ports loaded last.

在积载过程中,货物的配载位置是另一个需关注的问题。为了实现快装卸应当遵守下面的总体原则:航程中后到港的货物先装,先到港的货物后装。

3 And cargo must be evenly distributed vertically and longitudinally. If there is not an even distribution of cargo when the ship sails, with no compensation ballast, hogging or sagging may arise. Both hogging and sagging have an adverse effect on the hull, and impair the stability of the vessel.

货物必须在垂直方向和水平方向上均衡分布。船在航行期间,若货物积载不平衡又无压载补偿措施,船体会出现拱凸和凹陷现象而破坏船舶的稳定性。

4 The ship's deadweight and cubic capacity should be made best possible use. Generally 10 to 15 per cent of the total cubic capacity is allowed for broken stowage.

应充分利用船舶的载重量和舱容。一般来讲,亏舱率允许在10%至15%。

Vocabulary

factor ['fæktə]	n. 因素,要素,因数
stability [stə'biliti]	n. 稳定(性),稳度
seaworthiness ['si:wə:ðinis]	n. 适航性
injuriously [in'dʒuəriəsli]	adv. 伤害地,有害地
affect [ə'fekt]	vt. 影响,对…起作用
counteractive [ˌkauntə'ræktiv]	adj. 反对的,反作用的,抵抗的
foodstuff ['fu:dstʌf]	n. 粮食,食品
disposition [dispə'ziʃən]	n. 布置,配置,安排;部署
rotation [rəu'teiʃən]	n. 港序
vertically ['və:tikəli]	adv. 垂直地
longitudinally [lɔndʒi'tju:dinli]	adv. 纵向地
compensation [kɔmpen'seiʃən]	n. 补偿,赔偿,对消
hogging ['hɔgiŋ]	n. 弯[翘]曲,挠度,扭曲
sagging ['sægiŋ]	n. 下垂[沉,陷],松垂,垂度
impair [im'pɛə]	vt. 损害,伤害
midst ['midst]	n. 中部,中间
cubic ['kju:bik]	adj. 立方体的,立方的
broken stowage	亏舱

Exercises

1 Answer the following questions according to the text you have read.
(1) What are the factors should be considered during the stowing of cargo?
(2) How is the ship loaded in practice for her smooth movement through the water?
(3) What are the general principles of stowing cargo?

(4) How to prevent "double handling"?

(5) What would be happened if cargo is not distributed evenly throughout the ship?

2　Choose the best answer.

(1) In practice, it is advisable for the ship being loaded _____.
　　a) a little down by the bow
　　b) a little down the stern
　　c) heavily
　　d) lightly

(2) The ultimate purpose for the loading of ship is to ensure _____.
　　a) that either the or her cargo is damaged
　　b) that the ship as well as her cargo is not damaged
　　c) that both the ship and her cargo are damaged
　　d) that both the ship and her cargo are not damaged

(3) For cargoes such as grain, coal, ventilation is needed to prevent them from _____.
　　a) taint　　　　　　　　　　　b) sweat
　　c) pilferage　　　　　　　　　d) spontaneously combustion

(4) If all the cargo has been stowed fore and aft of the vessel, it may cause the vessel _____.
　　a) down by the head　　　　　b) down by the stern
　　c) hogging　　　　　　　　　d) sagging

(5) Four main factors to consider in the towage of cargo are _____.
　　a) deadweight, stability, security and segregation
　　b) cubic capacity, trim, stability and segregation
　　c) broken stowage, stability, security and segregation
　　d) broken stowage, stability, trim and security

3　Put into Chinese.

(1) Care should be given to the cargo to prevent it from damage or being injuriously affected.

(2) A proper segregation and stowage of different consignments for various ports must be made, to prevent delay in discharging and avoid double handling.

(3) The best possible use should be made of the ship's deadweight and cubic capacity.

(4) Good stowage is very important to the cargo work in ocean shipping business.

(5) General cargo are conveyed generally in cargo liners, provided with many decks, including tweendecks.

4　Put into English.

(1) 货物的积载对于船舶和货物的安全十分重要。

(2) 应当根据积载原则做好货物积载工作。

(3) 因为货物在航行中容易移动，所以必须捆扎好。

(4) 为防止船舶和货物受损，应当做好货物的分隔。

Project 3　Stowage of Cargo

(5)根据积载原则,重货不应堆在轻货上。

Dialogue

A：Chief Tally, are you free now?

B：Yes, what can I do for you?

A：I'd like to talk with you something about the stowage. First, In Hatch No.3 lower hold, the stevedores are loading wheat for Long Beach, Please tell them to put the outer bags across each other and keep the outside ones straight so that the bags may not fall during the voyage.

B：I've already told them to do that. Don't worry about it.

A：Secondly, the general cargo for Houston is to be stowed in Hatch No.3 lower hold fore part. Please tell the stevedores to block up the light packages inside and put the heavy ones outside, because we're going to load some other cargo on top at the next port.

B：All right. Is it necessary to keep a walking space in Hatch No.1 tweendeck?

A：Yes, please leave a 2-foot-wide walking space around the hatch square, and stow the cargo just to the white line, not over it.

B：But I'm afraid the space is not enough there.

A：In case the space is not enough, you can use more section in the Hatchway, but leave a small margin.

B：Alright.

A：In Hatch No.5, what are you going to load next?

B：We're going to load cotton piece goods for New York.

A：I see.

B：Can we stow it all over the lower hold?

A：Yes, but you have to take off the platform before loading the New York cargo.

B：Of course, the stevedores will make it level.

A：Also, Please stow the cargo as close as possible and right to the deckhead.

Program 2　Stowage Factor

The ideal economic result of a ship being fully loaded and used of its deadweight largely depends upon whether the stowage factor is taken into fully consideration.

The stowage factor is defined as the number of cubic feet (or cubic meters) required to stow one ton of a given cargo. It can be expressed in the following equation:

$$S.F = V/Q$$

Where $S.F$ is the stowage factor, V is the actual measurements of the cargo (cubic feet or cubic meters), Q is the weight of the cargo (ton).

It is a value that used to answer two important questions. First: when given a certain amount of cargo, what is the space that will be consumed in stowing it? Second: when given a certain volume of space, what is the number of tons, units, or pieces that will go into the space?

These two questions cannot be answered precisely, because the actual amount lies at the broken stowage resulting when the cargo is stowed. This latter value varies greatly. The space that contributes to the broken stowage is the space between containers of irregular shape, containers with curvature, space filled with dunnage, and the space over the last tier into which no cargo can be fitted for one reason or another. Broken stowage on uniform packaged commodities will average about 10%, that on general cargo will average about 25%. Both of these values may be affected by a number of variables.

When the broken stowage is taken into account, the calculation of the $S.F$ should be changed accordingly. The actual stowage factor is:

$$S.F = W/Q$$

Where W is volume consumed by the cargo stowed (cubic feet or cubic meters).

Q is the weight of the cargo stowed (ton).

As to the above two questions, a trustworthy actual stowage factor should be calculated prior to any attempts to estimate space or tons.

Notes

1 The ideal economic result of a ship being fully loaded and used of its deadweight largely depends upon whether the stowage factor is taken into fully consideration.

只有充分考虑积载因素才能判断一艘满载的和满载重量的船舶是否达到了理想的经济效果。

2 The space that contributes to the broken stowage is space between containers of irregular shape, containers with curvature, space filled with dunnage, and the space over the last tier into which no cargo can be fitted for one reason or another.

构成亏舱的舱容是指形状不规则的包装之间或带曲度的包装之间的空隙；是指塞入垫舱料的空隙；也是指在最高一层上面由于这样或那样的原因里面不适宜再装任何货物的空间。

3 These two questions cannot be answered precisely, because the actual amount lies at the broken stowage resulting when the cargo is stowed.

由于实际数量取决于装货时的亏舱，因而这两个问题难以准确回答。

4 Broken stowage on uniform packaged commodities will average about 10%, that on general cargo will average about 25%. Both of these values may be affected by a number of variables.

相同包装货物的亏舱率平均为10%，杂货的亏舱率平均大约为25%。这两个数值可受许多其他变量因素的影响。

Project 3　Stowage of Cargo

Vocabulary

stowage factor	积载因数
ideal [aiˈdiəl]	*adj.* 理想的,完美的
fully loaded	满载
depend upon/on	取决于;依赖
take into consideration	考虑到
cubic feet/meter	立方英尺/米
equation [iˈkweiʃən]	*n.* 方程式,等式,公式
amount [əˈmaunt]	*n.* 总数,总额
volume [ˈvɔljuːm]	*n.* 体积,容量
irregular [iˈregjulə]	*adj.* 不规则的;无规律的
curvature [ˈkəːvətʃə]	*n.* 弯曲(部分)
uniform [ˈjuːnifɔːm]	*adj.* 一致的,一样的
commodity [kəˈmɔditi]	*n.* 商品
average [ˈævəridʒ]	*n.* 平均数
trustworthy [ˈtrʌstˌwəːði]	*adj.* 值得信任的,可靠的

Exercises

1　Answer the following questions according to the text you have read.

(1) What is the stowage factor?

(2) How to calculate the stowage factor?

(3) What is the space that contributes to the broken space?

(4) Talk about some thing about the broken space.

(5) If the broken space is given, how to calculate the stowage factor?

2　Choose the best answer.

(1) The stowage factor is defined as _____.

　　a) how much cubic feet for a given cargo

　　b) how much space for a whole shipment

　　c) how much space for one ton of a certain cargo

　　d) how much space for different cargoes

(2) The actual amount of cargo loaded depends upon _____.

　　a) the broken stowage listed

　　b) the broken stowage calculated

　　c) the broken stowage given

　　d) the actual broken stowage

(3) The broken stowage will _____.

a) reduce the cabacity of a hold　　b) raise the cabacity of a hold

c) increase the cargo stowed　　d) damage the cargo stowed

(4) By the calculation of stowage factor, we can know _____.

a) how much cargo can be unloaded in a hold

b) the ship's deadweight

c) the amount of cargo can be stowed in a hold

d) the ship's draft

(5) The broken stowage should be made out _____.

a) in the process of loading　　b) before the start of the loading

c) betore the start of the discharging　　d) after the loading of a ship

3　Put into Chinese.

(1) The definition of the stowage factor points out that it is simply the specific volume of the commodity expressed in units of cubic feet per ton..

(2) When handling other bulk commodity such as ores, sulfur, and sugar, the only way that the stowage factor can be obtained is by weighing a known volume of the substance.

(3) The volume of the entire shipment and its gross weight or any part of the shipment can be used to calculate the stowage factor.

(4) Volume and weight information are readily available during the all the phases of the cargo of operation..

(5) We can calculate the density from the data given, but why not express the equation for stowage factor as one operation instead of two separate operations.

4　Put into English.

(1) 每艘船都会碰到能装多少货物的问题。

(2) 通过计算积载因素,我们可以估计一个舱的装货量。

(3) 装货中造成的实际亏舱差异很大。

(4) 亏舱应在编制船图前计算好。

(5) 货物的积载因素直接与货物的密度相关。

Dialogue

A：Hello, Chief-officer, very happy to see you again, it has been only about a week since your ship left here last time.

B：Yes, you are right, it's really a short time.

A：Well, Chief, looking through your import manifest, we know that you loaded 7 lots of general cargo at the last port Pusan Korea, is that so?

B：Correct, 7 lots altogether.

A：Before coming to you, I went to the deck to have a look at the cargoes inside your 3 holds. I happened to find that the cargoes in the holds seemed not to have been stowed in good order or in normal conditions. I mean that they'll be difficult to be unloaded. What's the reason for this?

B: Well, frankly speaking, we came up against strong winds during the voyage at sea. We were pitching and rolling for a long time and we could do nothing about it. I guess the cargo inside the holds have been avoidably shift to a certain extent. For that reason, we don't know exactly what the final result is like. I can't see the real situation in the holds now.

A: Yes, because of this, I suppose that some cargo, especially the drums on pallets, might have been listed and damaged. Since the stevedores can't discharge the cargo by forklift in a normal way, some of them must be moved and laid on pallet by hand prior to discharge. It not only takes a longer time than usual, but also costs more for laborers.

B: I see, it is a problem, but we could not control it, that was the force majeure.

A: Yes you are right. By the way, have you tendered the sea protest to the Harbour Officer?

B: Well, I think that's the captain's business, I am not clear about it.

A: OK, I'll ask your captain later, yes, that's another story. No, lets return to the topic of your cargo situation in the holds. According to my experience, the local port foreman will talk to you about it and then ask you to sign a sheet stating the difficult working operation for the cargo in the holds.

B: I see, but can we discharge all the cargoes without signing it?

A: It seems not. You see, under such a special circumstance, more stevedores will be used, additional costs will be incurred, and longer time must be taken. It is no doubt a difficulty for the port. I think, you have to sign, if not, the discharging will not be commenced and completed in time.

B: I understand. If so, I ought to report this to my captain.

Program 3　Stowage Plan

When loading a vessel there are many concerns must be taken into consideration, such as: how to lay out the ship so that she is assured to be seaworthy and safe during voyage? and how to ensure the cargos being stowed are in good order and condition, and will be discharged smoothly and economically in the rotation of destination ports? A tentative stowage plan is designed and made out to deal with these questions.

The tentative plan, made up from the loading list, shows the approximate amount in tons and numbers of packages expected to be placed in the indicated spaces.

The tentative plan usually provides for loading cargo bound for the last port of call first and the first port last. Meanwhile, heavy cargoes must be stowed on the bottom tiers.

The tentative plan will provide for the correct distribution of weight vertically and longitudinally throughout the ship, to ensure her general stability.

The tentative plan will reflect the correct segregation of cargoes. The problem of segregation is that of stowing the cargoes so that one cannot cause damage to another.

Finally, the tentative plan will provide for an amount of cargo to be stowed in each hold so that

no one hold will require an unproportional number of gang hours of work to discharge the cargo. This calculation will take into consideration the number of sets of cargo gear at each hold.

When the ship is completely loaded, the stowage of the cargo will resemble the tentative plan but will never be precisely in accordance with it. The numerous changes cannot be kept on the tentative plan so that it will serve as a final stowage plan.

The final stowage plan, turned reversely to the tentative plan, is used by the stevedores of the discharging port to plan the discharging operation. Moreover, the plan presents a picture of the stowage that is readily interpreted, and the officer sees the segregation immediately upon viewing the plan. So it plays as a guide for the ship's officers to cope with any emergency impairing the ship and the cargo carried during voyage.

Without an accurate, complete, and clear final stowage plan, there can be no efficiency in the discharging operation and the safety of the ship and the crew is impaired greatly.

Notes

1 The tentative plan, made up from the loading list, shows the approximate amount in tons and numbers of packages expected to be placed in the indicated spaces.

根据载货清单编制的配载图记载要装在指定位置的货物情况,包括货物的大约重量(吨)和件数。

2 The tentative plan usually provides for loading cargo bound for the last port of call first and the first port last. Meanwhile, heavy cargoes must be stowed on the bottom tiers.

按照配载图通常要求,运往后到港口的货物要先装,而先到港的货物后装。同时规定,重货必须堆在底层。

3 The tentative plan will provide for the correct distribution of weight vertically and longitudinally throughout the ship, to ensure her general stability.

配载图要求货物重量在全船上要在垂直方向上和水平方向上正确分布,以保证船舶的总体稳性。

4 Finally, the tentative plan will provide for an amount of cargo to be stowed in each hold so that no one hold will require an unproportional number of gang hours of work to discharge the cargo. This calculation will take into consideration the number of sets of cargo gear at each hold.

最后,配载图规定了任一货舱应装的货物量,以使任一货舱在卸载时所需的舱时量与其他货舱所需的舱时量成均衡比例。这一货物量的计算应考虑货舱所配备的货物起吊设备数量。

5 When the ship is completely loaded, the stowage of the cargo will resemble the tentative plan but will never be precisely in accordance with it. The numerous changes cannot be kept on the tentative plan so that it will serve as a final stowage plan.

装船完毕后,货物的积载情况会与配载图规定的相类似,但不可能完全一致,要对配载图做许多修改,通过修改使配载图成为最终积载图。

6 The final stowage plan, turned reversely to the tentative plan, is used by the stevedores of

the discharging port to plan the discharging operation; moreover, the plan presents a picture of the stowage that is readily interpreted, and the officer sees the segregation immediately upon viewing the plan. So it plays as a guide for the ship's officers to cope with any emergency impairing the ship and the cargo carried during voyage.

最终积载图的用途与配载图相反,用于卸货港的卸货操作;而且,最终积载图清晰地反映了船舶的受载情况,船舶驾驶人员一看图可立刻了解货物的分隔状况。因而可用于指导船舶驾驶人员处理航程中出现的紧急情况,防止对船舶和所载货物的危害。

Vocabulary

lay out	摆开,展示,布置,安排,投资
smoothly [ˈsmuːðlɪ]	adv. 平稳地
tentative stowage plan	预配图
bound for	开往,驶往,去哪里
meanwhile [ˈmiːnwail]	adv. 同时
resemble [riˈzembl]	vt. 相似,类似
in accordance with	与……一致,依照
operation [ˌɔpəˈreiʃən]	n. 操作
moreover [mɔːˈrəuvə]	adv. 而且;此外;再者
readily [ˈredili]	adv. 迅速地,轻易地,乐意地

Exercises

1 Answer the following questions according to the text you have read.
(1) What is the tentative plan?
(2) How does the tentative plan play in the process of loading the ship?
(3) How to stow the cargo so that the ship's general stability is gained?
(4) What is the final stowage plan?
(5) What function does the final stowage plan have?

2 Choose the best answer.
(1) The tentative plan _____.
　　a) eliminates confusion with the final stowage plan
　　b) shows the approximate amount of cargo to be loaded in each hold
　　c) expedites the total operation
　　d) requires an unproportional number of gang hours of work to discharge the cargo
(2) The tentative plan will reflect _____.
　　a) the actual stowage
　　b) the total operation
　　c) the correct distribution of the weight

d) the gang hours of work

(3) The tentative plan will provide for an amount of cargo in each hold so that _____.

    a) gang hours of work will be reduced for each hold

    b) gang hours of work will be equal for each hold

    c) gang hours of work will be estimated for each hold

    d) gang hours of work will be proportional for each hold

(4) If the cargo carried is for the first port of call it should _____.

    a) be loaded last   b) be loaded first

    c) be loaded in the lower hold   d) be loaded in the lower tweendeck

(5) The final stowage plan is used _____.

    a) in the process of loading

    b) in the process of discharging

    c) to calculate the amount of gang hours of work

    d) to distribute the cargo throughout the ship

3 Put into Chinese.

(1) The stevedores at the loading port must lay out the ship so that she is assured to be seaworthy and safe during voyage.

(2) It is very important to ensure the cargoes being stowed are in good order and condition, and will be discharged smoothly and economically in the rotation of destination ports.

(3) When the ship is completely loaded, the stowage of the cargo will resemble the tentative plan but will never be precisely in accordance with it.

(4) The correct way to prevent costly mistakes from occurring during the loading process is to lay out the ship as far in advance as possible.

(5) "Double handling" requires the shifting of cargo to get the load discharged and means added time and expense for the cargo operation.

4 Put into English.

(1) 配载图是根据载货清单事先制成的。

(2) 货物分隔的目的是防止货物相互损坏。

(3) 货物的重量应在水平和垂直方向上正确分布。

(4) 在编制配载图时,应考虑每个舱口的装卸索具。

(5) 最终积载图不同于配载图,它是用来指导卸船的。

Dialogue

A: Chief, is everything set for the loading now.

B: No, sorry, I can't say it is.

A: Why? what do you mean?

B: Please take a seat. Here is the stowage plan for the general cargo. The situation for the past two days has been quite all right. Nevertheless, I got some rough information from the tallyman this

Project 3　Stowage of Cargo

morning saying that another 50tons of chemical goods in bags and 100 tons of steelwire in boundless must be added to shipping orders No.4 and No.7 respectively.The tallyman told me that this is a common quest from these two shippers.

A:I see.What the tallyman said is true,in such case do you think it is possible for you to adjust the stowage plan in order to load this additional cargo on board?

B:It seems very difficult.

A:Why so?

B:Well,our sailing time is 18:00 hour this afternoon and now it's nearly 12 o'clock.The time is very tight,and we have already finished loading 80% of the whole general cargo.It is really to mend the plan,because we haven't enough space left.

A:Yes,that's sound reasonable,but could you try your best to help the shippers get around the problem? If you could manage it,this would be also beneficial to the ship owner.The more cargo you load,the more fright revenue the ship owner can get.

B:That's correct,but it is really a hard nut.

A:Well,let's talk about how we could mend the plan.Please pass it to me.

B:Here it is.

A:Thanks.We can see that there is no space for the extra cargo now,and we don't have time to shift what's been loaded.My idea is that you could load the additional cargo in both hatch No.2 and No.4 where there is still some space for them.These two lots of additional cargo are the ones to be unloaded at the second discharging port,so they can be handled at the same time as the same cargo in hatches No.1 and No.3.I think you can ask the foreman to do it in this way.If it's OK,the problem is solved.

B:Oh,a very good idea! It looks workable,thank you.I'll adjust the plan and ask the foreman and tallyman to load the cargo accordingly.

Program 4　Segregation

One of the basic requirements of the protection of cargo is the proper segregation of the various types.Segregation refers to the stowage of cargo in separate parts of ship so that one cannot damage the other by its inherent characteristics.Such as:wet cargoes must be kept away from the dry cargoes.Generally,certain areas of the ship will be specified for the stowage of wet items when the tentative plan is made.In the same way,other areas will be specified for dry cargoes,dirty or clean.

Although segregation is called for in the case of odorous and delicate cargoes,special sections are not specified for their stowage.Each time the ship is laid out,care must be taken not to make a serious mistake in this respect.Segregation of light and heavy cargoes is necessary with respect to their vertical position.Heavy items must always be given bottom stowage in any compartment.Finally,the stowage of any of the dangerous cargoes must be in strict accordance with the segregation re-

quired by the regulations concerned.

There are four kinds of segregation for the stowage of cargoes in terms of their counteractive nature.

(1) Cargoes that must not be stowed side by side. Fertilizer can't be stowed near the metallic products because they are directly counteractive in nature.

(2) Cargoes that are not allowed to be stowed in the same compartment. Such as rubber and oils. However, they are not prohibited being stowed in the different compartments in the same hold.

(3) Cargoes that cannot be stowed together in the same hold. Examples are fishmeal and sugar, rice and mercury. They cannot be stowed between the tweendeck and lower hold in one hold.

(4) Cargoes that are not allowed to be stowed in the neighboring hold. For example, the inflammable gas and the organic peroxide must be stowed separately at least one other hold.

Segregation must be given considerable significance in the stowage of cargo which would not only prevent cargo from damage but also facilitate the process of cargo handling.

Notes

1　Segregation refers to the stowage of cargo in separate parts of ship so that one cannot damage the other by its inherent characteristics.

货物的分隔是指按照货物的内在性质将不同的货物分开装在船舶不同的舱室使之相互之间不造成损害。

2　Although segregation is called for in the case of odorous and delicate cargoes, special sections are not specified for their stowage. Each time the ship is laid out, care must be taken not to make a serious mistake in this respect.

虽然要求进行分隔气味货和易污货，但对于它们是否积载在特定位置并不具体规定。对于这方面，在对船舶进行货物配载时应当予以重视避免发生严重错误。

3　Segregation of light and heavy cargoes is necessary with respect to their vertical position. Heavy items must always be given bottom stowage in any compartment.

对轻货和重货的积载有必要进行垂直分隔。重货在任何舱室内都应堆放在底层。

Vocabulary

refer to	参考,查阅;涉及,提到;指的是
inherent [inˈhiərənt]	adj. 固有的
characteristic [ˌkæriktəˈristik]	n. 特性,特征,特色
inherent characteristic	固有特性
odorous [ˈəudərəs]	adj. 有气味的
delicate [ˈdelikit]	adj. 精美的,精致的,精巧的
in this respect	在这方面,在这点上
with respect to	关于,至于

side by side	并排,并肩
metallic [miˈtælik]	*adj.* 金属的
metallic product	金属制品
compartment [kəmˈpɑːtmənt]	*n.* 区划,区分;间隔,部分;舱,室
mercury [ˈməːkjuri]	*n.* 汞,水银
organic peroxide	有机氧化物

Exercises

1 Answer the following questions according to the text you have read.
(1) What is the segregation of cargo?
(2) How to arrange the segregation between dry cargo and wet cargo?
(3) How to arrange the segregation between the heavy cargo and light cargo?
(4) What kinds of cargo can't be stowed in the same hold?
(5) What kinds of cargo can't be stowed in the neighboring hold?

2 Select the suitable words.
(1) Can you tell me _____ about the segregation?
　　a) any thing　　　　　　b) something
　　c) nothing　　　　　　　d) some thing
(2) You _____ better shift it away.
　　a) are　　　　　　　　　b) were
　　c) have　　　　　　　　 d) had
(3) As _____ the segregation, our stevedores will go it well.
　　a) in　　　　　　　　　 b) on
　　c) at　　　　　　　　　 d) for
(4) We usually stow drums in two tiers to prevent them from _____.
　　a) moving　　　　　　　b) move
　　c) to move　　　　　　　d) moved
(5) What _____ segregation?
　　a) of　　　　　　　　　 b) about
　　c) in　　　　　　　　　 d) on

3 Put into Chinese.
(1) Each time the ship is laid out, care must be taken not to make a serious mistake in this respect.
(2) Heavy items must always be given bottom stowage in any compartment.
(3) In order to avoid any damage, you have to make a good segregation between the two kinds of cargo.
(4) There are plenty of nets on board and you may use them when necessary.
(5) Cargoes with counteractive nature must be segregated well for preventing them from damage.

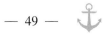

4　Put into English.

（1）做好货物的隔离是货物积载的一项重要要求。

（2）货物分隔的目的是防止货物相互损坏。

（3）气味货物和易污货物是不能堆放在一个舱室内的。

（4）进行货物积载时应考虑货物的具体特性。

（5）工人们正在考虑堆放橡胶的具体位置。

Dialogue

The Duty Officer(A) and the Forman(B) monitor the whole process of loading operation.

A：Hi,Forman.Please note：light cargo on top of heavy cargo and big cases before small one.

B：That's common practice.Yes,we're just doing like this.

A：You know we've got 180 containers to load on Wharf.No.3.Stow them as tightly as possible.

B：I see.Yes,anything else?

A：Well,I found some stevedores did it in wrong way.Cargo in Hold No.3 was improperly stowed.Please tell your men to restow it and choke them up again.

B：Oh,really? I think I have to go and take a look.

A：Some cases contain heavy and valuable machinery.Please handle with care.

B：No problem.I'll give special care to that.Look,Hatch No.2 is almost full.Shall we go on with Hatch No.1?

A：We've got a number of steel tubes for this voyage.As they are subject to shifting inside the holds,please stow them well and choke up both sides with rough boards.

B：Alright.Well,only 20 sets of cargo left now.I think the loading will complete in 1 hour.You may then proceed to special anchorage for dangerous cargo.

A：What are the drafts fore and aft now?

B：The draft are 7.4 meters forward and 7.2 meters aft.The ship is little down by the head.

A：True.So it is time to put reserved 150tons of bagged cargo in Hold No.5.

B：With this 150tons in Hold No.5,the ship will be down by the stern.

A：Yes.And as you know,too,it's good sailing a little down by the stern.

B：You are right.

A：Take caution against cargo shifting inside containers.Containers,especially those on deck,should be securely lashed with twist lock bridge fittings and strong wire cables,or they may be swept overboard at sea.

B：Sure.Our stevedores will follow up to the loading procedures.

Notes

Containers,especially those on deck,should be securely lashed with twist lock bridge fittings and strong wire cables,or they may be swept overboard at sea.

集装箱,尤其是甲板上的集装箱,应用钮锁桥装置和强力钢丝绳绑紧,否则会被风刮倒海里去。

Program 5　Separation

Separation is one of the essential measures to prevent consignments from being mixed up during loading and unloading.

Separation is defined as the materials used to separate blocks of cargoes by port and/or consignee. It is necessary to do so when the same type of cargo is destined for separate ports or for different consignees at the same port. Clear and definite separation makes the cargo easier to discharge in consignee blocks. In the same way the separation lessens the possibility of overcarrying the cargo.

Therefore, if the separation is omitted or incomplete, confusion is the result, and some cargo may be inadvertently left in the ship.

Some cargoes need no separation because they are different in nature and mistaken a container is impossible. For example, when discharging, bags of rice for one port and the adjacent cargo for the next port is barrels of flour, there is no possibility of mixing the rice and the flour. This may be termed natural separation.

The selection of separation and methods depends on the type of cargo carried. For example:

1. As to two lots of cargoes in the same container in one compartment and to be received by two consignees or for different ports, they can be separated by another cargo with different specification and distinct packing.

2. Nets or mats can be used as separation for the cargo in carton, case and bag. A simple way of separation for cartons or cases is to draw lines with poster paint on the surfaces.

3. Steel plates, bars, rails and lumber can be separated with paint of different colors.

4. For the cargoes in drums, planks or straws can be used for separation.

5. As bulk cargo is concerned, separation can be done by lying mats or canvas after trimming.

Good and proper selection of materials and methods of separation would lead to lowering the cost both in money and time, which would certainly facilitate the handling of cargo.

Notes

1　Separation is defined as the materials used to separate blocks of cargoes by port and/or consignee. It is necessary to do so when the same type of cargo is destined for separate ports or for different consignees at the same port.

隔票是指用不同的材料,按照货物的目的港和收货人,对不同票的货物进行分隔。对于同种类的货物,如果目的港不同或目的港相同但收货人不同,有必要对其进行隔票。

2　Clear and definite separation makes the cargo easier to discharge in consignee blocks. In the same way the separation lessens the possibility of overcarrying the cargo.

清晰明确的隔票可加快到港货的卸船。同样,隔票可减少错港货的发生。

3　As to two lots of cargoes in the same container in one compartment and to be received by two consignees or for different ports, they can be separated by another cargo with different specification and distinct packing.

对于两票货物,如果使用的容器相同且装在同一舱室内,但收货人和目的港不同,可使用另一种规格不同包装不同的货物进行隔票。

Vocabulary

separation [ˌsepəˈreiʃne]	n.隔票
mix up	混票
define [diˈfain]	vt.解释;给……下定义
block [blɔk]	n.一批;滑车;滑轮
overcarry	越港运输
omit [əuˈmit]	vt.省略;遗漏;忘记
confusion [kənˈfjuːʒən]	n.混淆
inadvertently [ˌinədˈvəːtəntli]	adv.不注意地
adjacent [əˈdʒeisənt]	adj.接近的,相邻的
flour [ˈflauə]	n.面粉;谷粉;粉末

Exercises

1　Answer the following questions according to the text you have read.
(1) What is the separation of cargo?
(2) How to make separation of cargoes for separate ports or different consignees?
(3) Is it necessary to make separation for all of cargo to be loaded on board? and why?
(4) What kinds of separation are applied for cargoes in cartons, cases or in bags?
(5) What is the simplest way to separate naked cargo, such as steel plates, rail or lumber?

2　Select the suitable words.
(1) The cargo must be clearly separated _____ planks.
　　a) with　　　　　　　　　　　　b) on
　　c) in　　　　　　　　　　　　　d) of
(2) In hatch No.2 lower hold there are a lot of materials for separation, _____ nets, planks, paint and tapes.
　　a) like　　　　　　　　　　　　b) such as
　　c) as　　　　　　　　　　　　　d) such that
(3) When _____ separation, we usually us materials such as nets and planks.
　　a) make　　　　　　　　　　　b) making
　　c) made　　　　　　　　　　　d) to make

Project 3　Stowage of Cargo

　　(4) The planks _____ from Ship Chandler are not enough.
　　　　a) ordered　　　　　　　　　　b) ordering
　　　　c) to order　　　　　　　　　　d) order
　　(5) If it _____ rained, we would have started loading.
　　　　a) haven't　　　　　　　　　　b) hasn't
　　　　c) didn't　　　　　　　　　　 d) hadn't

3　Put into Chinese.
　　(1) If the separation is omitted or incomplete, confusion is the result, and some cargo may be inadvertently left in the ship.
　　(2) You have to separate the big lots for the same port with colored tapes.
　　(3) Is the rotation of discharging ports shown on the cargo plan wrong?
　　(4) Is it necessary to separate the cargos for the same port or identical consignee?
　　(5) The separation must be well done to prevent the cargo being overcarried.

4　Put into English.
　　(1) 不同港口的货物必须用网隔开。
　　(2) 你们可以用各色胶带来分隔去同一港口的大票货。
　　(3) 这些货物不需要隔票，它们是运往同一港口的。
　　(4) 对于这些不同收货人的钢条，可用不同颜色的油漆进行隔票。
　　(5) 我们需要从船舶物料供应商那里订购足够的木板。

Dialogue

　　A: Chief, I've got something to talk with you. It is about the export cargoes to be loaded on board your ship.
　　B: I see, something for me to do now?
　　A: Yes, according to the export cargo manifest, there are 8 lots of cargo altogether from five different shippers. These cargoes can not be mixed with each other during loading. They must be separated either by plastic sheets and nets or by tarpaulins, as far as the smooth discharge and delivery of the cargoes at the discharging port are concerned, it is also beneficial for your ship, I think.
　　B: What you said is correct, I'm thinking about it, too. But I'm concerned about how many separation materials I need to take and who will pay the costs of the separation material.
　　A: That's it. If I'm not wrong, there are 3 holds on board your ship.
　　B: You are right, you see, there are two lots of bulk cargoes which will be loaded at the bottom of each hold, the rest—the other 6 lots of general cargo, will be loaded into 3 different holds.
　　A: Yes, because of this, the cargo separation becomes very necessary.
　　B: That's true, but who will be responsible for the costs of the separation materials?
　　A: That's a very good question and we have to clarify it before you take the separation materials. To the best of my knowledge, the charter agreement shows that the cost for cargo separation ma-

terials at the loading port, if any, will be covered by your charterer. You can ask your captain to confirm it later. Do you think the separation materials are enough?

B: Yes, I suppose so. I'll ask for more if not.

A: OK, Chief, as for better usage of the separation materials, you should count them in the spot and ask the foreman and stevedores to use them sparingly.

B: Very important reminder, many thanks. I'll ask my duty officer to take care of it at that time.

A: All right, Chief, if there are some changes, let's keep in contact and we can do any necessary adjustments. Anything else now?

B: So far no, thank you very much again.

A: You are welcome. Now it's time for me to make the arrangements for the separation materials. Bye-bye, Chief.

B: Yes, bye-bye.

Program 6 Dunnage

Dunnage is defined as the materials used to protect cargo and ship.

Dunnage is used to prevent cargo from contacting by free moisture which might be present in a hold due to the leak in the hull plating, an adjacent tank, deck, or openings into the hold, or heavy condensation. For the cargo stowed on deck or in the lower hold, at least two tiers of dunnage are required to be laid. The bottom tier laid fore and aft crossed to the drain wells of the ship is to provide the drainage, and the top tier to support the cargo which should always be perpendicular to the first tier and approximately be placed about five centimeters from it.

To free from the wetting with condensation in case of contacting with steel members, such as stanchions, frames, ladders, bulkheads, etc., vertical dunnage is placed between the cargo and all steel members. Mats, canvas and plastic papers are commonly used to cover such members.

Dunnage is also used to prevent condensation. It is placed in the cargo to help the circulation of air current. It is by thorough ventilation that high dew point air is removed from hold interiors, thus prevent condensation. The permanent dunnage attached to the frame of the ship is also an aid in ventilation. This dunnage is known as cargo battens or sweat battens.

Dunnage is also used to prevent crushing of cargo. Between the tiers of cargo is the dunnage placed to spread weight evenly so that pressure is equalized on lower tiers, and maintain levels. Dunnage is placed in the hold so that cargo shifting is prevented.

When stowing heavy lifts, dunnage with sufficient strength and measurements should be used to protect the deck or ceiling of the ship, such as steel plates, thick planks or square woods.

Also dunnage is used to prevent spontaneous heating. Some cargoes require dunnage to provide air channels through the stowed cargo block in order to carry away heat generated by the cargo.

Notes

1 Dunnage is used to prevent cargo from contacting by free moisture which might be present in a hold due to the leak in the hull plating, an adjacent tank, deck, or openings into the hold, or heavy condensation.

衬垫是用来防止货物与舱内的游离水分接触而损害。游离水分可由于船壳钢板、邻近水舱、甲板、或与货舱相通的出水口等的滴漏或水汽凝结等原因造成。

2 The bottom tier laid fore and aft crossed to the drain wells of the ship to provide the drainage, and the top tier to support the cargo which should be always be perpendicular to the first tier and approximately be placed about five centimeters from it.

底层垫舱板跨越疏水井纵向铺放形成排水通道,上层垫舱板相互间隔大约五厘米与底层相互垂直铺放,用来支撑货物。

3 To free from the wetting with condensation in case of contacting with steel members, such as stanchions, frames, ladders, bulkheads, etc., vertical dunnage is placed between the cargo and all steel members. Mats, canvas and plastic papers are commonly used to cover such members.

为了防止货物与船舶钢制结构件接触遭受汗湿,应在货物与刚结构件之间垂直铺放衬垫。钢结构件包括立柱、框架、梯子、和舱壁等;经常使用来覆盖钢结构件的衬垫有席子、帆布、塑料薄膜等。

4 Dunnage is also used to prevent condensation. It is placed in the cargo to help the circulation of air current. It is by thorough ventilation that high dew point air is removed from hold interiors, thus prevent condensation. The permanent dunnage attached to the frame of the ship is also an aid in ventilation. This dunnage is known as cargo battens or sweat battens.

货物的衬垫有助于空气的流通可用来防止水汽凝结。舱内的高露点的空气,通过全面的通风而排出舱外,使水汽不能凝结。船体构件上的永久性衬垫也有助于空气流动。这种永久性衬垫被称作护货板或防汗湿衬板。

5 Dunnage is also used to prevent crushing of cargo. Between the tiers of cargo is the dunnage placed to spread weight evenly so that pressure is equalized on lower tiers, and maintain levels. Dunnage is placed in the hold so that cargo shifting is prevented.

衬垫也用来防止货物受挤压损坏。置于货物各层间的衬垫可使货物重量均匀分散开来,使各下层货物受压相等,压力均衡。可在舱内货物中放置衬垫防止货物移动。

Vocabulary

dunnage [ˈdʌnidʒ]	n. 衬垫
moisture [ˈmɔistʃə]	n. 湿气,水分,水汽
due to	由于,应归于
opening [ˈəupniŋ]	n. 出水口
condensation [kɔndenˈseiʃən]	n. 凝结

fore and aft	纵向,从船头到船尾的
drain well	排水井
drainage [ˈdreinidʒ]	n.排水
perpendicular [ˌpəːpənˈdikjulə]	adj.垂直的
stanchion [ˈstɑːnʃən]	n.柱子
frame [freim]	n.骨架结构;框架,框子
dew [djuː]	n.露,露水
dew point	露点
permanent [ˈpəːmənənt]	adj.永久性的
cargo batten	舱壁护条;货舱护板
sweat batten	舱内防汗湿木板
square wood	方木
spontaneous [spɔnˈteinjəs, -niəs]	adj.自发的

Exercises

1 Answer the following questions according to the text you have read.

(1) What is the dunnage?

(2) What is the function of dunnage?

(3) How to use the dunnage when dealing with cargo stowed on deck or in the lower hold?

(4) Why is the dunnage put between the tiers of cargo?

(5) What is the reason that the dunnage is used to prevent cargo from spontaneous heating?

2 Choose the best answer.

(1) It is required that _____ of dunnage to be put for the cargo on deck or in the lower hold.

  a) one tier   b) more than one tier

  c) less than two tiers   d) no more than two tiers

(2) Sweat battens are used to _____.

  a) prevent leakage of cargo   b) avoid the cargo being tainted

  c) free the cargo from moisture   d) free the cargo from sweating

(3) The main purpose of putting dunnage in wheat is _____.

  a) to prevent the wheat from moving

  b) to avoid spontaneously heating in wheat

  c) to avoid the wheat being wet

  d) to avoid the wheat being tainted

(4) Steel members of a ship are covered with mats, which is the measure to _____.

  a) protect the ship   b) to prevent the cargo from sweating

  c) avoid the cargo being wetted   d) free the cargo from tainting

(5) Steel plates can be used as dunnage which mainly are applied to _____.

  a) bulk cargo   b) heavy lifts
  c) corrosive cargo   d) inflammable cargo

3 Put into Chinese.

(1) Dunnage is used to prevent cargo from contacting by free moisture which might be present in a hold.

(2) For the cargo stowed on deck or in the lower hold, at least two tiers of dunnage are required to be laid.

(3) When stowing heavy lifts, dunnage with sufficient strength and measurements should be used to protect the deck or ceiling of the ship.

(4) Because of the shortness of dunnage some of cargo on board tends to be damaged.

(5) Some dunnage must be inserted in the block of rice in order to prevent spontaneous heating.

4 Put into English.

(1) 垫舱可以防止货物和船舶受损。

(2) 应根据货物的特性来选择垫舱。

(3) 汗湿是造成货物损坏的原因之一。

(4) 应在货舱内铺上衬垫以防止货物移动。

(5) 铺在舱壁上的护货版有助于空气流通。

Dialogue

Duty Officer: Hi, Foreman. I'm the duty officer. May I have a talk with you?

Forman: Certainly. What can I help you?

Duty Officer: Have you finished covering the lower hold with plastics sheet as required?

Forman: Not yet, I'm afraid. Why, Anything wrong?

Duty Officer: Oh, no. But I'd like to stress here, don't miss any space for stowing the bagged cargo.

Forman: Take it easy, I'll go and check. Anything else?

Duty Officer: Yes. Before loading cargo into the lower hold, put 2 layers of dunnage materials. The first layer to be arranged athwartships and the upper tier, fore and aft.

Forman: Ok, I understand. What about the bilge and double bottom tanks?

Duty Officer: Such place must be covered with heavy planks in a criss-cross way. As for the protruding parts in the holds, just wrap them with mats to protect the cargo from sweat and chafe.

Forman: What shall we do with the cargo close to the bulkhead of engine room? It is too hot to stack cargo right against it.

Duty Officer: Quite right. So please make a small space between the bulkhead and the cargo for air circulation, and secure the cargo by filling in the space with planks.

Forman: It's a good arrangement. Double dunnage planks are laid in each lower hold with mats on top of them. Will it be the same with the tweendecks?

Duty Officer: No. As for the tweendecks, it'll be all right to put single dunnage and then the mats on top.

Forman: Yes, single dunnage first, then mats.

Duty Officer: Look here, the planks are laid too far apart. Please tell the stevedores to put them closer together, and then spread a piece of plastic sheet on top of the dunnage.

Forman: Ok, I'll ask them to do that immediately. Must we separate the different lots of cargo for the same port.

Duty Officer: Yes, of course. Every lots of cargo must be separated from each other. Besides, you should guard against mixing up cargo marks.

Forman: You mean we have adopt the method of lot separation?

Duty Officer: Exactly.

Forman: Ok, no problem. We'll take good care of this matter and separate the different lots of cargo with planks, mats or nets as required.

Duty Officer: All right. Thank you.

Project 4　Cargo Handling

Project Description

Traditionally, loading and unloading of cargo are prime tasks for ports, which involve various kinds of working and procedure and parties concerned. And the handling mode of different kinds of cargo such as general cargo, dry bulk cargo, liquid bulk cargo, heavy lifts and containers may vary greatly, which involves the applying of different ship's gear, tools, equipments and transferring carriers. Safety must always be taken into account first both for loading and unloading during the handling process.

Knowledge Objective

1　The preparation of cargo loading and the technology used in the process of loading.
2　The preparation of cargo unloading and the technology used in the process of unloading.
3　The kinds of general cargo and the equipments and tools used in the handling process.
4　The kinds of bulk cargo and the machinery used in the handling process.
5　The characteristics of dangerous cargos and the safety measures taken in handling of them.

Ability Objective

1　Have the ability to analyse the technology and make outline for the loading process.
2　Have the ability to analyse the technology and make outline for the unloading process.
3　Be able to select proper equipment and tools in dealing with different kinds of cargo in their handling.
4　Have a keen awareness of the characteristics of different kinds of dangerous cargo and know how to cope with them with proper safely measures accordingly.

Task

1　Make a technology scheme for the handling of general cargo.
2　Make a technology scheme for the handling of bulk cargo.
3　List safety measures respectively that must be taken when dealing with cargoes that are of explosive, inflammable, poisonous and corrosive natures.

Program 1　Loading and Unloading

Efficient loading and discharging is dependent on proper planning and correct procedure during actual operations.

Before loading commences, the stevedore office will make a program, based on the shipping order and the cargo plan drawn by Chief Mate of the ship, to organize dock workers, transferring carriers and handling equipments for loading, and have the cargo delivered in advance and located at the correct berth, clarified the schedule of loading for various consignments.

During loading it is necessary to observe the safety rules, to follow the planned loading schedule, to ensure correct timing of the cargo for loading, to ensure satisfactory handling of the cargo, to use the proper handling equipment, and to avoid damage to the cargo handled. After the loading is completed, an overall check is to make to ensure no cargo has been short shipped.

With respect to the discharging, a program, similar to that of cargo loading, called Discharging Technological Program should be made out in advance according to the type of cargo to be discharged based on the Loading List and stowage plan which are supplied by the Ship. A good program will considerably lower the labor intensity of stevedores, reduce the numbers of gang hours and raise the productivity.

Before the discharging commences, it should be made sure that storage space is fully arranged as well as stevedores, handling equipments, transferring carriers, etc.

Lack of adequate storage during discharging will reduce productivity, can cause congestion and may also result in damage to the cargo due to, for example, particularly high stacking.

During discharging, it is necessary to observe the safety rules, to use proper equipment and handling procedures, to avoid damaging the cargo, to provide continuity of work, to avoid direct discharge, and to provide a satisfactory registration and tally.

For the ship, the ship's gear must be get ready before loading or discharging. And it is necessary for the ship to provide a tentative plan before loading for proper distribution of cargo onto the board. Before discharging, the information about the ship and the cargo carried should be given, and a plan called stowage plan must be provided to instruct the discharging.

Notes

1　Before loading commences, The stevedore office will make a program, based on the shipping order and the cargo plan drawn by Chief Mate of the ship, to organize dock workers, transferring carriers and handling equipments for loading, and have the cargo delivered in advance and located at the correct berth, clarified the schedule of loading for various consignments.

在装船开始前，调度室根据装货单和大副编制的积载图制定装船计划，组织工人、安排运输工具和装船设备；提前将货物运达装船泊位，确定各种货物的装船计划。

2　With respect to the discharging, a program, similar to that of cargo loading, called Discharging Technological Program should be made out in advance according to the type of cargo to be discharged, based on the Loading List and stowage plan which are supplied by the Ship. A good program will considerably lower the labor intensity of stevedores, reduce the numbers of gang and raise the productivity.

对于卸船,一份类似于装船计划的被称作"卸船工艺规划"提前编制出来,该规划是根据待卸货物的种类、载货清单、船方提供的积载图编制的。好的工艺规划可显著的降低工人的劳动强度,减少工组数量并提高生产效率。

3 Lack of adequate of storage during discharging will reduce productivity, can cause congestion and may also result in damage to the cargo due to, for example, particularly high stacking.

在卸货过程中,若堆场不足,将会降低卸船效率,形成拥阻,并可由于货堆过高等原因造成货物残损。

4 During discharging, it is necessary to observe the safety rules strictly, to use proper equipment and handling procedures, to avoid damaging the cargo, to provide continuity of work, to avoid direct discharge, and to provide a satisfactory registration and tally.

在卸货过程中,要严格遵守安全规则,设备选用正确,工作程序合理,防止货物残损;要保证工作的连续性,避免直卸;货物情况要登记清楚,理货准确无误。

5 For the ship, the ship's gear must be get ready before loading or discharging. And it is necessary for the ship to provide a tentative plan before loading for proper distribution of cargo onto the board. Before discharging, the information about the ship and the cargo carried should be given, and a plan called stowage plan must be provided to instruct the discharging.

对于船方,在装船或卸船前应将船泊吊具准备好。在装船前,船方应提供配载图用于货物的正确配置。在卸船前,应提供船泊和所载货物的情况,并提供船舶积载图以指导卸船。

Vocabulary

Proper ['prɔpə]	adj.正确的,合适的
commence [kə'mens]	vt.开始
Shipping Order	装货单
cargo plan	积载图
Chief Mate	大副
observe [əb'zə:v]	vt.遵守
overall ['əuvərɔ:l]	adj.全部的,从头至尾的
short shipped	短装
Discharging Technological Program	卸船工艺规划
Loading List	载货清单
labor intensity	劳动强度
gang hour	工时

Exercises

1 Answer the following questions according to the text you have read.

(1) What does the efficiency of loading and unloading depend on?

(2) What should be done before the loading begins?

(3) What should be given notice during the operation of loading?

(4) What should be done before discharging?

(5) What should be done during discharging?

2 Choose the best answer.

(1) A _____ is required to make up before loading to organize the operation.

  a) program   b) loading list

  c) final cargo plan   d) manifest

(2) An overall check is imperative _____.

  a) before loading   b) during loading

  c) after loading   d) during discharging

(3) Loading List and stowage plan are made out and offered by _____ which are used to compile the program.

  a) the loading port   b) the discharging port

  c) the shipper   d) the carrier

(4) High stacking of cargo is caused by _____.

  a) low productivity   b) shortness of storage space

  c) lack of power   d) lack of adequate equipment

(5) A stowage plan is necessary for instructing _____.

  a) the carriage of cargo   b) the stowage of cargo

  c) the discharging of cargo   d) the loading of cargo

3 Put into Chinese.

(1) The stopping of the power supply will slow down the speed of loading.

(2) It is not advisable to drag slings during loading and unloading.

(3) The discharging will certainly be delayed in case the machinery is not full arranged.

(4) I'll tell the stevedores to leave the damaged cargo on board for your inspection.

(5) We have found some damaged cargo on deck, I'll inform the Shipper to repair or renew it at once.

4 Put into English.

(1) 不要超负荷,否则会造成严重事故。

(2) 看来需要对配载图做些调整。

(3) 在卸货时,如果发生什么事情,请及时与装卸队长联系。

(4) 不要在舱内任意拖关,那样会造成货物严重损坏。

(5) 应当移一些货到三舱以平衡舱时量。

Dialogue

Duty Office: Hi, Forman. Is all the cargo for our ship ready?

Foreman: Yes, I think so.

Duty Office: That's good. How many gangs are available today?

Foreman: Only 2 gangs at first due to shortage of hands, but I try to let you have 4.

Duty Office: Fine. When will the stevedores start loading?

Foreman: Any time. They are standing by on deck now.

Duty Office: If everything goes smoothly, when do you expect to finish loading?

Foreman: By Saturday, in 4 days, to be exact.

Duty Office: I see, thank you.

Foreman: Look at the stowage plan. Hold No.3 is your key hold, so 2 gangs for Hatch 3 and 2 for No.1 and 4.

Duty Office: How to you plan to load the ship, Foreman?

Foreman: We have a lot of cargo to load in this port. First we'll take in the general cargo here, then the dangerous cargo. The container will be handled last.

Duty Office: It sounds good. Please let your man to handle the dangerous cargo with care. Among 180 containers to be loaded on Wharf No.8, we have 2 heavy ones, 8 reefer containers; 12 dangerous containers; 2 odd-size containers and 4 over-height containers.

Foreman: We'll put a layer of plastics sheet over the lower hold before loading the bagged cargo, for the easy collection of sweepings after discharging.

Duty Office: That's a good idea.

Foreman: Duty Officer, look here, (pointing at the stowage plan) most cargo in Hold No.4 will be discharged at Singapore. The ship will be down by the head after the cargo is taken out there. You don't expect to occur, do you?

Duty Office: No, but we can pump in ballast water while discharging to keep balance.

Foreman: I see. By the way, have you got enough materials for lashing, dunnaging and separation? I hear there is a lot of deck cargo that needs lashing, too.

Duty Office: We've got enough materials on board. You can get them at will.

Foreman: I noticed that the Chief Officer reserved 150 bagged cargo. What for?

Duty Office: That'll be used to adjust the draft before loading completes.

Foreman: I'll tell my workers to pay proper attention to the ship's trim during loading.

Duty Office: And you'd better assign a deck-watching during loading to check the drafts fore and aft, especially when the ship is getting down to her load line.

Foreman: Yes. We should cooperate to ensure the ship's trim while loading. Look, the derrick is lifting the first sling of cargo from the wharf! The loading has begun.

Duty Office: Is that so?

Program 2 Handling of General Cargo

General cargo can be classified into several kinds according to the types of packing and forms

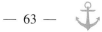

of package.

Bag cargo: such as bagged grain, bagged salt, bagged fertilizer and cement, etc. Bale cargo: such as baled cotton, baled tobacco.

Drum cargo: liquid goods can be carried in drum such as gasoline, rude oil, liquid chemical products, etc.

Case or carton cargo: hardware and canned goods are packed in case and cigarettes, foodstuff are packed in carton, etc.

Goods in basket, crate and jar: such as vegetable, fruits and preserved vegetable, sulfate, etc.

Naked or bundled cargo: pig iron, steel bars, aluminum ingot, lead ingot, steel pipe, etc. are naked, of which the steel bars, and pipes are naked and bundled.

Equipment and tools applied in handling general cargo vary based on the cargo handled and port natural condition and wharf facilities, etc.

Gantry crane, mobile crane, truck, forklift, straddle carrier, tractor and trailer are common quayside machinery in handling general cargo. For heavy lifts such as locomotive, concrete mixer, excavator, etc. floating crane, which has a large lifting capacity, will be applied for and then used. In addition, ship's equipment including winch, derrick, jumbo boom, etc. are mainly adopted in some ports in handling general cargo, such as ports in Japan and United States due to limitation of port conditions.

During the handling of the general cargo, a variety of slings will be made to cater for different kinds of general cargo. There are various tools for making slings, for example, rope slings, canvas slings, wire slings, chain slings, cargo tray and drum hooks. These slings are used for different cargoes: rope slings for bales, canvas slings for bags, wire slings for steels, trays for cases and cartons, and drum hooks for cargo in drums.

Proper and correct adoption of equipment and tools is very important in handling general cargo, which will not only facilitate the handling of cargo but also minimize the accident may occur during the process of handling.

Notes

1　Gantry crane, mobile crane, truck, forklift, straddle carrier, tractor and trailer are common quayside machinery in handling general cargo.

桥吊、吊车、货运卡车、叉车、跨运车、拖车和拖盘是杂货作业常见的码头机械。

2　For heavy lifts such as locomotive, concrete mixer, excavator, floating crane, which has a large lifting capacity, will be applied for and used.

对于重件，如机车、水泥搅拌机、推土机等就需申请和使用负荷量更大的浮吊进行作业。

3　During the handling of the general cargo, a variety of slings will be made to cater for different kinds of general cargo.

在杂货的装卸过程中，需做各种各样的货关以适应不同种类杂货作业的要求。

Project 4　Cargo Handling

4　There are various tools for making slings, for example, rope slings, canvas slings, wire slings, chain slings, cargo tray and drum hooks. These slings are used for different cargoes: rope slings for bales, canvas slings for bags, wire slings for steels, trays for cases and cartons, and drum hooks for cargo in drums.

有多种工具用来做货关,譬如,络绳吊索、帆布吊包、钢丝吊索、链式吊索、货盘、桶钩等。这些货关用于不同货物的装卸:络绳吊索用于捆包货、帆布吊包用于袋装货、钢丝吊索用于钢材、货盘用于木箱或纸箱、桶钩用于桶装货。

Vocabulary

rude oil	原油
jar [dʒɑː]	n.缸,罐,瓶
preserved vegetable	榨菜;泡菜;冬菜
sulfate ['sʌlfeit]	n.硫酸;硫酸盐
pig iron	生铁
aluminum ingot	铝锭
lead ingot	铅锭
gantry crane	龙门吊;龙门起重机
mobile crane	移动式起重机
straddle carrier	跨运车
quayside ['kiːsaid]	n.码头沿岸
concrete mixer	混凝土搅拌机
excavator ['ekskəveitə]	n.挖掘机;挖土机
floating crane	浮吊
cater ['keitə]	vt.迎合
rope slings	络绳吊索
canvas slings	帆布吊包
wire slings	钢丝吊索
chain slings	链式吊索
cargo tray	货盘
drum hooks	桶钩

Exercises

1　Answer the following questions according to the text you have read.

(1) What kinds of general cargo can you list based on the text?

(2) What kinds of equipment are used in the handling of general cargo?

(3) Can you list the equipment and tools that are commonly used in the handling of general cargo according to your experience?

(4) What kinds of ship's gear are used in the handling of general cargo?

(5) How to make slings to cater for the varieties of general cargo?

2 Choose the best answer.

(1) Cotton belongs to _____.
  a) bale item   b) box item
  c) case item   d) case item

(2) Hardware is usually packed in _____.
  a) carton   b) case
  c) bale   d) drum

(3) Concrete mixer is handled with _____.
  a) forklift   b) ship's derrick
  c) floating crane   d) forklift

(4) Making slings is applied to handle _____.
  a) liquid bulk cargo   b) dry bulk cargo
  c) general cargo   d) container

(5) Canvas slings are usually adopted when dealing with _____.
  a) baled cargo   b) drummed cargo
  c) bagged cargo   d) naked cargo

3 Put into Chinese.

(1) The dockers usually choose their tools according to the cargo packing.

(2) The ship's jumbo has been out of order. We have to apply for a floating crane.

(3) We usually use cargo trays to make slings for the handling of general cargo.

(4) All the tools in the tool house are not useful for making slings.

(5) The dockers use trucks, tractors and trailers for transferring the cargo from warehouses to ship's side.

4 Put into English.

(1) 原油和化工产品很多是用桶来装的。

(2) 具有大负荷量的浮吊通常申请用来卸重件。

(3) 我们通常用木货盘做关来装卸杂货。

(4) 桶装货你们怎样做关?

Dialogue

Duty Officer: Hi, Foreman. Please note: Light cargo on top of the heavy lifts and big cases before small ones.

Foreman: That's a common practice. Yes, we are just doing like this.

Duty Officer: You know we've got 180 containers to load on wharf No.5, stow them as tightly as possible.

Foreman: I see. Yes, any thing else?

Project 4　Cargo Handling

Duty Officer: Well, I found some stevedores did it in wrong way. Cargo in Hold No.2 was improperly stowed. Please tell your man to restow it and chock them up again.

Foreman: Oh, really? I think I have to go and take a look.

Duty Officer: Some cases contain heavy and valuable machinery. Please handle with care.

Foreman: No problem. I'll give special care to that. Look Hatch No.2 is almost full. Shall we go on with Hatch No.1?

Duty Officer: We've got a good number of steel tubes for this voyage. As they are subject to shifting inside the hold, please stow them well and chock up both sides with rough boards.

Foreman: Alright. Well, only 2 sets of cargo left now. I think the loading will complete in one hour. You may then proceed to the special anchorage for dangerous cargo.

Duty Officer: What are the draft fore and aft now?

Foreman: The drafts are 7.4 meters forward and 7.2 aft. The ship is a little down by head.

Duty Officer: True. So it's time to put the reserved 150 tons of bagged cargo in Hold No.5.

Foreman: With these 150 tons in Hold No.5, the ship will be down by stern.

Duty Officer: Yes. And as you know, too, it's good sailing a little down by the stern.

Foreman: Shall I hoist red flag B while loading the cargo?

Duty Officer: Right you are. The barge is coming. Tell your men to get ready.

Foreman: OK. Duty Officer, we've got drummed inflammable cargo to load on the tweendeck of Hold No.3. Am I correct?

Duty Officer: That's right. The drums ought to be stowed on end with bungs on top.

Foreman: Please get the fire-fighting apparatus ready in case of fire. Nobody is allowed to smoke in the working area.

Duty Office: The fire-fighting apparatus is ready. Have your men got masks and gloves? You know the cargo is poisonous.

Foreman: I'll attend to it, I assure you.

Program 3　Handling of Dry Bulk Cargo

There are two kinds of bulk cargo, that is dry bulk cargo and liquid bulk cargo. We are discussing the handling of dry bulk cargo. Coal, ore, fertilizer and grain are the main dry bulk cargoes. There are various types of equipment used in handling the dry bulk cargo including wagon dumper, screw unloader, grab gantry crane, chain bucket unloader, shiploader, trimmer, hold cleaner, belt conveyor, claimer, reclaimer, claimer-reclaimer, etc.

The coal or ore can be discharged by wagon dumper or screw unloader if it is carried by wagons, or by grab gantry crane or chain bucket unloader if it is carried by ship. Then the cargo discharged is received and transmitted to the storage yard by belt conveyor and piled by claimer. The dumper can be classified into two types based on the form of operation: the single-wagon dumper and the series-wagon dumper, the discharging rate of the former can reach 6000-8000t/h. The screw unloader is the aided device to the dumper which is used in the place where the dumper is inaccessible for the limited space or other limitations. The grab gantry crane is widely used in discharging of coal or ore which has a lifting capacity of 30-50t and with a discharging rate of 3000t/h. The chain bucket unloader is a continuous-discharging device which is of high working efficiency with less shifting and less swaying of arm, and due to its advantage of environment protection it is more preferred by modern ports. It has a discharging capacity of more than 3000t/h. Bulldozer—called hold cleaner is used after or during discharging which cleans up the leftover in the hold, and strengthens the discharging capacity of grab crane.

When loading, the ore or coal is fetched from pile-yard by reclaimer and transmitted by belt conveyor to a shiploader or train loader by which the ship or train is loaded. Grab gantry crane is less used today for directly loading.

Notes

1　There are various types of equipment used in handling the dry bulk cargo including wagon dumper, screw unloader, grab gantry crane, shiploader, chain bucket unloader, trimmer, hold cleaner, belt conveyor, claimer, reclaimer, claimer-reclaimer, etc.

用于装卸干散货的设备有多种多样包括：翻车机、螺旋卸车机、抓斗门机、装船机、链斗卸船机、平舱机、清舱机、皮带机、堆料机、取料机、堆-取料机等。

2　The dumper can be classified into two types based on the form of operation: the single-wagon dumper and the series-wagon dumper, the discharging rate of the former can reach 6000—8000t/h.

翻车机可根据其作业方式分为单车翻车机和多车翻车机，前者卸车效率可达每小时6000吨至8000吨。

3　The screw unloader is the aided device to the dumper which is used in the place where the dumper is inaccessible for the limited space or other limitations.

螺旋卸车机辅助翻车机作业。用于翻车机因空间限制或其他条件限制而难以发挥作用的条件下。

4　The chain bucket unloader is a continuous-discharging device which is of high working efficiency with less shifting and less swaying of arm, and due to its advantage of environment protection, is more preferred by modern ports.

链斗式卸船机是一种连续卸船装置。由于不需频繁的移动和摆臂因而工作效率高，并由于具有防环境污染的优势，更多的被现代化港口采用。

5　Bulldozer—called hold cleaner is used after or during discharging which cleans up the leftover in the hold, and strengthens the discharging capacity of grab crane.

被称作清舱机的推扒机，在卸船过程中或结束后用于清理货舱中的余留货物。有利于提高抓斗门吊的工作效率。

Project 4 Cargo Handling

Vocabulary

dry bulk cargo	干散货
ore[ɔː(r)]	n.矿石;矿砂
wagon dumper	翻车机
screw unloader	螺旋卸车机
grab[græb]	n.抓斗
grab gantry crane	抓斗门机
shiploader	装船机
chain bucket unloader	链斗卸船机
trimmer['trimə]	n.平舱机
hold cleaner	清舱机
belt conveyor	皮带机
claimer ['kleimə]	n.堆料机
reclaimer [ri'kleimə]	n.取料机
claimer-reclaimer	堆-取料机
single-wagon dumper	单车翻车机
series-wagon dumper	多车翻车机
inaccessible [ˌinæk'sesəbl]	adj.达不到的;不能进入的
bulldozer ['buldəuzə]	n.清舱机
pile-yard	堆场

Exercises

1 Answer the following questions according to the text you have read.

(1) What is the dry bulk cargo based on the text?
(2) What kinds of equipment are used in the handling dry bulk cargo?
(3) How to discharge coal or ore according to the text?
(4) What is the dumper, and its working rate?
(5) What is the chain bucket unloader?

2 Fill out the blanks with suitable words or terms based on the text.

(1) Dry bulk cargo and _____ bulk cargo are two kinds of _____.
(2) If coal or ore is carried by wagons, it can be discharged by _____.
(3) If the coal is carried by ship it can be discharged by _____ or _____.
(4) The cargo discharged is received and transmitted to the storage yard by _____ and piled by _____.
(5) The discharging rate of the _____ can reach 6000-8000t/h.
(6) The _____ is the aided device to the dumper which is used in the place where the

dumper is inaccessible for the limited space or other limitations.

（7）The _____ is a continuous-discharging device which is of high working efficiency.

（8）_____ is used after or during discharging which cleans up the leftover in the hold.

3　Put into Chinese.

（1）Usually, the dry bulk cargo will be trimmed after the completion of discharging.

（2）Shiploader coupled with belt conveyor is used to load ore from pile ground into a ship.

（3）Wagon dumpers are of high working efficiency when discharging coal in a train.

（4）The grab gantry crane is widely used in discharging of coal or ore which has a lifting capacity of 30-50t and with a discharging rate of 3000t/h.

（5）Bulldozer being put into ship holds by quay crane is used to clean up the leftover during or after discharging.

4　Put into English.

（1）根据干散货的装载工具,可选用相应的装卸设备来卸。

（2）皮带机可用于多种干散货的转运。

（3）堆取料机是一种方便的机械,既可用于干散货的装,也可用于卸的过程。

（4）链斗卸船机具有较高的卸船效率,同时又有环保效果。

（5）抓斗门机的起吊能力可达30~50吨,经常用于矿石的装卸。

Dialogue

Foreman：Chief, what kind of cargo will you discharge?

Chief Office：General cargo, including some heavy lifts. Can you manage to work five hatches simultaneously?

Foreman：No problem. What cargo will be discharged first?

Chief Office：The cases under B/Ls No.1-No.5 will be discharged first.

Foreman：How many cases can we load for each sling?

Chief Office：No more than 20 cases. Please tell the tallyman to count sling by sling.

Foreman：All right,

Chief Office：To avoid any possible list, Please pay attention to the discharging rate at both sides.

Foreman：I'll keep an eye on that matter. What shall I do if trim happens during discharging?

Chief Office：You may ask the Carpenter to pump in or out the ballast water to adjust it in time.

Foreman：I see.

Chief Office：Foreman, look at the stevedores over there. They are dragging bags with hooks!

Foreman：I am sorry for that.

Chief Office：You'll be held responsible for cargo damage if they go on using hooks.

Foreman：Sure. I'll go and ask them not use them any more, but can you please have the derrick readjusted? You see it is not in position.

Chief Office: I'll arrange for the bosun to readjust the derrick immediately.

Bosun: What can I do for you, Foreman?

Foreman: The derrick is too high. Will you please lower it for me?

Bosun: Of course. Do you want me to lower it handsomely or cheerily?

Foreman: A little handsomely, please. Just plumb the set of cargo and pick it up from the hold. The set will go to the wharf side.

Bosun: OK. Is it all right to swing the starboard boom a little outboard?

Foreman: Yes, be slow and steady in landing the load. Please top the port boom inboard to plumb the next set of cargo, over the hatchway.

Bosun: Yes. We'll adjust it at once. Don't stand under the sling of cargo. It is dangerous. The sling might hit you when it comes down.

Program 4 Handling of Dangerous Cargo

Cargoes which are of an explosive, inflammable, poisonous and corrosive nature are called dangerous goods. In order to avoid any accident, special attention should be paid to the handling of them. So far as explosives are concerned, they must not be loaded until all other cargo has been placed on board. Generally, the port authorities prevent the handling of explosives at piers near a port's concentration of facilities. The ship will usually proceed to an anchorage and pick up the explosive shipment from a barge. The space for stowing the shipment must be left accessible.

At intermediate ports of call during the voyage, explosives must not be worked at the same time as other cargo. They should be discharged first at the port of destination.

Inflammable liquids, when stowed on deck, must all be on one side of the ship's centerline. The 25-foot clearance from lifeboat stations and entrances to quarters is also required. Inflammable liquids must not be stowed closer than 20 feet to bulkheads that are heated, such as the boiler room or galley bulkhead. This requirement does not prevail if the heated bulkhead is efficiently insulated.

Poisonous cargoes, when packed in fiberboard boxes, should be stowed under deck, or, if they are stowed on deck, must be so protected that at no time are they exposed to the weather or to the sea-water. In order to avoid contamination, all cargoes of this nature must be stowed separated from or away from foodstuffs. After discharge, spaces used for the carriage of poisonous cargoes must be inspected for contamination. A space which has been contaminated must be properly cleaned and examined before used for other cargoes, especially foodstuff.

Stowage of containers of corrosive liquids must in such a manner that the cargo can be observed easily. When corrosive liquids are stowed on deck, any leakage must be able to drain into a scupper leading directly over the side. Glass carboys of such liquids must not be stowed more than two tiers high.

Segregation required for corrosive cargo should be obvious. It must not be stowed in the same

compartment with explosives, and it should be well separated from foodstuffs and cargo being of an organic nature.

Notes

1 So far as explosives are concerned, they must not be loaded until all other cargo has been placed on board. Generally, the port authorities prevent the handling of explosives at piers near a port's concentration of facilities. The ship will usually proceed to an anchorage and pick up the explosive shipment from a barge. The space for stowing the shipment must be left accessible.

对于易爆货物,只有在其他货物装船完毕后才能装船。通常,港口当局不允许在港口设施集中的码头上进行易爆货物的作业。船舶通常行驶到锚地,从驳船上将货物装上船。堆装易爆货物的场地必须留有通道。

2 The 25-foot clearance from lifeboat stations and entrances to quarters is also required. Inflammable liquids must not be stowed closer than 20 feet to bulkheads that are heated, such as the boiler room or galley bulkhead. This requirement does not prevail if the heated bulkhead is efficiently insulated.

易燃物品的堆放须与救生船放置点和船员舱入口处保持25英尺距离空间。易燃液体的堆放必须与受热舱壁相隔不小于20英尺,例如锅炉房或厨房舱壁。但是,若舱壁绝缘良好,上述要求可不考虑。

3 Poisonous cargoes, when packed in fiberboard boxes, should be stowed under deck, or, if they are stowed on deck, must be so protected that at no time are they exposed to the weather or to the sea-water.

用纤维板箱包装的毒性货物,应当装在甲板下,若装在甲板上,必须保护好使之任何时候都不暴露于空气中或海水。

4 Stowage of containers of corrosive liquids must in such a manner that the cargo can be observed easily. When corrosive liquids are stowed on deck, any leakage must be able to drain into a scupper leading directly over the side.

腐蚀性液体容器的装载应当易于观察。当腐蚀性液体货装在甲板上时若发生泄漏,保证能通过排水孔直接排出船外。

Vocabulary

explosive [iks'pləusiv]	adj.易爆炸的,有爆炸性的
inflammable [in'flæməbl]	adj.易燃的
poisonous ['pɔiznəs]	adj.有毒的
corrosive [kə'rəusiv]	adj.腐蚀(性)的,侵蚀性的
concentration [ˌkɔnsen'treiʃne]	n.集中
accessible [ək'sesəbl]	adj.易接近的,可进入的
intermediate [ˌintə'mi:djət]	adj.中间的

Project 4　Cargo Handling

centerline ['sentəlain]	n.中心线
clearance ['kliərəns]	n.间隙,距离
proceed [prə'si:d]	v.前进;行进
anchorage ['æŋkəridʒ]	n.锚地
barge [bɑ:dʒ]	n.驳船
prevail [pri'veil]	v.流行,盛行
insulate ['insjuleit]	vt.隔离;使孤立
contamination [kən,tæmi'neiʃən]	n.污染;污物
inspect [in'spekt]	vt.检查,检阅,检验
glass carboy	玻璃酸瓶

Exercises

1　Answer the following questions according to the text you have read.

(1) What are the dangerous cargoes?
(2) How to deal with the explosive cargo?
(3) What must be done when handling the inflammable cargo?
(4) How to handle the poisoning cargo?
(5) What measures should be taken when dealing with the corrosive cargo?

2　Make judgment based on the text.

(1) We call the goods which are of an explosive, inflammable, poisonous and corrosive nature dangerous goods.

(2) Explosive goods should be loaded after all other cargo has been placed on board.

(3) The explosives should be discharged last at the port of destination.

(4) Inflammable liquids must not be stowed closer than 15 feet to bulkheads that are heated, such as the boiler room or galley bulkhead.

(5) Poisonous cargoes must be kept away from the foodstuff.

(6) Inflammable liquids must not be stowed in the same compartment with the explosives at any condition.

(7) Glass carboys of corrosive liquids must not be stowed more than three tiers high.

(8) Corrosive cargo must not be stowed in the same compartment with explosives.

3　Put into Chinese.

(1) When dealing with dangerous goods, safety measures must be carried out.

(2) Stevedores working with dangerous goods are discussing the protective steps for the process of handling.

(3) We should well aware the care marks before handling these kinds of goods.

(4) Smoking is prohibited on board during the handling of dangerous goods.

(5) Chief Officer should be held responsible for the security of both the ship and the cargo on board.

4 Put into English.

(1)在卸危险货物时,一定要采取保护性措施。

(2)在危险性货物上面不要堆放其他货物。

(3)请把这个货舱清洗一下,我们要在里面装食品。

(4)请把这些货物移开,不要挡住排水孔。

(5)这票货物已经检查过了,请把它们放在这边。

Dialogue

A: We're going to discharge dangerous goods this morning. I found many drums on he aft deck. Are they for this port?

B: Yes. Don't forget to discharge them ashore.

A: But the drums are very rusty and the marks are rather indistinct. Will you trace them from your boat notes?

B: As I remember, these drums are belong to B/L No.3. they are packed with gasoline, a kind of inflammable cargo, you know.

A: Yes. We have to be careful with them. Chief, besides the gasoline, where are the other dangerous goods?

B: Oh, we have plenty of them on board, for example, the bromine on the fore deck, which is of corrosive nature; the acetylene in Hatch No.1 tweendeck, an inflammable cargo, and the DDT technical powder in Hatch No.2, a strong poisonous cargo. Please tell your stevedores to handle them carefully.

A: Don't worry about that. They'll certainly take safety measures to discharge the dangerous cargo.

B: That's fine. Well, when will you discharge the gasoline and acetylene?

A: We'll discharge them direct into trucks sometime tomorrow afternoon.

B: Can you start earlier?

A: No, we have to wait the trucks.

B: Then why not pile them up in the godown or on the wharf yards for the time being?

A: You know they are easy to catch fire. According to the Port Regulations, it's absolutely forbidden to keep them in the deck.

B: I see. By the way, please tell your stevedores not to smoke during discharging.

A: They know smoking is prohibited when discharging dangerous goods.

B: Good.

Project 5 Cargo-tallying Service

Project Description

The ship tally is indispensible if claims are to be avoided, both when loading and unloading. It is started with mark-sorting based on Shipping Order or Import Manifest; and in the process, it is imperative to deal with problems arisen such as mixed-up of cargo, short-landed or over-landed, cargo damaged and sweepings, etc. when conducting the tallying. And proper counting measure adopted according to the features of cargo being tallied and practical conditions is essential for correctness, time-cost saving and money-cost saving.

Knowledge Objective

1 How to realize the fairness and equality in tallying work.
2 The general range and the process of tallying work.
3 The application of tallying papers and the roles being played.
4 The role of mark-assorting.
5 The measures taken to prevent cargo from being mixed up.
6 The main ways of counting for different kinds of cargo.
7 The measures dealing with the over-landed and short-landed cargo.
8 How to handle the damaged cargo and sweepings in tallying work.

Ability Objective

1 Have the ability to handle properly the problems in tallying with principle of fairness and equality.
2 Being capable of filling out and applying correctly the tallying papers.
3 Assuring of dealing with troubles during tallying such as mark-assorting, cargo being mixed up, damaged cargo, over and / or short-landed cargo and sweepings.
4 Have the ability to apply properly the methods of counting based on the features of cargo and practical conditions.

Task

Assumed that a kind of bagged cargo is discharging ashore:
1 Apply the principles of tallying to deal with disputes, if any.

2　Choose and apply correct tallying papers catering to this kind of cargo in the process of tallying.

3　Handle properly problems arisen during the process of discharging such as cargo mixed up, cargo damaged, cargo over or/and short-landed, etc.

4　Choose correct counting method suitable to this kind of cargo.

Program 1　Ocean Shipping Tally

One of the most important parts in the business of foreign trade and ocean shipping is tallying. It plays its role between the shipper and carrier to justify the figure and condition of the cargo handled.

The fairness and equality are the inherent nature of tallying which must be observed to guarantee the interests of parties concerned. The observation of fairness and equality is realized by:

(1) Seek truth from facts. Tallying is done independently with no consideration and concession of any unjustifiedrequirement or hint or restrain from any party involved. The result of tallying is drawn only from practical condition of cargo tallied based on facts.

(2) Cargo delivery by ship's rail. Delivery of Cargo must be made by shipside. The risk and responsibility to the cargo concerned between the dcliverer and receiver begin or end by ship's rail.

(3) Clean tally papers. In accordance with the international shipping practice, the carrier must sign relevant documents when the cargo has been loaded on board or unloaded onto ashore. Once the result of tallying is acknowledged and signed by the entrusting party no amendment is allowed to change at will.

Nowadays, the tallying work is done by the tallying agency entrusted, and the services that the tallying agency renders may often range from counting to the inspection of the damage or loss of cargo, instruction of the cargo stowage, mark-sorting, preparation of shipping documents, etc. Moreover, the tallying agency not only renders services for the entrusting party but also acts as a witness of the third party confirming the order and condition of cargo handled.

The scope of tallying business varies. Package-cargo tallying, container tallying, barge carrier tallying and bulk-cargo vessel tallying are involved with the respect of types of cargo and vessels.

Notes

1　The fairness and equality are the inherent nature of tallying which must be observed to guarantee the interests of parties concerned.

公平公正是理货工作的本质要求，在理货工作中必须予以保证，以维护当事方的利益。

2　Tallying is done independently with no consideration and concession of any unjustified re-

Project 5　Cargo-tallying Service

quirement or hint or restrain from any party involved.The result of tallying is drawn only from practical condition of cargo tallied based on facts.

理货工作要采取独立自主的原则,要求理货人员在理货工作中必须做到不受任何一方的约束、授意和暗示,不迁就任何一方的不合理要求。以货物的事实为依据,事实求是地完成理货。

3　Delivery of Cargo must be made by shipside.The risk and responsibility to the cargo concerned between the deliverer and receiver begin or end by ship's rail.

货物的交付必须在船边进行。交接双方对货物的风险和责任始、止于船舷。

4　In accordance with the international shipping practice,the carrier must sign relevant documents when the cargo has been loaded on board or unloaded onto ashore.Once the result of tallying is acknowledged and signed by the entrusting party no amendment is allowed to change at will.

按照国际航运惯例,当货物装船或卸船完毕承运人应当签署相关的单证。一旦理货结果为委托方所认可且签字就不得随意修改。

5　Moreover,the tallying agency not only renders services for the entrusting party but also acts as a witness of the third party confirming the order and condition of cargo handled.

并且,理货代理不仅要为委托方提供服务,而且要作为第三方证人证明所理货物状况是否良好。

Vocabulary

shipper ['ʃipə]　　　　　　　　　　n.托运人;货主
carrier ['kæriə]　　　　　　　　　　n.承运人
justify ['dʒʌstifai]　　　　　　　　vt.证明
guarantee [ˌgærən'tiː]　　　　　　vt.保证,担保
independently [ˌindi'pendəntli]　　adv.独立地
concession [kən'seʃən]　　　　　　n.让与;让步
relevant ['relivənt]　　　　　　　　adj.有关的
entrust [in'trʌst]　　　　　　　　　vt.信任,委托
render ['rendə]　　　　　　　　　　vt.提供
witness ['witnis]　　　　　　　　　n.目击者;证人
scope [skəup]　　　　　　　　　　n.范围

Exercises

1　Answer the following questions according to the text you have read.
(1)What principles should be observed for tallying work?
(2)How to carry out the principles?
(3)How to judge the risk and responsibility to the cargo?
(4)Which party is responsible for singing the tallying papers?

(5) What are the roles played by tallying agency?

2 Fill out the blanks with suitable words or terms based on the text.

(1) Tallying plays its role between the _____ and _____ to justify the figure and condition of the cargo handled.

(2) The fairness and _____ are the inherent nature of tallying which must be observed to guarantee the interests of _____.

(3) The risk and responsibility to the cargo concerned between the deliverer and receiver begin or end by _____.

(4) The result of tallying is drawn only from _____ of cargo tallied _____.

(5) The _____ must sign relevant documents when the cargo has been loaded on board or unloaded onto ashore.

(6) Once the result of tallying is acknowledged and signed by the entrusting party _____ is allowed to change at will.

(7) The tallying work and services are usually done by the _____ entrusted.

(8) The tallying agency acts as a _____ confirming the order and condition of cargo handled.

3 Put into Chinese.

As cargo in modern harbor is moved from one point to another—from warehouse or shed…to ships,…etc.—command of their governance moves simultaneously.

And the job of making clear the position of responsibility in connection with cargo movement—number of items moved, item type, the proper affixing of marks, inspection to determine whether damage to cargo has occurred during movement, the making up of documents associated with delivery, etc.—is called tallying.

4 Put into English.

(1) 公平公正是理货工作的一项基本原则。

(2) 我们应当努力维护各当事方的利益。

(3) 请把你们的运输单证准备好，我们要核对一下。

(4) 对不起，我们只能按实事求是的原则处理这票货。

(5) 请问你们船长在哪，我们需要他在这单证上签字。

Dialogue

A: Hello, Agent, how are you?

B: Very well, thank you. Anything I can do for you?

A: The chief tally came to me this morning informing me that he would put some remarks on some import cargo tally report.

B: Really? Why?

A: He told me that one wooden case for B/L No.P-009 was found damaged when discharged from the ship. Some of the wooden planks on the left side are broken for some reason, so he intended to make some remark on the damage report and ask me to sign it.

B:I see.Is the damage slight or serious?

A:Not serious,I think.

B:Did you agree with him about this?

A:No,because I didn't think it a serious problem,we could ignore it.

B:And what is the opinion of the chief tally at that time?

A:He said that it was a fact,and he insisted on putting some remark on the damage report.

B:That sound logical and correct.Where is the wooden case now?

A:It's still on the deck at starboard side.

B:Can I have look at it?

A:Yes,let's go now.Here it is.

B:Where is the damage then?

A:Oh,on this side.

B:Yes,it is true,some planks are broken.Do you know how this happened,Chief?

A:To tell you the truth,I don't know exactly.

B:But as the chief officer in charge of that cargo handling,you must be well aware of the cargo situation at the loading port.

A:Yes,that's correct,but I really have no idea of the reason for the damage.What's more ,it is not serious,so I don't think it necessary for the tallyman to make some remark about it.

B:I agree with you,Chief,it isn't serious.However,to stand on his side,it's his duty to count the cargo and check its quality.If anything abnormal occurs,the tallyman will of course come to you to discuss the matter.In addition,the import cargo discharged from your ship is usually transferred to an open yard or a warehouse before being delivered to the consignee.If there isn't a remark about the damaged cargo signed by you the port side would have some difficulty delivering the cargo to the consignee.Have you thought of this possibility,chief?

A:Well,agent,frankly speaking,I hadn't considered this.I was only considering it from my own point of view.

B:So if you don't sign it,the chief tally would be in a difficult position when the damaged cargo is conveyed to the warehouse.The warehouse may not even accept it from the ship because the damage occurred before discharging.

A:I see.I'll go to the chief tally right away to sign the damage report.

Program 2　Papers of Tally

　　The papers of tallying are the primitive records which state the actual figure and conditions of the cargo carried that is being delivered at the port.The tallying- paper is drawn by the tallymen who directly operate or witness the whole process of the shiftiness of cargo at the delivery point be-

tween ship and port, and are acknowledged and signed by the parties concerned, which hence play a role as the proof with lawful effect.

The application of the tallying-paper spreads broadly. In the movement process of cargo it involves warehousing, loading/unloading, shipping, supervising, settlement of exchange bill, insurance, claims, etc. With respect of interested parties of cargo it is related to consignor, port, vessel, Customs Office, bank, insurance company, consignee, etc.

The role of the tallying-paper playing mainly involves: the proof of figure or condition of cargo to be delivered and received between the carrier and shipper or the holder of B/L; the evidence and reference catering for the case of claims or maritime peril; the basis for port operation in cargo handling, and for consignee to take delivery of goods; the evidence that whether or not the shipment contract has been put into effect by buyer or seller.

The subjects that the tallying-paper is required to submit to differ based on the papers' functions and the business nature of the parties concerned. Tally sheet, On-the-spot Record, Stand-by Time Record, Daily Report, Tally Certificate, Stowage Plan, Cargo Hatch List are required to submit to the Ship; Over-landed and Short-landed Cargo List, Damaged Cargo List are given to the Ship, port, consignee, and sent to ship-owner by agent. The agent, on behalf of the interest of the ship-owner, to whom the Tally Certificate, Over-landed and Short-landed Cargo List and Damaged Cargo List are to be provided.

Notes

1 The papers of tallying are the primitive records which state the actual figure and conditions of the cargo carried that is being delivered at the port. The tallying- paper is drawn by the tallymen who directly operate or witness the whole process of the shiftiness of cargo at the delivery point between ship and port, and are acknowledged and signed by the parties concerned, which hence play a role as the proof with lawful effect.

理货单证是反映船舶载运货物在港口交接当时的数量和状态的实际情况的原始记录。理货单证是由直接参与或亲自目睹货物在船、港交接处的理货人员编制的,且取得当事方承认的,因而具有法律证明效力。

2 The application of the tallying- paper spreads broadly. In the movement process of cargo it involves warehousing, loading/unloading, shipping, supervising, settlement of exchange bill, insurance, claims, etc. With respect of interested parties of cargo it is related to consignor, port, vessel, Customs Office, bank, insurance company, consignee, etc.

理货单证的应用范围非常广泛,在货物的流通过程中,涉及仓储、装卸、监管、结汇、保险、索赔;涉及货物的各个关系人,包括发货人、港口、船舶、海关、银行、保险、收货人等。

3 The role of the tallying-paper playing mainly involves: The proof of figure or condition of cargo to be delivered and received between the carrier and shipper or the holder of B/L; the evidence and reference catering for the case of claims or maritime peril; the basis for port operation in cargo handling, and for consignee to take delivery of goods; the evidence that whether or not the

shipment contract has been put into effect by buyer or seller.

理货单证的作用主要包括:作为货物在承运人与托运人或提单持有人之间交接数字和状况的证明;在处理索赔或海事案件中作为证据和参考;是港口货物作业和收货人接收货物的依据;是买卖双方是否履行业务合同的证明。

4 The subjects that the tallying-paper is required to submit to differ based on the papers' functions and the business nature of the parties concerned. Tally sheet, On-the-spot Record, Stand-by Time Record, Daily Report, Tally Certificate, Stowage Plan, Cargo Hatch List are required to submit to the Ship; Over-landed and Shortlande Cargo List, Damaged Cargo List are given to the Ship, port, consignee, and to ship-owner by agent. The agent, on behalf of the interest of the ship-owner, to whom the Tally Certificate, Over-landed and Short-landed Cargo List and Damaged Cargo List are to be provided.

接受理货单证提供的对象,依据单证的功用和相关方的业务性质不同而不同。理货单、现场记录单、待时记录、日报表、理货证明书、积载图、舱单等须提供给船方;货物溢短单、货物残损单需分别提供给船方、港方和收货人并由代理送交船东;需向船东的代理人提供理货证明书、货物溢短单和货物残损单。

Vocabulary

primitive ['primitiv]	adj.原始的
hence [hens]	adv.因此,所以
lawful ['lɔːfəl]	adj.合法的,法定的
application [ˌæpliˈkeiʃən]	n.使用,运用,应用
settlement ['setlmənt]	n.解决;支付,结帐
consignor [kənˈsainə]	n.发货人,寄件人
consignee [kɔnsaiˈniː]	n.收货人
submit [səbˈmit]	vt.提交
Tally sheet	理货单
On-the-spot Record	现场记录
Stand-by Time Record	待时记录
Daily Report	日报表
Tally Certificate	理货证明书
Cargo Hatch List	舱单
Over-landed and Short-lande Cargo List	货物溢短单
Damaged Cargo List	货物残损单

Exercises

1 Answer the following questions according to the text you have read.

(1) What are the papers of tallying?

(2) What application do the papers carry out?

(3) What is the role of the tallying-paper?

(4) What are the interested parties of cargo?

(5) What are the kinds of tallying-paper?

2　Fill out the blanks with suitable words or terms based on the text.

(1) The papers of tallying are the _____ which state the _____ and conditions of the cargo carried that is being delivered at the port.

(2) The tallying- paper is drawn by the _____.

(3) The papers of tallying play a role as the _____ with lawful effect of the cargo's order and condition.

(4) The papers of tallying must be acknowledged and signed by _____.

(5) With respect of interested parties of cargo it is related to _____, port, vessel, Customs Office, bank, _____, consignee, etc.

(6) The agent, on behalf of the interest of _____, to whom the Tally Certificate, Over-landed and Short-lande Cargo List and Damaged Cargo List are to be provided.

(7) The tallying-paper is an evidence and reference catering for the _____ or maritime peril.

3　Put into Chinese.

(1) Having finished discharging, the Chief Tallying made out the Damaged Cargo List for the Chief Officer to sign.

(2) Meeting with a typhoon, the ship rolled and pitched so heavily during the voyage and damage to cargo might happen.

(3) The Chief Officer asked the Chief Tally to sign the On-the-Spot for the mixed-up stowage of the cotton piece goods.

(4) We can't agree to cut down the short-landed figure by half. If you don't believe our tallied figure, you can apply for retally.

(5) Tallying charges shall be additionally collected on difficult conditions according to the descriptions of the cargoes tallied.

4　Put into English.

(1) 我可以向你证明装货港的理货数字是不可靠的。

(2) 你不要把事情看得太严重了，溢多或短缺货物在理货上是常有的事。

(3) 如果重理数字与原来的数字不符合，重理费用由我们理货公司承担。

(4) 货物装卸时，理货员应及时与值班船员联系解决各舱口产生的问题。

(5) 理货工作已完成，请在这份理货证明书上签字。

Dialogue

A: Chief, here are some tally papers for you to sign. This is the Over-landed and Short-landed Cargo List.

B: What's result?

A: 2 cases of auto parts are over-landed and 50 pieces of copper bars short-landed.

B: The overage is O.K. But 50 pieces of copper bars short. That's impossible.

A: The shortage is based on fact. You can't refuse to sign.

B: If you reduce it by 50%, that's to say, deduct 25 pieces from the total, I'll sign.

A: I'm sorry there's no bargain. As tallymen, we always respect the facts and do business on principle.

B: We know that you are practical and act on principle. However, the shortage is too much. I have to put remarks, anyhow.

A: What remarks?

B: Under such circumstances I usually put remarks "In dispute".

A: What do you mean by it?

B: Now you see, there are 2 different figures, one from you and the other from the loading port. Which one is correct is unknown. We're not in agreement on that point. So the shortage of the cargo is in dispute. That's it.

Program 3 Tallying Cargo

Tallying cargo means "to check" or "to keep a record" of all cargo loaded into or discharge from a vessel. It is an essential part of cargo work in order to prevent claims, sometimes illegitimate, upon the ship for short discharge. As is often the case, there are many channels through which consignments have to pass before eventually reach the ship for loading or eventually reach the consignee after discharging.

The tallying of the cargo should be made in a alphabetically indexed books, one for each hatch and each port of discharge, and should consist of records for all marks and numbers of the goods, description, quantity, and disposition of stowage within a compartment.

As a ship's responsibility does not begin or end until the cargo crosses the rail, tallying should be made on board the vessel and not, as often happens, ashore in the warehouses or on the wharf.

It is customary for the shipper and/or the consignee to provide their own tally clerks, whereas it is practice for the warehouse authorities to provide their own clerks when handling general cargo. Whatever the system may be, comparison should always be made at the end of the day between the ship tally and shore tally, and any difference immediately investigated. It may even be necessary to retally a consignment if the discrepancy is large. And inspection should be carried out to determine whether any damage to cargo has occurred during movement, and documents associated with delivery, etc. are to be made out.

While tallying a general cargo, it is suggested that greater efficiency will be obtained by tall-

ying in the compartment where the sling is "broken open". By so doing, it is comparatively easy to obtain all marks and numbers to supervise and note the disposition of stowage. The latter point is helpful when compiling the cargo plan. In tallying a bale or bagged cargo, the slings should contain the same number of bales of bags, which is so called "making slings in fixed form and fixed quantity", in order that each sling may be checked easily as it crosses the rail.

Notes

1 As is often the case, there are many channels through which consignments have to pass before eventually reach the ship for loading or eventually reach the consignee after discharging.

通常的情况是,货物在最终运至船边装船之前或卸船后最终到达收货人手中之前,需要经过多个环节。

2 The tallying of the cargo should be made in a alphabetically indexed books, one for each hatch and each port of discharge, and should consist of records for all marks and numbers of the goods, description, quantity, and disposition of stowage within a compartment. inspection to determine whether damage to cargo has occurred during movement, the making up of documents associated with delivery, etc.

货物的计数(理货)应当在按字母顺序编排的本子上进行,每一个舱口和每一个卸货港一本,理货还应当包括货物的标志、号码、货名、数量和舱内堆放位置的记录。

3 Whatever the system may be, comparison should always be made at the end of the day between the ship tally and shore tally and any difference immediately investigated. It may even be necessary to retally a consignment if the discrepancy is large.

无论采取什么样的理货方式,一天的理货工作结束后,船上的理货结果和岸上的理货结果都应当进行比较,如有差异应立即进行调查。若差异过大,可能有必要进行重新理货。

4 While tallying a general cargo, it is suggested that greater efficiency will be obtained by tallying in the compartment where the sling is "broken open". By so doing, it is comparatively easy to obtain all marks and numbers to supervise and note the disposition of stowage.

当计理杂货时,在货舱中进行效率会更高,这是由于在货舱中"货关"打开的缘故,而且能比较容易地记录货物标志和号码,监督和记录货物的积载位置。

5 In tallying a bale or bagged cargo, the slings should contain the same number of bales of bags, which is so called "making slings in fixed form and fixed quantity", in order that each sling may be checked easily as it crosses the rail.

在对捆包货或袋装货进行计数时,每一货关中应当有相同数量的捆包或袋子,这种做关方式被称作"定型定量做关",这样,当每一货关越过船舷时容易进行核实。

Vocabulary

illegitimate [ˌiliˈdʒitimit]   adj. 非法的,违法的
eventually [iˈventjuəli]   adv. 最终,最后

Project 5 Cargo-tallying Service

alphabetically [ˌælfəˈbetɪk(ə)li]	adv.按字母顺序地
index [ˈɪndeks]	n.索引，目录
consist of	由……组成
ashore [əˈʃɔː]	adv.在岸上，在陆上
customary [ˈkʌstəməri]	adj.通常的，习惯的，惯例的
tally clerk	理货员
comparison [kəmˈpærɪsn]	n.比较，对照
investigate [ɪnˈvestɪɡeɪt]	vt.研究；调查
discrepancy [dɪsˈkrepənsi]	n.差异，不一致
determine [dɪˈtɜːmɪn]	vt.决定，决心
occur [əˈkɜː]	v.(事件等)发生
obtain [əbˈteɪn]	vt.获得，得到
compile [kəmˈpaɪl]	vt.汇集，编辑，编制

Exercises

1 Answer the following questions according to the text you have read.
(1) What is the tallying cargo?
(2) Where should be the tallying made?
(3) When is the retallying necessarily made?
(4) Where is the right place in which tallying is made more effectively?
(5) What records should be included in tallying?

2 Fill out the blanks with suitable words or terms based on the text.
(1) Tallying is an essential part of cargo work in order to prevent _____, sometimes _____, upon the ship for short discharge.
(2) The tallying of the cargo should be made in a alphabetically indexed books, one for _____ and _____ of discharge.
(3) A ship's responsibility does not begin or end until the cargo crosses the _____.
(4) Whatever the tallying system may be, comparison should always be made at the end of the day between the _____ and _____.
(5) It may even be necessary to _____ a consignment if the discrepancy between the ship tally and shore tally is large.
(6) While tallying a general cargo, it is suggested that greater efficiency will be obtained by tallying in the _____.

3 Put into Chinese.
(1) These cases have been examined and recognized original damage. It was you that signed the Record on the Spot.
(2) Don't mix stevedores' damage with original. Otherwise I won't sign the Damaged Cargo List.

(3) The Chief Officer is afraid that both the figure of the loading port and that of the discharging port are not correct.

(4) The cargo is tallied by three sides at the discharging port, that is, the tallyman, the lighterman and the warehouse keeper.

(5) In tallying, the term "In dispute" generally refers to the disagreement between the Ship and the Port about the tally figure.

4　Put into English.

(1)大副在"货物残损报告"上作了批注,大意是甲板货物由发货人承担风险。

(2)货物运到目的地后,理货人员会在卸船前记下所有货物批注情况。

(3)你们的数字与装卸港的数字不一致,请再核对一下。

(4)对我来说,你"根据提单"的批注是不能接受的,因为我们的理货数字是以实卸数为依据的。

(5)请将这个数字与装货单上的数字核对一下,看一看问题出现在哪里。

Dialogue

A: Do you have any special requirements for tallying?

B: Nothing particular. Please tell your tallymen to pay more attention to the packing, otherwise, it'll cause much trouble on delivery.

A: Yes, but all of our export cargo is thoroughly examined before shipment. If not up to the standard, the cargo is not allowed to export.

B: That's fine. Nevertheless, I'm still afraid your stevedores might damage the cargo during the process of loading.

A: Please don't worry. I'll tell the stevedores to handle it carefully. In case they damage any cargo we'll have it changed or repaired. Furthermore, we'll pick out the damaged cargo in holds or in the slings, if there is any.

B: That's fine. Another thing, the exact quantity of the whole shipment should be guaranteed.

A: Undoubtedly, the cargo is not allowed to ship on board without passing 4 parties, namely, the shipper, the customs officer, the warehouse keeper, and the tallyman. So the quantity of cargo is definitely correct.

B: I trust you.

A: By the way, when do you think it convenient to hand in the Mate's Receipts for your signature?

B: How about signing them after loading?

A: That won't do. The Shippers want each Mate's Receipt to be signed right after the cargo concerned is loaded. I suggest signing them in bathes.

B: That'll do. By the way, will you let me know something about your tallying method?

A: Sure. We usually arrange one tallyman for each gang. His duty is to check figures, sort marks and inspect any possible damage to cargoes. The warehouse keepers do the same in the warehouses or on the open yards. Furthermore, all the slings for big lots of cargo are made in fixed form and fixed quantity so as to facilitate counting.

B: I see.

Program 4 Mark-Assorting

Sorting marks is the primary work for the tallymen. Essentially, the task of mark-assorting is to clear up the main marks and the attribution of cargo so as to make identification of the shipping marks and attribution of the mixed-up or unidentified cargoes based on the Export Shipping Order or the Import Manifest. Mark-assorting is considered to be the scratch of tallying by which the truth and accurateness of tallying-figure can be guaranteed, and constructed a significant link of assuring the quality of traffic.

The roles of the mark-assorting are as following:

The premise condition of completion of cargo-counting. Prior to counting cargo, the tallyman must identify the main marks of cargo in accordance with the Export Shipping Order or the Import Manifest to justify the belonging of the cargo so as to make sure whether or not there is any cargo over-landed or short-landed according to the tally figure.

The premise condition of the identification of cargo damaged. Whatever damaged cargo is found it is impossible to deal with it without make identification of its main marks and belonging.

The security of improving the quality of traffic. As to the cargo exported, it is to be loaded lot by lot according to the tentative cargo plan, and properly stowed and segregated. As to the cargo imported, it is to be discharged by lots according to the imported manifest and original stowage plan, and placed on standard block. As to the cargo being stowed in chaotic condition with unclearly separation, the order of batches and the number of lots must be obtained.

Whatever loading or unloading, the tallymen must check the main marks of cargo handled carefully against respective shipping documents, and instruct the stevedores to load or unload lot by lot.

The efforts of mark-assorting can be minimized by alert stevedoring whatever in loading or discharging which would certainly lead to lowering the cost both in money and time.

Notes

1 Essentially, the task of mark-assorting is to clear up the main marks and the attribution of cargo so as to make identification of the shipping marks and attribution of the mixed-up or unidentified cargoes based on the Export Shipping Order or the Import Manifest.

根本上说，分票就是依据出口装货单或进口舱单中的货物的主标志和归属，分清混票或隔票不清的货物的运输标志和归属。

2 Mark-assorting is considered to be the scratch of tallying by which the truth and accurate-

ness of tallying-figure can be guaranteed, and constructs a significant link of assuring the quality of traffic.

分票是理货工作的起点,是确保理货数字准确的基本保证,是保证货运质量的重要一环。

3 Prior to counting cargo, the tallyman must identify the main marks of cargo in accordance with the Export Shipping Order or the Import Manifest to justify the belonging of the cargo so as to make sure whether or not there is any cargo over-landed or short-landed according to the tallying figure.

在理数之前,首先要按出口装货单或进口舱单分清货物的主标志,以明确货物的归属,然后才能根据理货数字,确定货物是否有溢短。

4 As to the cargo being stowed in chaotic condition with unclearly separation, the order of batches and the number of lots must be obtained.

对积载混乱、隔票不清的货物要分清批次和票数。

5 Whatever loading or unloading, the tallymen must check the main marks of cargo handled carefully against respective shipping documents, and instruct the stevedores to load or unload lot by lot.

在装卸过程中,理货员必须对照着相应的运输单证核对货物的主标志,指导工人的装卸工作。

6 The efforts of mark-assorting can be minimized by simply alert stevedoring whatever in loading or discharging, which would certainly lead to lowering the cost both in money and time.

无论是装货或卸货,我们可通过认真细致的工作就可将分票任务尽量减少,这必将降低经济成本和时间成本。

Vocabulary

assort [əˈsɔːt]	vt. 把……分类
sort marks	分标志
attribution [ˌætriˈbjuːʃən]	n. 归属
identification [aiˌdentifiˈkeiʃən]	n. 识别,证实,核对
shipping marks	运输标志
Export Shipping Order	出口装货单
Import Manifest	进口舱单
premise [ˈpremis]	n. 前提
original stowage plan	原始积载图
chaotic [keiˈɔtik]	adj. 混乱的,无秩序的
batch [bætʃ]	n. 成批;一宗,一批
alert [əˈləːt]	adj. 警惕的;留心的

Exercises

1 Answer the following questions according to the text you have read.

(1) What is the mark-assorting?

(2) What is the task of mark-assorting?

(3) What is the roles of the mark-assorting?

(4) How to ensure the security of the quality of traffic?

(5) What is the significance of reducing the work in mark-assorting?

2　Fill out the blanks with suitable words or terms based on the text.

(1) The task of mark-assorting is to clear up the _____ and the _____ of cargo.

(2) Mark-assorting is considered to be the _____ by which the truth and _____ of tallying-figure can be guaranteed,.

(3) Prior to counting cargo, the tallyman must identify the _____ of cargo in accordance with the Export Shipping Order or the Import Manifest.

(4) Whatever damaged cargo is found it is impossible to deal with it without making identification of its _____ and _____.

(5) As to the cargo exported , it is to be loaded lot by lot according to the _____.

(6) As to the cargo imported, it is to be discharged by lots according to the _____ and _____.

3　Put into Chinese.

(1) The tallyman should check up the main marks of cargo lot by lot against the shipping order.

(2) To ensure the quality of cargo carried the tallymen must make the mark sorting carefully.

(3) We should make sure that the shipping makes is in accordance with that in the shipping order.

(4) If anything related to the cargo handled is unclear, it is advisable to contact the shipper.

(5) The stevedores should be under the instruction as to handle the cargo lot by lot and deliver itaccurately.

4　Put into English.

(1)请核对一下这票货的运输标志。

(2)这票货的运输标志不清,因而不能装船。

(3)请告诉工人们按票装船。

(4)请与发货人联系确定其是否决定更换主标志。

(5)要做好分票工作以提高货运质量。

Dialogue

A:Chief,I got your import manifest from our import section yesterday.I found that you had three loading ports and 11 lots general cargo.Is that correct?

B:Yes,right.We start from a port in Malaysia,then we went to Saigon in Vietnam,and we called at Kaohsiung in Taiwan,so we have 11 lots of general cargo.

A:I understand.Now I have a question,do you think that all the different cargoes in your three holds were separated clearly at the last three ports?

B:Sorry,the cargoes were not separated,but I don't think it matters much.

A:Well,it is important,because it concerns the discharging operation.

B:How is that? I am a bit puzzled.I think after we open the hatch covers,the stevedores can start their discharging.It is very simple and there appears to be no any difficulty or problem.

A:Umm,the situation is probably not as you have described.If the separation of your cargo is notobvious,the stevedores can not distinguish and discharging the mixed cargoes lot by lot and later they don't know how to store the different cargoes for different consignees.The tallyman can not tally the mixed cargoes lot by lot either.

In a word,the discharging operation will become complicated and the discharging time will be longer.

B:Perhaps you are right,but I still think that the stevedores can unload the cargoes in the usual way.

A:Sorry,it is wrong.If the cargoes is not separated very well during loading ,the stevedores here can not discharge the cargo easily.It might be possible to unload the cargo this way but there would be confusion on the wharf if even 5% of them are mixed up.There would be additional work for the stevedores to separate them before the consignees could take them away.

B:I see.Well what shall I do them in such case?

A:As far as I know,the foreman will ask you to sign a sheet as the application for sorting the mixed cargoes and the stevedores will sort them by hand during the discharging.

B:Under this circumstances,I have to report to my captain and explain to him the whole situation,then I'll sign the sheet for the foreman.

A:OK,I suggest you arrange for your duty officer to cooperate with the foreman and the tallyman during the discharge.Whenever they find some mixed cargo,your duty officer is to make a record on the spot together with the tallyman inside the holds.With this first hand record,you can finally sign the tally report correctly.

B:That's a good idea,I'll follow it.

Program 5　Mixed-up of Cargo

Mixed-up of cargo means the mixture of different cargoes which prevents the cargo from being unloaded properly and orderly in the discharging port.

Cargo with different lots being stowed together and mixed up would prevent the discharging from high efficiency and would lead to discrepancy in the process of tallying,which must be avoided as can as possible.

There are many causes which result in the cargoes being mixed up.

(1)The cargo in the loading port is not stowed strictly in accordance with the stowage plan that is prepared and provided by the ship.

(2)The cargo is not properly distributed over on board by the ship.

(3) The separation is not well done or the dunnage is not provided sufficiently and correctly by the ship.

(4) Some cargo has been discharged or loaded in the midway of rotation.

(5) Cargo is discharged carelessly and not accord with the rules in the discharging port.

(6) Operational mistakes or negligence happen during the process of tallying.

Occurrence of cargo being mixed up can be minimized by alert operation and check.

When loading, the tallymen should closely supervise the process of loading and instruct the stevedores make proper stowage, separation and dunnage of cargo, load and clear up the cargo lot by lot, assemble the small lots in a certain place; make a clear separation between big lots that are in same packing but in different marks; separate the cargoes that are for different destinations; and stow the cargo according to the rotation of discharging ports, that is, discharging first the one that is loaded last and the last the first. When discharging, tallymen must be alert in monitoring the discharging, making the discharging and settlement of cargo lot by lot, preventing the cargo remained in the hold from mixing up. For the cargoes having been mixed, no efforts should be saved to assort the marks while discharging, and if the efforts fail, remedy must be done so as to assort the marks ashore.

Notes

1 Cargo with different lots being stowed together and mixed up prevents the discharging from high efficiency and would lead to discrepancy in the process of tallying, which must be avoided as can as possible.

不同票的货物混装在一起阻碍卸货效率的提高，并且影响理货的准确性。这种情况应当尽量避免。

2 When loading, the tallymen should closely supervise the process of loading and instruct the stevedores make proper stowage, separation and dunnage of cargo, load and clear up the cargo lot by lot, assemble the small lots in a certain place; make a clear separation between big lots that are in same packing but in different marks; separate the cargoes that are for different destinations; and stow the cargo according to the rotation of discharging ports, that is, discharging first the one that is loaded last and the last the first.

装船时，理货人员要严格监督装船过程，指导工人正确地积载、隔票和垫舱；按票装船，一票一清，零星小票货物集中堆放；同包装不同标志的大票货物和不同港口的货物要分隔清楚；要按卸货港顺序装船，先卸后装，后卸先装。

3 When discharging, tallymen must be alert in monitoring the discharging, making the discharging and settlement of cargo lot by lot, preventing the cargo remained in the hold from mixing up.

当卸货时，理货人员认真监督理货过程，按票理货和结单，防止舱内后卸货物混票发生。

4 For the cargoes having been mixed, no efforts should be saved to assort the marks while discharging, and if the efforts fail, remedy must be done so as to assort the marks ashore.

对混票货物应尽量做到边卸边分票,如做不到,应当采取措施在卸货后岸上分清。

Vocabulary

mixture ['mikstʃə]	n. 混合,混淆
midway ['mid'wei]	n. 中途,半路,中间
be accord with	与……一致
negligence ['neglidʒəns]	n. 疏忽,粗心大意,忽视
monitor ['mɔnitə]	vt. 监视,监听,监督
remain [ri'mein]	vi. 保持,逗留,剩余
effort ['efət]	n. 努力,成就
remedy ['remidi]	n. 补救,纠正

Exercises

1 Answer the following questions according to the text you have read.

(1) What is the mixed-up of cargo?

(2) What is the consequence of the mixed-up of cargo?

(3) What is the causes of the mixed-up of cargo?

(4) How to prevent the mixed-up of cargo from happening during loading?

(5) How to prevent the mixed-up of cargo from happening during discharging?

2 Fill out the blanks with suitable words or terms based on the text.

(1) Mixed-up of cargo means the _____ of different cargoes which prevents the cargo from being _____ properly and orderly in the discharging port.

(2) Cargo with different lots being _____ and mixed up would prevent the discharging from high _____.

(3) Prior to counting cargo, the tallyman must identify the _____ of cargo in accordance with the Export Shipping Order or the Import Manifest.

(4) The cargo in the loading port is stowed strictly in accordance with the _____ prepared and provided by the _____, which may not lead to the mixture of cargoes.

(5) The separation is not well done or the _____ is not provided sufficiently and correctly by the _____ would result in the cargoes being mix

(6) The cargo should be stowed according to the rotation of discharging ports, that is, discharging _____ the one that is loaded last and the last the _____.

3 Put into Chinese.

(1) The cargo of different lots is not clearly identified which leads to improper separation.

(2) We must pay much attention to the mixture of cargoes which is the main course of mistakes in tallying.

(3) The tallymen should contact the duty man of the ship to have a check when they find any

Project 5　Cargo-tallying Service

mixture of cargoes exists.

(4) The tallymen should supervise the process of loading and instruct the loading of cargo lot by lot.

(5) We should make clear as to who is responsible for the mixture of cargoes.

4　Put into English.

(1) 混票在货物作业过程中是经常发生的事情。

(2) 理货人员应当正确处理货物的混票问题。

(3) 货物混票会严重地影响货物作业效率

(4) 货物的混票与隔票不清是有区别的。

(5) 我们卸货港对货物混票不负责任。

Dialogue

A:Chief,here is the On-the-Spot Record for the mixed up stowage of the cotton in Hatch No.2.Please sign.

B:Sorry,I can't sign.I've already put remarks in the Shipping Orders.

A:What remarks have you put down?

B:"All cotton mixed up at the loading port".Here are the Shipping Orders.

A:I see.But you should sign the record to certify the fact,anyway.

B:You Chief Tally are a go-between.Since you've signed it,it is no longer necessary for me to sign.

A:According to the Business Regulation of our company,in case there is any mixed-up stowage of inward cargo,the Chief Tally should make out a Record on the Sport for the Ship to sign.

B:If so,I'll sign it,however,I must put remarks to cover my shipowners.

A:What's it.

B:Similar to the remarks in the Shipping Orders.

A:That'll do.By the way,we found the mixed up of bagged urea under Bill of Lading No.2 and 4 in Hatch No.3.

B:Yes,that's true.Well,please tell your tallymen to sort out the marks in the holds during discharging.

A:It'll take considerable time to sort out the marks clearly in the holds.

B:Then.What's your suggestion.

A:The best way to sort them out ashore,I suppose.

B:Good.Then who'll be responsible for the sorting charges?

A:According to the Business Regulations of our company ,expenses thus incurred shall be borne by the Ship.

B:I think the charterer will be responsible for it.

A:That's depends on the terms stipulated in the Charter-party.

Program 6　Counting

Tally work consists in the counting, and the counting is the basic task of tallymen and is provided as a ruler to measure the quality of tally work.

Counting is done by the tallymen who work by the shipside, in the hold or on the deck of the ship. The tallymen tick slings, count packages in the sling and summarize the figures of cargo handled during the loading or unloading of ship.

There are several ways of counting, and which way to be selected to use depends on the type of cargo being tallied. Among them are:

Chip-allotting Counting: A chip is given to each of the slings, and all of the chips having been sent are to be collected and counted after work to determine the figure of the cargo tallied. This method of counting is applied when the cargo sling is made in fixed form and fixed quantity.

Sling-ticking Counting: Counting the number of packages sling by sling, which is used universally.

Label-attached Counting: Each of the slings is attached with a label made of metal or plastic with order number on it. This method of counting can be also used universally.

Ticket-filling Counting: The ticket is made in duplication with Series No. on it. Filling the ticket according to the numbers of package in a sling, and one is hold by the deliverer and the receiver respectively. The total figure of cargo is attained based on the tickets collected. This way of counting is adaptable to all kinds of cargo.

Block-ticking Counting: Figures of cargo is obtained by counting the packages in blocks. The block refers to the block of cargo that is made in fixed shape based on standard and placed in the dock warehouse or pile-ground. This method can be used as an auxiliary means in certain cases which is not suitable to the foreign trade cargo.

Number-jotting Counting: Jotting down the Package No. of each piece of cargo, which is taken as a basis to calculate the figure of cargo. Normally, a Package No. is printed on the packing of cargo presenting a piece of cargo especially for the complete set of equipment.

Automatic Counting: A scientific device is adopted as counting tool and connected to the handling machinery. Nowadays, on most cases, an automatic counter is mounted on a belt conveyor. This way of counting is a great step toward science and modernization for the tally work.

Notes

1　Tally work consists in the counting, and the counting is the basic task of tallymen and is provided as a ruler to measure the quality of tally work.

理数是理货工作的核心内容,是理货员的最基本的工作,也是衡量理货质量的尺度。

2　The tallymen tick slings, count packages in the sling and summarize the figures of cargo

handled during the loading or unloading of ship。

理货人员在船舶的装卸过程中,记录起吊货物的钩数,点清钩内货物细数,计算装卸货物的数字。

3 Chip-allotting Counting:A chip is given to each of the slings,and all of the chips having been sent are to be collected and counted after work to determine the figure of the cargo tallied. This method of counting is applied when the cargo sling is made in fixed form and fixed quantity.

发筹理数:对每钩货物发一支筹码,工作结束后,凭筹码计算货物数字,这种方法适用于可定型定量做关的货物。

4 Sling-ticking Counting:Counting the number of packages sling by sling,which is used universally.

划钩理数:逐钩点清货物数字,称为划钩理货。这种方法适用于各种货物。

5 Label-attached Counting:Each of the slings is attached with a label made of metal or plastic with order number on it.This method of counting can be also used universally.

挂牌理货:对每钩货物挂一个金属或塑料小牌,上面有顺序编号。这种计数方法适用于各种货物。

6 Ticket-filling Counting:The ticket is made in duplication with Series No.on it.Filling the ticket according to the numbers of package in a sling,and one is hold by the deliverer and the receiver respectively.The total figure of cargo is got based on the tickets collected.

小票理数:小票是一种有顺序编号的两联单。按每钩货物数字填发小票。交接双方各持一联。凭票计算货物数字。

7 Block-ticking Counting:Figures of cargo is obtained by counting the packages in blocks. The block refers to the block of cargo that is made in fixed shape based on standard and placed in the dock warehouse or pile-ground.This method can be used as an auxiliary means in certain cases which is not suitable to the foreign trade cargo.

点垛理数:按垛点清货物数字。垛是指在码头库场按一定要求堆码成型的货物。在某些情况下作为理数的辅助手段,不适于外贸运输货物。

8 Number-jotting Counting:Jotting down the Package No.of each piece of cargo,which is taken as a basis to calculate the figure of cargo.Normally,a Package No.is printed on the packing of cargo presenting a piece of cargo especially for the complete set of equipment .

抄号理数:抄录每件货物的号码,据此以计算货物的数字。一般货物的包装上都印有货物的件号,一个号码代表一件货物,尤其是成套设备。

Vocabulary

shipside ['ʃipsaid]	n.船边
tick slings	记关
summarize ['sʌməraiz]	vt.概括,总结
Chip-allotting Counting	发筹理数
Sling-ticking Counting	划钩理数

universally [juːniˈvɜːsəli]	adv. 普遍地
Label-attached Counting	挂牌理货
Ticket-filling Counting	小票理数
Block-ticking Counting	点垛理数
auxiliary [ɔːgˈziljəri]	adj. 辅助的,补助的
Number-jotting Counting	抄号理数
Automatic Counting	自动理数
device [diˈvais]	n. 装置,设备

Exercises

1 Answer the following questions according to the text you have read.

(1) What is the counting of cargo?

(2) How many kinds of counting, and what are they?

(3) What is the chip-allotting counting?

(4) What is the sling-ticking counting?

(5) What is the ticket-sending counting?

2 Fill out the blanks with suitable words or terms based on the text.

(1) The counting is the basic task of tallymen and is provided as a _____ to measure the _____ of tally work.

(2) The tallymen _____ slings, _____ packages in the sling and _____ the figures of cargo handled during the loading or unloading of ship.

(3) Chip-allotting is applied when the cargo sling is made in _____ and _____.

(4) The method of ticket-sending is that the total figure of cargo is attained based on the _____.

(5) In block-ticking, the block refers to the block of cargo that is made in _____ based on standard and placed in the dock _____ or pile-ground.

3 Put into Chinese.

(1) The tallymen should be alert and hold sense of responsibility in the work of counting.

(2) The method of counting depends on the types of cargo and the operation of cargo.

(3) What kinds of counting do you apply in your tally work?

(4) The method of counting varies according to the types of cargo handled.

(5) In fact, there is no any kind of method of counting is absolutely correct.

4 Put into English.

(1) 计数是一项重要的理货工作。

(2) 理货人员应当根据实际情况采用正确的计数方法。

(3) 发筹理数方法适用于定型定量做关的货物。

(4) 自动计数方法并不是绝对不出错误的。

(5) 好的计数方法既要方便实用又要正确可靠。

Project 5 Cargo-tallying Service

Dialogue

A: Hello, are you going to ticking slings with me?

B: Yes.

A: You don't trust me ticking, do you?

B: Of course, I do. But it is our master who sends me here.

A: I understand. Now let me introduce myself. My name is Wang, I'm the tallyman of this hatch. May I know your name?

B: My name is Smith, John Smith. I'm quartermaster.

A: Are you from Canada, Mr. Smith?

B: No, I was born in England. After I got married, I moved to Canada. Now I'm living in Montreal.

A: Have you ever been to China before?

B: Yes, I've been here twice. You Chinese people have made great progress.

A: We've really made remarkable achievements in our construction for the past few years. But we still have a long way to go. Well, the discharging of urea will start soon. Let's get ready.

B: Oh, Mr. Wang, I forgot to bring some paper with me. Would you mind giving me a few blank tally sheets?

A: Not at all. Here you are.

B: Thank you.

A: Have you ever ticked slings before?

B: Yes, it's a simple and easy job, isn't it?

A: Not exactly. If you miss out one sling, the tally figure will be inaccurate. Therefore ticking slings correctly isn't an easy job, I should say.

B: Yes, you are right.

A: Look here comes the first sling. It's 20 bags: 8 on this side, 8 on the other and 4 on top. Is that right?

B: Yes, that's right. Do the stevedores make slings in fixed quantity?

A: Yes, they always make slings in fixed form and fixed quantity.

B: I see.

A: Look, this sling contains only 19 bags.

B: Let me count... Yes, you are right. Why is this sling short of one bag?

A: Let me ask the signal man.

B: (the tallyman comes back) What did he say?

A: He says one bag falls while the sling is going up. They'll make up for it in the next sling. Now look, here comes the sling. It's 21, isn't it?

B: Yes, it is.

A: How many slings have you ticked up to now?

B: Let me see. 5, 10, 15 and 3, altogether 18 slings. Is that right?
A: Yes, that's right.

Program 7 Short-landed and Over-landed Cargo

As regarding to loading or unloading a ship, the Shipping Order or Import Manifest is taken as an unique base and proof for cargo tallying, as well as to the shipment of cargo. The figure of cargo having been tallied must be checked against these two shipping documents to determine whether the cargo is "over" or "short". In the loading port, the consignment must be checked up to see whether or not it is in accordance with that of Shipping Order, and in the discharging port, to see whether or not it is in accordance with that of Import Manifest.

There are many factors contribute to the "short" or "over".

(1) The consignor might have delivered the cargo to the warehouse, pile-ground or shipside without in accordance with the figure stated in the S/O, or the marks of cargo delivered and the marks shown in the S/O do not accord well together.

(2) In loading port, the whole lot or part lot of cargo is neglected without being loaded on board, and the cargo being not demanded is taken to load on board. In another case, the cargo for one destination is taken to load amidst the cargo for another destination.

(3) In discharging port, some of cargo might have been left behind or mistaken into the cargo for different port due to the facts that the stowage of cargo on board is in a chaotic condition, separation is not clearly made, and the place does not accord with that shown on the stowage plan, etc.

(4) Some of the cargo that might be discharged in later port has been taken ashore currently, or some that ought to have been discharged has been left behind on board on the midst of rotation of ports called due to improper operation such as cargo mixing-up in holds, unclear separation, undue stowage, etc. Moreover, pilferage, sea peril during the voyage contribute to the "over" or "short" as well.

(5) The amount of cargo is not received correctly owing to the faults made by the receiver or is not in strictly accordance with that stated on Import Manifest or on the Bill of Lading.

(6) Faults happen during the operation of tallying for the reason or another made by the tallymen.

If any cargo over-landed or short-landed happens it will result in a seriously adverse affect to the ship, especially in the case of short-landing for the ship will be held responsibility for the indemnity for the shortage of the cargo.

Notes

1 As regarding to loading or unloading a ship, the Shipping Order or Import Manifest is taken as an unique base and proof for cargo tallying, as well as to the shipment of cargo.

在船舶装卸货物时,装货单和进口舱单是理货的唯一凭证和依据,也是船舶承运货物的凭证和依据。

2 The figure of cargo having been tallied must be checked against these two shipping documents to determine whether the cargo is "over" or "short".

理出的数字结果必须与这两个货运单进行对照,来确定货物是否溢多或短少。

3 In loading port, the whole lot or part lot of cargo is neglected without being loaded on board, and the cargo being not demanded is taken to load on board. In another case, the cargo for one destination is taken to load amidst the cargo for another destination.

在装货港,整票或部分货物遗漏未装,将不该装船的货物误装上船,或将不同目的港的货物装在其他目的港货物的中间。

4 Some of the cargo that might be discharged in later port has been taken ashore currently, or some that ought to have been discharged has been left behind on board on the midst of rotation of ports called due to improper operation such as cargo mixing-up in holds, unclear separation, undue stowage, etc. Moreover, pilferage, sea peril during the voyage contribute to the "over" or "short" as well.

在中途港装卸货物时,将舱内货物搞混乱,或货物隔票不清、积载不当,致使不该卸船的货物卸下船,或该卸的没卸下船。货物被盗或航行期间发生海难也是造成货物溢、短的原因。

Vocabulary

unique [juːˈniːk]	adj. 独一无二的,独特的,稀罕的
demand [diˈmɑːnd]	vt. 要求,需求
amidst [əˈmidst]	prep. 在……当中
undue stowage	积载不当
sea peril	海难
owing to	由于,因……之缘故
Bill of Lading	提单
indemnity [inˈdemniti]	n. 赔偿,保障,

Exercises

1 Answer the following questions according to the text you have read.
(1) What is the over-landed or short-landed cargo?
(2) How to check the cargo to determine whether or not it is over-landed or short-landed?
(3) What should the consignor do to avoid the "over" or "short" happening?
(4) Can you list some causes that lead to the cargo being over-landed or short-lande?
(5) Could you put forward some suggestions to avoid the cargo being over-landed or short-landed?

2 Fill out the blanks with suitable words or terms based on the text.

(1) The figure of cargo having been tallied must be checked _____ these two _____ to determine whether the cargo is "over" or "short".

(2) In the loading port, the consignment must be checked up to see whether or not it is in accordance with that of _____.

(3) In the discharging port, to see whether or not it is _____ that of _____.

(4) The consignor might have delivered the cargo to the warehouse, pile-ground or shipside without in accordance with the figure stated in the _____.

(5) If any cargo over-landed or short-landed happens it will result in a seriously _____ affect to the _____.

3 Put into Chinese.

(1) To my knowledge, we can never use sweepings to make up for the short-landed cargo.

(2) The figures of cargo discharged from the respective hatches do not correspond to those on the cargo plan.

(3) It gives us an impression that the tally figure of the loading port is not reliable.

(4) The shipping marks of this lot of cargo are unclear, we wouldn't lord it in this situation.

(5) I think that there is some cargo being mistaken onto the board due to the mismanagement of warehouse department.

4 Put into English.

(1) 我发现你们工人时而把残损货物混装上船。

(2) 你不要把事情看得太严重了,溢多和短缺货物在理货中是常有的事情。

(3) 你们没有按装货单上载明的数字将货物送到船边。

(4) 我发现装上船的货物的积载位置与积载图上的位置不符。

(5) 你们把不该装船的货物带上船,该装船的货物没能全部装上。

Dialogue

A: Hi, Chief, glad to see you again. Everything is OK for the discharging.

B: Yes, everything is OK, except for some over-landed cargo.

A: What, what did you say, Chief?

B: I sad that some cargo was over-landed from my ship this morning.

A: I see. What kind of cargo? Please describe in details.

B: Yes, my second officer was asked to see the chief tally when he was on duty this morning. The chief tally told him that 2 bundles of steel pipe and 8 drums of chemical goods were over-landed.

A: But how the tallyman prove that it was over-landed?

B: My second officer at that time asked me the same question, too. The tallyman then showed him the following manifest. For Bill of Lading NO.SK-11, the correct figure of the pipe bundles should be 80, but actually it is 82, 2 more than the manifest indicates. And for Bill NO.P-07, the right figure of the drums should be 150, but in fact it is 158, just one pallet more.

A: Now I understand. But did your second officer count them himself?

B: Yes, he did, and the figures were correct.

A: Did the chief tally finally sign the tally paper and give you a copy later?

B: Yes, here it is. Please have a look.

A: All right. Did you report it to your captain?

B: I certainly did. He said he should report the case to our agent for his opinion. And he said it would up to you to decide.

A: Well, from my experience, such cases are usually settled in the following way: 1. the over-landed cargo is carried back by the original ship to the original loading port for retune to the original shipper. 2. the over-landed cargo can be taken back by some other ship to the original shipper in the future. , if the shipper still wants the cargo. 3. If the shipper, even if he knows the story, doesn't want to get the cargo back, he may sell it the consignee and get some money from him later. 4. The shipper, in a future contract, sends the consignee the same cargo by deducting the figure of cargo over-landed this voyage, so that the shipper can offset his loss in the future agreement with the consignee.

B: Oh, Agent, it is very complicated. I've never done anything like this. But now I at least see how it should be dealt with. As I told you a few minutes ago , our captain would on the owner's behalf authorize you—our agent to settle the problem. I think, you may begin arrange things.

A: That's all right, but I have to get your captain's writing authorization before we start.

B: No problem, his approval will be forthcoming.

A: Simultaneously I need your tally report copy, your stowage plan, over-landed cargo report and your manifest, so that I may contact your owner for his opinion.

B: OK, I'll get all of these ready for your soon.

A: Thanks. I'll retune for them in about an hour. Good-bye.

Program 8 Dealing with the Over-landed and Short-landed Cargo

There are many factors that lead to the happening of the short-landed and over-landed cargo, which should be coped with appropriately so as to guarantee the quality of tally work.

When handling the exported cargo, the tallymen should instruct loading the cargo according to the figure shown on the Shipping Order, and if any cargo with overage is found, the cargo is not allowed to be shipped. In case that the shipper insists on the shipping of the cargo, only after an alteration to the S/O is made by him do the shipment can be proceeded. In case of shortage, it is obliged for the tallymen to contact the shipper and urge him to complement the cargo in shortage based on the figure on the S/O. In the event that no complementary goods can be put into, the whole lot of the cargo shall be canceled, or to be short shipped if an amendment to the S/O has been made by the shipper. And if no cancellation of cargo or no amendment to the S/O is made, the tallyman is obliged to make remarks on the S/O based on the figure actually tallied.

When handling the imported cargo, the tallymen should instruct discharging the cargo in accordance with the figure stated on Import Manifest. For the cargo with overage or shortage, an Over-landed and Short-landed List should be made out; as to the package being apart, effort should be made to put the parts being off together forming the original one, and if the efforts fail, the package being apart should be treated as "package-short, parts-over"; as to the cargo with marks missing or mismatching, it should be treated as the over-landed; in regard of the identical consignment with different lots, a conformation about the overage or shortage should be made by parties concerned and then an attempt should be made in offsetting between the overage and the shortage, and if the overage or shortage can not be eliminated after the offsetting, the consignment in question is ought to be treated as over-landed or short-landed cargo.

Notes

1 In case that the shipper insists on the shipping of the cargo, only after the formality of alteration to the S/O is made by him do the shipment can be proceeded.

如发货人坚持要求装船,应由发货人办理更改装货单手续后,方可装船。

2 In the event that no complementary items can be put into, the whole lot of the cargo shall be canceled, or to be short shipped if an amendment to the S/O has been made by the shipper.

如无货物可补,应将整票货物退关,或由发货人办理装货单的更改后装船。

3 And if no cancellation of cargo or no amendment to the S/O is made, the tallyman is obliged to make remarks on the S/O based on the figure actually tallied.

如货物未被退关或者装货单也未修改,则理货人员应按理货数字批注装货单。

4 As to the package being apart, effort should be made to put the parts being off together forming the original one, and if the efforts fail, the package being apart should be treated as "package-short, part-over"; as to the cargo with marks missing or mismatching it should be treated as the over-landed; in regard of the identical consignment with different lots, a conformation about the overage or shortage should be made by parties concerned and then an attempt should be made in offsetting between the overage and the shortage, and if the overage or shortage can not be eliminated after the offsetting, the consignment in question is ought to be treated as over-landed or short-landed cargo.

对散件的货物,应尽量折合成原件,如做不到,可按短件溢支处理;对无标志或标志不符的货物,按溢卸货物处理;对不同票的相同货物,经相关方确认后,可溢短相抵,如仍有溢短,再按溢短货物处理。

Vocabulary

deal with   安排,处理

Project 5 Cargo-tallying Service

appropriately [əˈprəupriitli]	adv. 适当地
alteration [ˌɔːltəˈreiʃən]	n. 变更,改变
be obliged to	不得不
mismatching [ˈmisˈmætʃiŋ]	n. 失配,不匹配,失谐
treat as	把……看作……
in regard of	关于……,至于……
offset [ˈɔːfset]	n. 抵消;补偿
eliminate [iˈlimineit]	vt. 除去,消除

Exercises

1 Answer the following questions according to the text you have read.

（1）What should the tallymen do when dealing with the exported cargo?

（2）What should the tallymen do in case of shortage of cargo?

（3）In what case that the tallymen should make remarks on the S/O?

（4）What should the tallymen do when handling the imported cargo?

（5）What should be done if the overage or shortage can not be eliminated after the offsetting?

2 Fill out the blanks with suitable words or terms based on the text.

（1）When handling the exported cargo, the tallymen should instruct loading the cargo according to the _____ shown on the _____.

（2）In case of shortage, it is obliged for the tallymen to contact the _____ and urge him to complement the cargo _____ based on the figure on the S/O.

（3）In the event that no complementary goods can be put into, the _____ of the cargo shall _____.

（4）When handling the imported cargo, the tallymen should instruct _____ the cargo in accordance with the figure stated on _____.

（5）If the overage or shortage can not be eliminated after the offsetting, the _____ is ought to be treated as over-landed or _____ cargo.

3 Put into Chinese.

（1）As to the urea, I'd like to set off the sweepings bags against the shortage.

（2）I take it for granted that the figure of the loading port is correct and that of your port is wrong.

（3）According to the Charter-party terms, the responsibility of the carrier shall commence from the time when the goods are loaded on board the ship and shall cease when they are discharged from the ship.

（4）Once the shortage of cargo is found we'll inform the duty officer to look up.

（5）The ship should be held responsibility for the cargo over-landed.

4 Put into English.

（1）装船时,发现货物有短缺,应由发货人进行处理。

(2)我认为收货人一定会根据事实与发货人解决这个问题的。

(3)进口货物、出口货物、不同目的港、不同票的货物不应当堆在一起。

(4)我们应当保证货物的安全和质量,不发生货物的短装和短卸。

(5)理货人员应当事实就地处理理货数字。

Dialogue

A: Good morning, Chief Checker. Have you finished discharging?

B: Yes, just finished.

A: What's outturn?

B: Everything is O.K. except for the lead ingots and the sisal.

A: What's wrong?

B: The lead ingot is short-landed in bundles and over-landed in pieces.

A: Give me the figures respectively?

B: 75 bundles are short and 3825 pieces are over. Here's the Short-landed and Over-landed Cargo List. I wonder why there are so many loose pieces.

A: It's due to insufficient of space. The stevedores at the loading port untied several score of bundles in order to fill the broken space with the loose pieces.

B: I see.

A: Then can you set off the overage against the shortage?

B: I can't tell. Because the number of pieces of each bundles is not shown on the manifest.

A: That's the point.

B: But don't worry about that. I believe the consignee will contact the shipper to settle that matter.

A: The consignee will take it for granted that the shortage is true. So I'd better put the remarks "Ship not responsible for the shortage".

B: As the ship is the carrier of the cargo, it seems unreasonable to put such remarks. Meanwhile I don't think the consignee will accept it.

A: But on my part, I have to cover my owner's interests, otherwise, I'm to blame for it.

B: Chief, you ought to have a better understanding of our Chinese tallymen. We never cheat in our business. I'm sure the consignee will deal with matter according to the fact. If the figure of the lead ingots is correct, he will definitely not lodge any claims against the shipowner. Please take it easy.

B: I see. Then what about the figure of sisal?

A: We found 18 bales of sisal short-landed.

B: 18 bales short! Is it possible?

A: But that is the actual figure we've tallied out.

B: 18 bales is not a small number. Frankly speaking, I feel doubtful about the figure.

A: I know it's not a small figure. So we've check it repeatedly.

B: Well, how many bales of sisal make a sling?

A: 6 bales. We always make a sling in fixed form and fixed quantity.

B: But I'm afraid your tallymen may miss 3 slings on tally sheet by chance, because 18 bales are just equivalent to 3 slings.

A: No, you haven't guess it. The shortage doesn't come out of 1 hatch but from 3 hatches, that is 7 bales from Hatch No.2, 9 from Hatch No.4 and 2 from Hatch No.3 respectively.

B: Your explanation sounds all right. But I'm afraid…

Program 9   Checking the Damage

The cargo damaged can be broken down as follows: (1) Original Damage: the cargo being damaged is found on board before discharging. (2) Stevedores' Damage: referring to the cargo that damaged during the loading and unloading. (3) Accidental Damage: the damage of cargo is caused during handling by accidental incident beyond foreseeable. (4) Natural Disaster Accident Damage: Owing to the force majeure, the cargo is damaged during loading and unloading. The damages mentioned above present in various forms of cargo condition, which constitute the major task of tallymen in their work, such as: breakage, stains (dirt-stain, water-stain, oil-stain, etc.), wet with water, rusty, mould stained, etc. appearing on the package or on the surface of cargo.

In the process of damage checking, tallymen must be impartial, make judgment on the fact basis and fulfill their duties in accordance with the principle. The requirements for damage checking are listed as follows:

(1) A clear distinction must be made between the original damage and the stevedores' damage, and reject the cargo being damaged.

(2) Determining the position of the original damage in the hold, their figures and the extent of damage; making out the On-the-Spot Record and asking for the signature of the Ship.

(3) Determining the figures of the stevedores' damage and the extent of them, making out the On-the-Spot Record and signed by the Foreman of the gang.

(4) The tallymen make a collection of the On-the-Spot Record and on the basis of it, fill out the Damaged Cargo List.

(5) The responsibility for the damaged cargo must be specified as to who is to blame for the damage. For example, in regard to the original damage, the Ship is to take the blame; as for the stevedores' damage, it is obligatory on the Port to take the responsibility.

As regards the export cargo, if any cargo damaged is found and no permission is allowed for its loading, and if the damage is found in any hold during loading, it is bound to being discharged whatsoever. And as for the import cargo, if, the Ship would be asked for inspection, and an On-the-Spot Record should be worked out stating the figure, stowage position, and the extend of the damaged cargo so that the damage can be discharged ashore after recognition and signing by the Ship.

Notes

1   Accidental Damage: the damage of cargo is caused during handling by accidental incidents beyond foreseeable.

意外事故残损:是指装卸过程中因各种潜在因素造成意外事故导致货物的残损。

2   Natural Disaster Accident Damage: Owing to the force majeure, the cargo is damaged during loading and unloading.

货物在装卸过程中,由于不可抗拒力造成的货物残损。

3   The responsibility for the damaged cargo must be specified as to who is to blame for the damage.

责任必须明确,确定谁是残损货物的责任方。

4   For example, in regard to the original damage, the Ship is to take the blame; as for the stevedores' damage, it is obligatory on the Port to take the responsibility.

例如,对于原残,船方要对残损负责,至于工残,则应由港方负责。

5   And as for the import cargo, if, the Ship would be asked for inspection, and an On-the-Spot Record should be worked out stating the figure, stowage position, and the extend of the damaged cargo so that the damage can be discharged ashore after recognition and signing by the Ship

对于进口货物,若发现残损,应要求船方进行检查,并编制现场记录单,记载残损货物数字、积载部位、和残损情况,取得船方确认后再卸下船。

Vocabulary

Original Damage	原残
Stevedores' Damage	工残
Accidental Damage	意外事故残损
Natural Disaster Accident Damage	自然灾害(不可抗力)造成的残损
force majeure	不可抗力
impartial [im'pɑːʃəl]	adj.公平的;平等相待的;无偏见的
extent [iks'tent]	n.范围,限度,程度
obligatory [ɔ'bligətəri]	adj.义务的,必须的,强制性的
permission [pə(ː)'miʃən]	n.许可

Exercises

1   Answer the following questions according to the text you have read.

(1) How to classify the damage cargo?

(2) What is the major task of tallymen in their work dealing with the damaged cargo?

(3) What are the requirements for damage checking?

(4) As for the original damage, who should be held responsible for the damage?

Project 5 Cargo-tallying Service

(5) With respect to the stevedores' damage, who is to take the responsibility?

2 Fill out the blanks with suitable words or terms based on the text.

(1) The original damage refers to the cargo being damaged _____ before _____.

(2) The stevedores' damage refers to the cargo that damaged during the _____ and _____.

(3) The accidental damage means that the damage of cargo is caused during _____ by _____ beyond foreseeable.

(4) The natural disaster accident damage means that the cargo is damaged during loading and unloading owing to the _____.

(5) As for the import cargo, if any damaged cargo is found, the _____ would be asked for inspection, and an _____ should be worked out.

3 Put into Chinese.

(1) It is quite evident that the cargo was damaged before discharging because the traces of the damage are old ones.

(2) If there is any argument between the ship and the tallymen about the damaged cargo, we usually submit the case to the cargo surveyor for decision.

(3) Damage to the cargo on deck is often found particularly when a ship encountered bad weather.

(4) Though deck cargo is loaded at the shipper's risk yet the ship has to certify the damage condition.

(5) The damage occurred after discharging and before delivery to receivers should be reported separately.

4 Put into English.

(1) 很明显，由于积载不良，货物受到了损坏。

(2) 从残损的痕迹可以看出，这是原残，我们不应当负责。

(3) 没有必要把工残写在现场记录上，因为这与你们船方无关。

(4) 我们应当将工残和原残严格地区分开来。

(5) 看来，唯一的解决办法是将此事提交给商检人员决定了。

Dialogue

The Tallymen(A) is talking with the Chief Officer(B) about the dealing with the damaged cargo.

A: Chief, here's the On-the-Spot record. Please sign it.

B: Let me have a look first. Why, 18 bundles of steel plates stained by urea and 15 cases of liquid nitrogen container planks broken. I can't believe that. As far as I know, all the cargo is undamaged at the loading port. Possibly you haven't distinguished the original damage with the stevedores'.

A: I'm not fully aware of what happened at the loading port. I merely mean the present state of the cargo on board the ship.

B:Stevedores' damage may arise in the process of loading and discharging. That's the common sense. The cargo I received on board at the loading port was all in apparent good order and condition. So it's evident that the cargo was damaged by your stevedores.

A:It's true that the stevedores may damage some cargo during discharging. In that case we will never charge it to your account. But here the stained plates and the broken cases are apparently original damaged. They were examined by the ship's personnel on duty. If you have any doubt, you can ask them about it.

B:As to the stained plates, the fault lies with you, not with me.

A:What evidence can you present to justify your views?

B:You've already seen all the steel plates in the holds properly covered with canvas and polythene paper. But your stevedores towed the slings roughly. Upon this the damage was removed from the steel plates. That's why some plates were stained by the urea from torn bags.

A:What you say is not convincing at all. You see, the rust on the stained plates is not a thin layer. It's obvious that such a thick covering of rust can only be formed in a long time. For our part the dockers swept the urea as soon as they found it on the plates during discharging.

B:Well, let's submit the case to the cargo surveyor.

A:All right.

Program 10 Sweepings

Sweepings is a segment of cargo off away from the original packing (or packaging) during loading or unloading which can not be counted as actual cargo handled. There are several causes resulting in the sweepings.

(1) The packing of the cargo is not sea-worthy in long transit and unendurable for the requirement of cargo handling, which makes packing broken or torn leading to the sweepings.

(2) Sweepings may occur by rough, careless handling or due to unsuitable devices applied in cargo handling.

(3) The facts that facilities in the hold are not well equipped or positioned, or cargo is not-properly stowed, or sea peril occurs, all of which may contribute to the sweepings' happening due to breakage or tearing of the packing.

Sweepings can't be repacked with original packing, instead, must be placed into the spare bags, and markings must be made to prevent mixing up with the intact goods. As to the sweepings from different lots of cargo or the different varieties of sweepings from one kind of cargo, they can't be put together and placed into the same bags.

Sweepings should be cleaned up and put into spare bags before discharging onto the place appointed.

The torn bags, empty of cargo, should be counted as the cargo handled based on the shipping marks; the sweepings bags, however, must not be treated as the original bags.

Ordinarily, the Ship would acknowledge and sign the paper stating the figure of the sweeping bags while signing the originally damaged cargo. The sweepings bags from the stevedores' damage should be deducted while asking for the ship to sign the paper.

The weight of the sweepings bags should be made approximately the same as the original bags. The spare bags must not be mixed up with the torn bags or empty bags. One point should be noted that the spare bags is exclusively used for sweepings filling and not used otherwise.

Notes

1 Sweepings is a segment of bulk cargo off away from the original packing(or packaging) during loading or unloading which can not be counted as actual cargo handled.

地脚货是装卸过程中从原包装内散漏出来的不能按实际装卸货物计数的散装货物。

2 The packing of the cargo is not sea-worthy in long transit and unendurable for the requirement of cargo handling, which makes packing broken or torn leading to the sweepings.

货物包装不适应海上长途运输和装卸操作要求发生破损，形成地脚货。

3 Sweepings can't be repacked with original packing, instead, must be placed into the spare bags, and markings must be made to prevent mixing up with the intact goods. As to the sweepings from different lots of cargo or the different varieties of sweepings from one kind of cargo, they can't be put together and placed into the same bags.

不能将地脚货重新装入原货物包装内，应灌入备用袋内，且作出标记，以防与完好货物相混淆。对于不同货类的地脚货，以及同货类不同品种的地脚货，都不能混装入同一备用袋内。

4 Ordinarily, the Ship would acknowledge and sign the paper stating the figure of the sweepings bags while signing the originally damaged cargo. The sweepings bags from the stevedores' damage should be deducted while asking for the ship to sign the paper.

通常，船方签认原残数字的货物，一般同时签认地脚灌包数。在提请船方签认地角灌包数时，应注意扣除工残所造成的地脚包数。

Vocabulary

sweepings ['swiːpiŋz]　　　　　　　　n.地角货，扫舱货
segment ['segmənt]　　　　　　　　　n.段，片，部分，节
unendurable [ˌʌnin'djuərəbl]　　　　　adj.不能容忍的，不能持久的
rough [rʌf]　　　　　　　　　　　　adj.粗暴的；无礼的
deduct [di'dʌkt]　　　　　　　　　　vt.扣除，减去
approximately [əprɔksi'mətli]　　　　adv.大约，大致，近于
exclusively [ik'skluːsivli]　　　　　　adv.专门地

Exercises

1 Answer the following questions according to the text you have read.

(1) What is sweepings?

(2) What are the causes of sweepings?

(3) How to deal with the sweepings?

(4) How to handle the torn bags?

(5) How should the ship deal with the sweepings bags?

2 Fill out the blanks with suitable words or terms based on the text.

(1) Sweepings is a segment of cargo off away from the _____ packing(or packaging) during loading or unloading which can not be counted as _____ handled.

(2) Sweepings can't be repacked with _____, instead, must be placed into the _____, and markings must be made to prevent mixing up with the intact goods.

(3) The torn bags, empty of cargo, should be counted as the cargo handled based on the _____; the sweepings bags, however, must not be treated as the _____.

(4) The sweepings bags from the stevedores' damage should _____ while asking for _____ to sign the paper.

(5) The weight of the sweepings bags should be made approximately the _____ as the original bags. The _____ must not be mixed up with the torn bags or empty bags.

3 Put into Chinese.

(1) The discharging has been finished, there is some sweepings left on the lower hold.

(2) To my knowledge, we can never use sweepings to make up for the short-landed cargo.

(3) The figures of cargo discharged from respective hatches do not correspond to those on the cargo plan.

(4) There some torn bags in the lower hold of Hatch No.3 which lead to the occurrence of sweepings.

(5) We can't offset the short-landed urea bags by the sweepings bags.

4 Put into English.

(1) 包装不良可能造成地脚货的发生。

(2) 工残和原残造成的地脚货不容易区分。

(3) 正确处理地脚货是理货人员的一项重要工作。

(4) 本航次由于恶劣天气造成了很多破袋。

(5) 不能使用地脚货来抵消短缺的货物。

Dialogue

A talk about the discharging between a Duty Officer(A) and a Forman(B)

A: There are a quite a lot of sweepings in the lower hold and in the tweendeck as well.

B: Yes.It's unavoidable in discharging bagged cargo.What shall will do with it?

A: They must bagged first and then taken ashore.According to the Charter Party, all the sweepings should be delivered to the consignee because they form part of his cargo.

B: That's right.I'll send some stevedores to collect the sweepings.

A: Foreman, have you found any damaged cargo by now?

B: Not yet.But how should we dispose of the damaged cargo if there is any?

A: just put aside and tell me in detail where and how the cargo was damaged.Then we can determine who's is to be responsible for the damage.

B: OK.I'll do as you say.

A: (A little later) Forman!

B: Yes? What's wrong?

A: Oh, nothing wrong.I want to know when the discharging will be completed.

B: Now there is only a few slings of cargo remaining inside the hold.The 5 hatches can be finished by 10 this evening at present discharging rate.

A: Good.It's taken only 4 days since the starting of operation.I think we'll be able to begin loading tomorrow as schedule.

B: No problem, it seems.

A: Thank you and all your stevedores very much.

B: Well, I just expect a better cooperation in loading tomorrow.

A: Me too.

Project 6　Container-tallying Service

Project Description

Containerization is a system of intermodal freight transport using intermodal containers, which have standardized dimensions, and its handling system is completely mechanized. All containers are numbered and tracked using computerized systems.

As a system, containerization contains a series of working procedure and technology which serve and guarantee the containerization proceeding in good order and condition.

Knowledge Objective

1　Familiar with the advantages of containerization.
2　The rules of goods laid out inside containers.
3　The procedure of interchange of FCL and LCL.
4　Thetechnology of container-handling.
5　The relevant documents of container load goods.
6　The basis of container tallying.
7　The techniques of tallying for import and export containers.
8　The technology of container-damage-checking.

Ability Objective

1　Know what kind of equipments should be used to handle containers in different occasion.
2　Have the ability to stuff diverse cargoes into container correctly based on their characteristics correspondingly.
3　With FCL and LCL, you should know the correct interchange requirements and methods respectively.
4　Be capable of selecting proper technology of container-handling according to the practical conditions of working place.
5　Have the ability to know what sort of documents should be used to define the responsibility towards the container in the channel it passes.
6　Have a clear idea about the basis of container-tallying for imported and exported containers.
7　Have the ability to perform checking the containers damaged.

Task

Assumed that there are a certain amount of containers to be stuffed and then exported from Qingdao Port:

1 Apply right technique and method to stuff containers according to the characteristics of the goods being handled.
2 Make a good arrangement forthe interchange of FCL and/or LCL.
3 Take appropriate technology for the container handling.
4 In the process, choose and fill out relevant documents.
5 Perform the tallying of the containers without mistakes.
6 Properly deal with the container damaged, if any.

Program 1 Containerization

Containerization is preferred over the conventional modes of transportation which fundamentally takes the place of liner bulk cargo transportation in twenty years.

The main advantages of containerization are listed as following:

(1) Containerization can considerably increase the cargo-handling productivity. The adoption of the mechanical and automatic means accelerates the loading and unloading of containers. The rate of container-handling has reached 50 TEU/h.

(2) Containerization can reduce the cargodiscrepancy and damage: Thanks to the protection of container with high-strength and water-proof and door-to-door transportation, the missing and damage of cargo during moving is evidently eliminated.

(3) Containerization has realized quick transit between ships and other transportation. Therefore, it is very high efficient method not only for marine transportation but also for inland transportation.

(4) Containerization can largely reduce the overall cost and expense of transportation. The reduction is not only shown in freight cost (packing cost, storage cost, tally fees, etc.) but also in cargo-handling costs.

There are various kinds of machinery employed in the handling of container.Such as container gantry crane, container trucks and chassis (semi-trailer), straddle carrier, container forklift, rubber-tired gantry crane (RTG), rail-mounted gantry crane (RMG), front-handling stacker, etc.

The container gantry crane (portainer) is used to discharge containers from ships, and then the containers are transferred to storage yard by semi-trailer.Straddle carriers are used to transfer containers between marshalling yard and ships.Containers are stacked by forklifts or front-handling stackers, and can be transferred between different transportation by RMG or RTG on the yard.

Containers can be divided into several types according to their applications.They are dry cargo container, bulk container, reefer container, open-top container, plat form based container, open container, tank container and car container, etc.

Notes

1 Containerization is much preferred over the conventional modes of transportation which fundamentally takes the place of general cargo liner in twenty years.

集装箱运输与传统的运输方式相比有很大的优越性,在20年间基本取代了杂货班轮运输。

2 Containerization can considerably increase the cargo-handling productivity. The adoption of the mechanical and automatic means accelerates the loading and unloading of containers.

集装箱运输极大的提高了货物的装卸效率。采用机械自动化设备加快了集装箱的装卸速度。

3 Containerization can reduce the cargo discrepancy and damage. Thanks to the protection of container with high-strength and water-proof and door-to-door transportation, the missing and damage of cargo during moving is evidently eliminated.

集装箱运输可以减少货损货差.由于采用了高强度、水密封的箱体保护和门到门的货物运输方式,使货物在运输中的丢失和损坏大大降低。

4 Containerization can largely reduce the overall cost and expanse of transportation. The reduction is not only shown in freight cost (packing cost, storage cost, tally fees, etc.) but also in cargo-handling costs.

集装箱运输可大大降低总成本和运输费用。包括:运输费(包装、储存费,理货费等)和货物装卸费。

5 There are various kinds of machinery employed in the handling of container. Such as container gantry crane, container trucks and chassis (semi-trailer), straddle carrier, container forklift, rubber-tired gantry crane (RTG), rail-mounted gantry crane (RMG), front-handling stacker, etc.

有多种机械设备可用来装卸集装箱,例如:集装箱龙门起重机、集卡和集装箱半拖挂车、跨运车、集装箱专用叉车、轮胎式龙门吊、轨道式门式起重机、集装箱正面吊运起重机等。

Vocabulary

containerization [kən,teinərai'zeiʃ ən]	n.集装箱化
fundamentally [fʌndə'mentəlɪ]	adv.首要地;基本地,根本地
accelerate [æk'seləreit]	vt.加速,促进
reduction [ri'dʌkʃ ən]	n.减少,缩影,变化
semi-trailer [semɪ'treɪlə]	n.半拖挂车
marshalling yard	前方堆场
rubber-tired gantry crane(RTG)	轮胎吊,轮胎式龙门吊
rail-mounted gantry crane(RMG)	轨道式门式起重机

front-handling stacker	集装箱正面吊运起重机
dry cargo container	干货集装箱,干杂货集装箱
bulk container	散货集装箱,散装集装箱
reefer container	冷冻集装箱,冷藏集装箱
open-top container	开顶集装箱
plat form based container	框架集装箱
open container	开敞集装箱,敞式货柜
tank container	罐式集装箱
car container	汽车集装箱

Exercises

1 Answer the following questions according to the text you have read.
(1) Why can containerization considerably increase the cargo-handling productivity?
(2) Why can containerization reduce the cargo discrepancy and damage?
(3) How does containerization realize quick transit between ships and other transportation?
(4) How does containerization largely reduce the overall cost and expanse of transportation?
(5) How is the container handled?

2 Fill out the blanks with suitable words or terms based on the text.
(1) Containerization is preferred over the _____ of transportation which fundamentally takes the place of _____ transportation in twenty years.
(2) Owing to the protection of container with _____ and water-proof and _____ transportation, the missing and damage of cargo during moving is evidently eliminated.
(3) Containerization is a very high efficient method of transportation not only for _____ transportation but also for _____ transportation.
(4) The container gantry crane (portainer) is used to discharge containers from _____, and then the containers are transferred to storage yard by _____.
(5) Containers _____ by forklifts or front-handling stackers, and can be transferred between different transportation by _____ or _____ RTG on the yard.

3 Put into Chinese.

Containerization—the packing of conventional general cargo or bulk cargo material into large, standardized, reusable containers for more efficient shipment—is one of the most significant developments experienced in the transportation industry in many years. Improved in efficiency in cargo handling, more economical terminal operation and improved protection for cargo against weather, damage and pilferage—all of these are made possible by the development of containerization. It may very well be the key to a whole new era in cargo transportation.

4 Put into English.
(1) 对航运业影响最深远是集装箱运输的发展。
(2) 集装箱适用于杂货,因为杂货与散货相比在形状、大小上更为多样化。

(3)由于集装箱运输具有安全、经济和高效率等优点,它不仅被船东所接受,也为发货人所接受。

(4)采用集装箱运输使运输变得更安全、更迅速、更准确、更经济。

(5)集装箱化运输可减少货损货差和提高货物的装卸效率。

Dialogue

A: Good morning, Chief. We're going to discharge containers this afternoon. Will you please let me have all the relevant papers?

B: Yes, here you are.

A: What papers?

B: They are the import manifest, the container load plan, the numerical container list and the bay plan.

A: Thank you, Chief. Are there any dangerous cargo containers on board?

B: No, but we've carried some special containers, that is, 30 reefer containers and 24 flat rack containers with heavy lifts on them. Here's the reefer container list. Don't forget to cut off the electricity supply before discharging the reefer containers.

A: OK, I'll tell the stevedores to attend to it. Chief, have you any exception list?

B: No. we didn't find any trouble with the containers.

A: Good. But some damage might have arisen during the voyage, I suppose.

B: I suppose not. We had beautiful weather when leaving Alexandria. It wasn't till on the Indian Ocean that we met with storm. However, it did no damage to the containers because they had been specially lashed. In case you find anything wrong, contact me, please.

A: That's fine. Chief, are all the containers on board for this port?

B: No, not all for Shanghai. There're some for Qingdao and Dalian. Don't take any of them ashore.

A: Take it easy, Chief! We'll have 2 tallymen for each gang. One of them will work on deck, checking the discharging sequence. He'll pay attention to it.

B: Fine. How many gangs are you going to start with this afternoon?

A: 2 gangs.

B: What time?

A: 3 o'clock.

B: What's efficiency of your portainers?

A: 20 vans per hour.

B: Not bad. We have altogether 485 vans for this port. Will the discharging be finished before 6 tomorrow morning?

A: I expect so.

B: Very good. I'll tell the sailors to get everything ready.

(afterwards)

A: Chief, in accordance with the bay plan, there should be 15 Shanghai vans in Bay No.17, but we've found only 14 there. One van is short. Its container number is COSU4211.

B: Did you find any van with the number of SCXU6938, which is not shown on the list.

A: Let me trace it from the papers (A few minutes later). Oh, yes, it is for Singapore. Chief Checker, pleas tell your stevedores to leave it on board. I'll sign you a record for you.

B: I see. Another thing, Chief, we found 2 vans with their seal missing and one van badly bruised. Will you sigh the record, too?

A: All right.

Program 2 Laying-out of Goods Inside Containers

With the development of the containerization, the variety of cargo with different types, packing, characteristics carried by the container has extended considerably, which increases not only the risk of cargo damage but also the breakdown of the handling equipments due to improper handling and stowage of cargo in the container.

The followings are rules that should be noted when stuffing the containers:

(1) Stowing sections should be divided. The goods with strong packing and the heavy packages are required to be stowed on the bottom tires. That is the heavy goods must not be stowed over the light ones.

(2) Correct distribution of weight. The goods should be evenly distributed within the container vertically and longitudinally to prevent the risk of deformation and accidents during operation.

(3) The tiers number of the block of goods are to be considered based on the strength of packing. And cushions are required to put between tiers to reduce the possibility of crushing.

(4) Proper segregation of different goods must be made. Cargo which is fragile, taints very easily, is subject to leakage, scratches easily, has strong odors, or is liable to sweat, requires proper segregation.

(5) Making full use of the cubic capacity of the container. The goods within the container are required to stow compactly with the least void which not only can make full use of the capacity of the box but also prevent goods from collision.

(6) Much attention must be paid to the goods around the door of the container. Measures must be taken to the tightness of the goods in this position after completion of the stuffing and give careful inspection before shutting the door in order to avoid collapse of the goods around the door, which once happened and caused injury and even death of during unstuffing.

(7) Dunnages must be clean and dry, otherwise, damage to the cargo may occur.

(8) The selection of specifications of containers should be based on the types, features, packing of cargo, and containers are to be used must be in accordance with the international standard and be inspected and obtain the certificates issued by the inspection authorities.

Notes

1 Stowing sections should be divided.The goods with strong packing and the heavy packages are required to be stowed on the bottom tires.That is, the heavy goods must not be stowed over the light ones.

应当划分货区。包装坚固和重件货应当放在箱子底部。即重不压轻。

2 Correct distribution of weight.The goods should be evenly distributed within the container vertically and longitudinally to prevent the risk of deformation and accidents during operation.

箱内货物重量的正确分布。货物无论是在垂直高度上还是在水平方向上都应均匀分布，以防止箱子变形和操作时的故障发生。

3 The tiers number of the block of goods are to be considered based on the strength of packing.And cushions are required to put between tiers to reduce the possibility of crushing to the under cargo.

货物的堆码层数应根据货物的包装强度决定。另外，为使箱内下层货物不被压坏，应在货物堆码之间垫入缓冲材料。

4 Proper segregation of different goods must be made.Cargo which is fragile, taints very easily, is subject to leakage, scratches easily, has strong odors, or is liable to sweat, requires proper segregation.

要做好不同货物之间的隔离。具有下列性质的货物如：易碎、易沾染、易泄漏、易刮伤、有强烈气味、易汗湿等货物需要进行良好的隔离。

5 Much attention must be paid to the goods around the door of the container.Measures must be taken to the tightness of the goods in this position after completion of the stuffing and give careful inspection before shutting the door in order to avoid collapse of the goods around the door, which once happened and caused injury and even death during unstuffing.

必须对箱门附近的货物多加注意。在装箱完毕后应对箱门附近的货物进行紧固，在关箱门前需进行仔细检查以防货物倒塌。以往曾发生过拆箱时发生货物倒塌造成人员伤亡的情况。

6 The selection of specifications of containers should be based on the types, features, packing of cargo, and containers are to be used must be in accordance with the international standard and be inspected and obtain the certificates issued by the inspection authorities.

应根据货物的种类、性质、包装选用不同规格的集装箱，选用的集装箱应符合国际标准经严格的检查，并具有检验部门发给的合格证书。

Vocabulary

improper [imˈprɔpə]   *adj.*不合适的
stuff [stʌf]   *vt.*装填

deformation [ˌdiːfɔːˈmeiʃən]	n. 变形
cushion [ˈkuʃən]	n. 缓冲
fragile [ˈfrædʒail]	adj. 脆的, 易碎的
scratch [skrætʃ]	n. 擦伤
sweat [swet]	v. 汗湿
void [vɔid]	n. 空间, 空白, 空隙
collision [kəˈliʒən]	n. 碰撞, 冲突, 抵触
collapse [kəˈlæps]	n. 崩溃, 倒塌
specification [ˌspesifiˈkeiʃən]	n. 规范, 规格
feature [ˈfiːtʃə]	n. 特征; 特色; 特性

Exercises

1 Answer the following questions according to the text you have read.

(1) Why is it important to have a good layout inside the container?

(2) How to divide the stowing section of goods inside the container?

(3) How to distribute the weight of goods inside the container?

(4) Why must the proper segregation of different goods be made?

(5) Why the cubic capacity of the container should be full used of?

2 Fill out the blanks with suitable words or terms based on the text.

(1) The goods with strong packing and the _____ are required to be stowed on the _____.

(2) The goods should be _____ distributed within the container vertically and longitudinally to prevent the risk of _____ and accidents during operation.

(3) The rule of the stowing is that: the _____ goods must not be stowed over the _____ ones.

(4) The tiers number of the block of goods are to be considered _____ the strength of _____.

(5) Measures must be taken to the _____ of the goods around the door after completion of the stuffing and give careful inspection before _____.

3 Put into Chinese.

(1) Chief Officer, how many 20' container and 40' container are there on board?

(2) Are there any additional containers on board?

(3) Chief Officer, this container is over-length 1 meter and over-wide 1.3 meter.

(4) We have carried some special containers, that is, 30 reefer containers and 24 flat rack containers with heavy lifts in them.

(5) All the loaded vans are available on the marshalling yard.

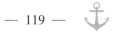

4　Put into English.

(1)这航次我们要运装多少空箱？

(2)注意,请把重箱装在空箱下面。

(3)装船马上就要开始了,行位图准备好了吗？

(4)这个集装箱的铅封已失落,我们不能接受,只得退关。

(5)如发现残损集装箱,请与当班副联系。

Dialogue

A:Good evening,Chief-officer.

B:Hi,Chief-tally,why are you coming here again at such a late time?

A:Well,it is an urgent matter and it's important for you to deal with it immediately.

B:What is it then?

A:It's something concerning the 21 containers discharged ashore this afternoon.These containers were wrongly carried here,and they are not for this port,but for port of Tianjin.This is why I rushed here to let you know it as soon as possible.They will need to be reloaded on board your ship without further trouble again for your sailing time.

B:Yes,our sailing time is 22:30 hours tonight,you see,it is nearly 7 o'clock p.m.and we are extremely busy now.I don't think the time left will be enough for this additional operation as we still have many containers for normal discharging and loading.

A:Yes,I'm aware of this situation,but they must be reloaded before your departure. This is an order from the ship's owner.

B:I see.Still I am not clear why we have to do so.The manifest shows clearly that the destination for them is this port,so what's wrong with it? I'm confused now.

A:All right,Chief,I now can't put it in detail,but it is because of the error of the last port agent.We've just received a correction by E-mail from the agent of last loading port indicating that these 21 containers must be reloaded again for Tianjin port.Of course,it is not your fault.

B:Oh,I see.The point is that the time is really very short.Do you think it possible to postpone the sailing time a little bit,say,another 2 or 3 hours?

A:It is a good idea.I'll discuss it with the port side and see if I can get it postponed if not, you'll have to complete the handling in time without delaying your ship.Now lets do it like this, you go to see the foreman to talk him with it,and I will go to have a discussion with the chief foreman in his office.Lets meet again in 20 minutes.

B:Very good,thanks.

A:OK,starting make some preparations now for your departure.

B:All right,I will.

A:Good,see you soon.

B:See you soon.

Program 3 Interchange of Container Load Goods

The containerization is to integrate the break bulk cargo into an unit(container) which then is to be transported by ship or other carriers. Except for the port which can serve as the spot of delivery and transshipment for containerization, the inland deport can also play the role.

As for the FCL(full container load), the consignor will take charge of stuffing, counting, filling out the CLP(container load plan) and making seal. Usually, there are only two parties that take charge of the FCL, the one is consignor and the other consignee. The carrier will undertake the duty of receipt and delivery of the unit which is under good condition and seal being intact. At present, the Container Liner operates the shipment of the FCL.

As regard to the LCL(less than container load), the carrier is responsible for the stuffing, counting, filling out the CLP and making seal at the CFS. The goods in the LCL involve several consignors and consignees. The carrier is in charge of taking and delivery of the goods in LCL which are in good condition and seal being intact. Nowadays, the LCL Shipment Operator operates the shipment of LCL.

The spot of delivery is the place where the goods are delivered from the carrier to the receiver, the risk and expenses are divided based on the terms of shipping contract. At present, the goods in the container are delivered at the spots such as: ship's rail or hook/tackle, container yard (CY), CFS, and other places(door) appointed by parties concerned.

The variety of the delivery spots creates the variety of the delivery methods. As mentioned above, there are four places where the container load goods are delivered, which, therefore, can develop 16 varieties of delivery methods(1.door to door, 2.door to CY, 3.door to CFS, 4.door to tackle, 5.CY to door, 6.CY to CY, 7.CY to CFS, 8.CY to tackle, 9.CFS to door, 10.CFS to CY, 11.CFS to CFS, 12.CFS to tackle, 13.tackle to door, 14.tackle to CY, 15.tackle to CFS, 16.tackle to tackle). In practice, in the seaborne container transport, the delivery methods CY/CY and CFS/CFS are more preferable, the former is for the Container Liner and the latter for the LCL Shipment Operator.

Notes

1 The containerization is to integrate the break bulk cargo into an unit(container) which then is to be transported by ship or other carriers. Except for the port which can serve as the spot of delivery and transshipment for containerization, the inland deports can also play the role.

集装箱运输是将散件货物汇成一个运输单元,使用船舶等运输工具进行的运输方式。除了港口作为货物交接和换装的地点,还可设置陆路交接、换装站点。

2 As for the FCL(full container load), the consignor will take charge of stuffing, counting,

filling out the CLP(container load plan) and making seal. Usually, there are only two parties that take charge of the FCL, that is, one consignor and one consignee. The carrier will undertake the duty of receipt and delivery of the unit which is under good condition and seal being intact. Nowadays, the Container Liner operates the shipment of the FCL.

对于整箱货,货方负责装箱、计数、填写装箱单,并加封志。通常只有一个发货人和一个收货人。承运人承担在箱体和封志完好状态下接受和交付整箱货的义务。当前,班轮公司主要从事整箱货的货运任务。

3　The spot of delivery is the place where the goods are delivered from the carrier to the receiver and the risk and expenses are divided based on the terms of shipping contract. At present, the goods in the container are delivered at the spots such as: ship's rail or hook/tackle, container yard(CY), CFS, and other places(door) appointed by parties concerned.

货物运输中的交接地点是指根据运输合同,承运人和货方交接货物、划分责任和风险和费用的地点。目前,集装箱运输中的货物的交接地点有船边或吊钩、集装箱堆场、集装箱货运站和其他双方约定的地点。

4　The variety of the delivery spots creates the variety of the delivery methods. As mentioned above, there are four places where the container load goods are delivered, which, therefore, can develop 16 varieties of delivery methods.

集装箱货物的交接地点不同就会有不同的交接方式。如上所述,集装箱货物有四种不同的交接地点因而可产生16种不同的交接方式。

5　In practice, in the seaborne container transport, the delivery methods CY/CY and CFS/CFS are more preferable, the former is for the Container Liner and the latter for the LCL Shipment Operator.

在实践中,海运集装箱货物的主要交接方式为:场到场和站到站。场到场是班轮公司通常采用的交接方式;站到站是集装箱经营人通常采用的方式。

Vocabulary

integrate [ˈintiɡreit]	vt.集成、整合
break bulk cargo	件杂货
inland deport	陆路交接点
FCL (full container load)	整箱货
CLP (container load plan)	装箱单
undertake [ˌʌndəˈteik]	vt.承担;接受;承办
seal [siːl]	n.铅封
LCL (less than container load)	拼箱货
CFS (Container Freight Station)	集装箱货运站
(CY container yard)	集装箱堆场

seaborne container transport 海运集装箱运输

Exercises

1 Answer the following questions according to the text you have read.

(1) Who is responsible for the FCL in terms of stuffing, counting, filling out the CLP and making seal?

(2) Who take charges of the duty of receipt and delivery of the container which is under good condition and seal is intact?

(3) Who operates the shipment of the FCL at present?

(4) As regard to the LCL, who is responsible for the stuffing, counting, filling out the CLP and making seal at the CFS?

(5) Who operates the shipment of LCL?

2 Fill out the blanks with suitable words or terms based on the text.

(1) Usually, there are only two parties that take charge of the FCL, that is, the one is _____ and the other _____.

(2) The goods in the container are delivered at the spots such as: ship's rail or hook/tackle, container yard(CY), _____, and other places(door) appointed by _____.

(3) The _____ is in charge of taking and _____ of the goods in LCL.

(4) The _____ will undertake the duty of receipt and _____ of the unit which is under good condition and seal being intact.

(5) In practice, in the seaborne container transport, the delivery methods _____ and _____ are more preferable.

3 Put into Chinese.

(1) The container will be discharged at the apron of the wharf to check whether it is in good order or damaged.

(2) During discharge, we found one damaged container in Hatch No.3. Obviously, the bruise is original damage. Would you certify the fact and sign?

(3) Please mark the safety draft scale and fore and aft full draft of the vessel in the stowage plan.

(4) The number of these container disagree with those shown on the plan. Is it possible that they have been mixed up or misplaced?

(5) Please inform the Duty Officer to take off the electric sockets for all reefer containers.

4 Put into English.

(1) 卸船的空箱较多,这是集装箱残损记录,请签字。

(2) 15 点左右卸船结束,何时装船请等待通知。

(3) 请告诉我,选港货集装箱在装载时有什么要求?

(4) 请告诉你们的船员,装危险品集装箱时,不要在甲板上吸烟。

(5) 这些冷藏集装箱是到鹿特丹的吗?

Dialogue

A: Hi, Chief, how about the loading situation, everything good now?

B: In general, it is OK, but still there are some problems.

A: Is that so? What are they?

B: Yes, I have to adjust the bay plan I finished yesterday.

A: Why so?

B: I was notified directly by the shipper of B/L No.K-006 that 7 containers previously planed to load in hatch No.3 have been cancelled for some reason. But you see, they have already been loaded on board the ship. In the mean time, the another agent from the container department of your company faxed me that 135 additional empty containers will be loaded on board. This is, I like to say, a really sudden change as for as the loading situation in this port is concerned.

A: Hmm, I see, that's right. You must make some adjustment of the bay plan. By the way, have you got any idea about how to mend it?

B: Yes. For the 7 containers to be cancelled they are to be discharged again from the ship, though it is a little troublesome. For the additional 135 empty containers, they have to be loaded on deck and inside hold No.4 respectively due to the need for rotation.

A: All right. But I would like to suggest you have a talk with the Chief-tally and the foreman about the details of working operations to ensure the ship's smooth handling.

B: Thank you for reminding of this. I'll do it like what you say.

A: And, Chief, would you please give me one copy of the new bay plan, when I come here again later?

B: Of course, I would.

A: Now, the last point I want to mention is the total time for loading. The previous total time for your loading and unloading without such change is about 20 hours, since the conditions have now changed, it will surely be longer. Therefore, please put this factor into your whole consideration, and try your best to do the operation smoothly to assure the ship's departure on time.

B: Yes, you are right, it is very important. Don't worry, I'll keep your words in mind and complete it without failure.

Program 4 Container-handling Technology

Proper selection of container-handling technology will not only save the expenses spent in the utilization of handling equipment and personnel but also raise the productive efficiency. There are two main schemes of technology applied in the container handling.

(1) Portainer—Straddle Carrier Technology Scheme

In this scheme, the operation of "Ship—Stacking Yard" is carried out as such: the container is discharged from ship by the portainer (container gantry crane) onto the ground of the quayside and then taken to the appointed slot in the marshalling yard by the straddle carrier, during which, the operations of Yard—Yard, Yard—Container Truck, and Yard—Cargo Distribution Station, etc. is done by the straddle carrier.

The utilization of straddle carrier with its flexibility and multi-function can increase the handling rate of the portainer and shorten the period of operation, and implement by itself many tasks such as self-claiming, carrying, stacking and loading & unloading vehicles, etc.

(2) Portainer—Transfer Crane Technology Scheme

The use of the transfer crane may be in the type of rubber-tired gantry crane (RTG) or rail-mounted gantry crane (RMG). At present, for the Chinese ports, the rubber-tired gantry crane is preferably applied.

As the gantry crane, for this scheme, can not make interchange of the container directly with the portainer, the full-trailer is added in this scheme, that is, the container is carried horizontally to and fro by the full-trailer between quayside and stacking yard, between marshalling yard and rear stacking yard, and between stacking yard and cargo distribution station.

As the gantry crane is able to make higher stacking of the container, large amount of containers stowed can be obtained per unit area, and owing to a compact stowing of containers can be made within the span of the gantry crane without walking space left, a higher utilization rate of the area can be made, both of which is of remarkable significance to a terminal with limited floor area of yard.

The adoption of the schemes of container-handling technology should take into account of the conditions of the terminal's facilities and the concerns of whether the scheme is practical and economical for the terminal.

Notes

1 In this scheme, the operation of "Ship—Stacking Yard" is carried out as such: the container is discharged from ship by the portainer (container gantry crane) onto the ground of the quayside and then taken to the appointed slot in the marshalling yard by the straddle carrier, during which, the operations of Yard—Yard, Yard—Container Truck, and Yard—Cargo Distribution Station, etc. is done by the straddle carrier.

在该方案中,"船—场"作业是由装卸桥将集装箱从船上卸到码头前沿地面上,然后用跨运车再把集装箱搬运到集装箱场地的指定箱位上。其中,"场—场"、"场—货运站"、"场—集装箱集卡"、"场—货运站"等作业,均可由跨运车承担。

2 The utilization of straddle carrier with its flexibility and multi-function can increase the handling rate of the portainer and shorten the period of operation, and implement by itself many tasks such as self-claiming, carrying, stacking and loading & unloading vehicles, etc.

跨运车具有机动灵活、功能多样的特点,这提高了集装箱桥吊的工作效率,节省了作业时间。跨运车具有自取、搬运、堆垛以及装卸车辆等多种功能。

3　As the transfer crane, for this scheme, can not make interchange of the container directly with the portainer, the combination of full-trailer is added in this scheme, that is, the container is carried horizontally to and fro by the full-trailer between quayside and stacking yard, between marshalling yard and rear stacking yard, and between stacking yard and cargo distribution station.

　　由于龙门起重机不能直接与装卸桥配合交接集装箱,所以这个方案还需要配牵引车挂车。即在码头前沿和堆场之间,前方堆场和和后方堆场之间,堆场与货运站之间需要配牵引车挂车作水平搬运集装箱之用。

4　As the gantry crane is able to make higher stacking of the container, large amount of containers stowed can be obtained per unit area, and owing to a compact stowing of containers can be made within the span of the gantry crane without walking space left, a higher utilization rate of the area can be made, both of which is of remarkable significance to a terminal with limited floor area of yard.

　　由于龙门起重机堆箱层数多,因此单位面积堆存量大;由于该机跨度内可紧密堆垛,不留通道,因此堆场面积利用率高。这在陆域较小的码头上特别显得重要。

Vocabulary

utilization [ˌjuːtilaiˈzeiʃən]	n.利用,使用,应用
raise [reiz]	vt.提高
scheme [skiːm]	n.计划,规划,方案
portainer [ˈpɔːteinə]	n.集装箱码头起重机,集装箱岸吊
slot [slɔt]	n.箱位
implement [ˈimplimənt]	n.工具,器具,手段
	vt.实现,使生效,执行
flexibility [ˌfleksəˈbiliti]	n.机动性,适应性,灵活性
interchange [ˌintəˈtʃeindʒ]	vt.交换,互换
horizontally [ˌhɔriˈzɔntli]	adv.地平地,水平地
to and fro	连续往返地;来回地
full-trailer	全挂车
stacking yard	集装箱堆场
cargo distribution station	货运站

Exercises

1　Answer the following questions according to the text you have read.

(1) What is the Portainer—Straddle Carrier Technology Scheme?

(2) What are the advantages of the utilization of straddle carrier?

(3) What is the handling machinery for the operations of Yard—Yard, Yard—Container Truck, and Yard—Cargo Distribution Station, etc?

Project 6 Container-tallying Service

(4) What is the Portainer—Transfer Crane Technology Scheme?

(5) What machinery is added in the Portainer—Transfer Crane Technology Scheme?

2 Fill out the blanks with suitable words or terms based on the text.

(1) In Portainer—Straddle Carrier Technology Scheme, the operation of "Ship—Stacking Yard" is carried out as such: the container is discharged from _____ by the portainer (container gantry crane) onto the _____ of the quayside.

(2) The utilization of straddle carrier with its _____ and multi-function can increase the _____ of the portainer and shorten the period of operation,

(3) The use of the transfer crane may be in the type of _____ (RTG) or _____ (RMG).

(4) As the gantry crane is able to make _____ of the container, _____ of containers stowed can be obtained per unit area.

(5) Owing to a _____ of containers can be made within the span of the gantry crane without walking space left, a higher _____ of the area can be made.

3 Put into Chinese.

(1) We usually use container trucks and chassis (semi-trailer) to transfer containers.

(2) All the containers are in good order on board, because they had been specially lashed.

(3) We found two vans with their seals missing and one van badly bruised. Please sign it.

(4) This stevedoring company is a modernized container terminal.

(5) Our company offers service of the utmost quality to customers from all of the world.

4 Put into English.

(1) 在卸冷冻箱之前,不要忘了切断电源。

(2) 我们每工班每条作业线可卸280标准箱。

(3) 大副,残损集装箱是卸上岸,还是留在船上让你检查?

(4) 配载计划员正在编制装船积载图,请稍等片刻。

(5) 现在船左倾,我们将装右侧集装箱。

Dialogue

A: Chief, I've got something urgent to talk with you. When I went to the tallyman's room a while ago, I was told by the chief tally that one import 40 feet reef container has some problem with temperature. To be exact, it failed to reach normal temperature minus 18 degree below zero. Do you know the reason?

B: Really? I've received no information about it. Why don't we go to the tallyman's room now together to ask him about the story?

A: Sounds good, let's go.

(in the tally-room)

B: Hello, sir, how is the discharging going? I heard that one 40 feet reefer container had some problem with temperature, is that true?

C: Yes, you are right. During the discharging, one of our tallyman on the last working shift found that the temperature of the reefer container under B/L 246 from Seoul Korea was only minus 13 degrees, not minus 18 degrees. So our tallyman checked it again with your third officer and he had nothing to say and signed the record. Here it is, you see.

B: Oh, like that. My third officer didn't mention it to me. And now he's off duty. Anyway since my duty officer signed it himself, I certainly admit it. But the problem is why did it happen? I really don't understand.

C: Chief-officer, do you think all of your reefer container sockets worked flawlessly or is it possible that the power supply stopped during the navigation?

B: No, I assure you that's not possible.

A: Chief, is it probable that some socket might be shocked suddenly for whatever reason, and that you might not find out about it in time?

B: I don't know exactly.

A: Or that something might have taken place at the loading port prior to your receiving it?

B: I'm sorry to say I cant remember it clearly. I believe we'll have to examine all the above possibilities, I hope by doing so we can find where the problem lies.

C: OK, it's very nice. Now shall we unload it on the wharf, Chief? No matter what you won't prevent unloading, will you?

B: Absolutely, not. Please believe me.

A: All right, Chief-tally. It ought to be connected to the yard socket as soon as the said reefer container is discharged on land.

C: Correct, I am going to inform the foreman of it.

B: Thanks for your arranging everything so well.

Program 5 Documents of Container Load Goods

As container load goods are moved through several channels, the command of their governance moves simultaneously before finally reaching their respective receivers, which involves many documents defining the responsibility towards the container in the corresponding channels.

(1) Dock Receipt (D/P)

In modern seaborne transport, the containerization plays the exceeding role. In order to simplify the formality, the clustering-bill dock receipt acts as the consignment note for container load goods. Meanwhile, the clustering-bill dock receipt is usually made up by freight forwarder and sent to shipping company or its agent for booking space, hence the consignment note is virtually a Booking Note. The bills of D/P mainly include expense-claim notice bill, shipping order bill, copy of D/P for Chief Mate, the original D/P bill and back bill of distribution, etc. The shipping company or its agent will write down the vessel's name, the voyage, the series

No. on the consignment note if the booking is accepted, and stamp on the shipping order bill to reconfirm the booking. The copy of D/P for Chief Mate will be delivered by the harbour office to Ocean Shipping Tally Company before loading and make delivery of goods based on it after completion of loading.

(2) Equipment Interchange Receipt (EIR)

EIR is a ticket for the user, carrier, and the keeper of the container to interchange box and equipment when container "in" or "out" the dock or CY. It is a ticket for interchange and also for grant as well.

Freight forwarder will obtain the EIR from the ship when he has completed the booking and been granted the shipping order.

There are many functions that the EIR plays in the export of the container load goods, the main role of which is to act as a base for the consignor (or freight forwarder) to fetch the empty vans from CY and move the loaded vans onto aboard. The other bills of the EIR consist of the inspection records of the container "in" or "out" the CY upon whether the empty or loaded vans in good order and condition to clarify the responsibility of the parties concerned.

(3) Container Load Plan (CLP)

The CLP is a paper that lists the goods packed into the box with full particulars such as description, quantity, types, characteristics, etc. CLP is the mere paper that gives the full information regarding the goods in a container.

(4) Goods-Delivery Record

In practice, Goods-Delivery Record has been prevailingly adopted for container liner instead of the Bill of Lading used in bulk general cargo, and plays an equivalent role as the B/L which includes: goods-received notice, bill of lading, expenses bill, record of delivery, etc.

Notes

1 As container load goods are moved through several channels, the command of their governance moves simultaneously before finally reaching their respective receivers, which involves many documents defining the responsibility towards the container in the corresponding channels.

集装箱货物在最终抵达收货人之前要经过多个环节，其物权的责任也同时跟着转移，这一过程就涉及到许多单证以确定相应环节的责任范围。

2 In modern seaborne transport, the containerization plays the exceeding role. In order to simplify the formality, the clustering-bill dock receipt acts as the consignment note for container load goods. Meanwhile, the clustering-bill dock receipt is usually made up by freight forwarder and sent to shipping company or its agent for booking space, hence the consignment note is virtually a Booking Note.

现代海上班轮运输以集装箱运输为主，为简化手续即以场站收据作为集装箱货物的托运单。"场站收据"联单现在通常是由货代缮制交船公司或其代理订舱，因此托运单也就相当于订舱单。

3 The bills of D/P mainly include freight notice bill, shipping order bill, copy of D/P for Chief Mate, the original D/P bill and back bill of distribution, etc. The shipping company or its agent will write down the vessel's name, the voyage, the series No. on the consignment note if the booking is accepted, and stamp on the shipping order bill to reconfirm the booking.

D/P 联单主要包括:运费通知、装船单、场站收据副本大副联、场站收据正本、配舱回单等。船公司或它的代理人接受订单后在托运单上加添船名、航次及编号,并在货运单上盖章,表示确认订舱。

4 EIR is a ticket for the user, carrier, and the keeper of the container to interchange box and equipment when container "in" or "out" the dock or CY. It is a ticket for interchange and also for grant as well.

集装箱"发放设备交接单"是集装箱进出港区、场站时,用箱人、运箱人、管箱人之间交接集装箱及设备的凭证,它既是一个交接凭证,又是一个发放凭证。

5 The CLP is a paper that lists the goods packed into the box with full particulars.

集装箱装箱单是详细记载集装箱内货物情况的单证。

Vocabulary

governance [ˈgʌvənəns]	n. 统治,统辖,管理
simultaneously [siməlˈteiniəsli]	adv. 同时地
respective [risˈpektiv]	adj. 各自的,分别的
corresponding [ˌkɔrisˈpɔndiŋ]	adj. 对应的,相应的
Dock Receipt(D/P)	场站收据
simplify [ˈsimplifai]	vt. 简化;使简易;使单纯
clustering-bill dock receipt	场站收据联单
freight forwarder	货代
Booking Note	订舱单
Equipment Interchange Receipt(EIR)	设备交接单
empty vans	空箱
loaded vans	重箱
mere [miə]	adj. 仅仅的,只不过的
Goods-Delivery Record	交货记录单

Exercises

1 Answer the following questions according to the text you have read.
(1) Who is the maker for the clustering-bill dock receipt?
(2) How the copy of D/P for Chief Mate is delivered after completion of loading?
(3) What is the role of the Equipment Interchange Receipt(EIR)?
(4) What is the Container Load Plan(CLP)?

Project 6 Container-tallying Service

(5)What is Goods-Delivery Record?

2 Fill out the blanks with suitable words or terms based on the text.

(1)In order to simplify the _____,the clustering-bill dock receipt acts as the _____ for container load goods.

(2)The clustering-bill dock receipt is usually made up by _____ and sent to shipping company or its agent for _____.

(3)The copy of D/P for _____ will be delivered by the harbour office to _____ before loading.

(4)Freight forwarder will obtain the EIR from the _____ when he has completed the booking and been granted the _____.

(5)In practice,Goods-Delivery Record has been prevailingly adopted for _____ instead of the Bill of Lading used in _____.

3 Put into Chinese.

(1)I'm sorry,Chief,I found there is a platform container where packages on the container load list do not conform to those on the inward manifest.

(2)These containers in Bay No30 disagree with your stowage plan with one over-landed.How did it happen?

(3)We are waiting for the transshipment containers from the feeder barge being loaded to this voyage.

(4)The shipper told us that one of his containers should be shut out.So we are looking for it.

(5)Chief,these containers to Hong Kong have no place to be loaded.Would you please tell me how to drag them to another Bay?

4 Put into English.

(1)右舷的集装箱需移一些到左舷,因为船向右倾了。

(2)看来吊具需要更换,有没有备用的?

(3)桥吊发生了故障,暂时不能作业。

(4)轨道式龙门吊正在修理,用轮胎式堆箱。

(5)我们应当根据事实编制现场记录。

Dialogue

A:Have you heard that 2 containers fell down and got damaged during unloading last night?

B:Yes,I have,but I have no idea about the details of the story.Could you please tell me more about it?

A:Certainly,here is the story.When I have just gone on duty and I suddenly heard some faint but heavy sound from the direction of the deck,and I rushed out of the room and hurried to the deck where I saw two containers had been seriously damaged.

B:Did any person tell you how it happened like this?

A:Yes,the Chief－tally said that when one container had been lifted out of hold No.3 and it

was in the mid-air, it became difficult to be controlled because of its unusual height. Therefore it hit another container below it, which fell down from the top of other containers to the deck. The container in the air got damaged and fell down onto the deck.

B: I see. What about the cargo inside? Was it damaged?

A: I couldn't see the cargo inside, so I don't know exactly whether it was damaged, too.

B: OK, we'll check it later. What did you do then, Chief?

A: I asked the chief tally to write me a damage report with his signature on it. I also asked the foreman on duty to sign it and then reported the matter to the captain.

B: That's good, Chief. What are you planning to do next?

A: Well, I am not clear how to deal it best. I don't have much experience of this kind of problem. Can you give some advice?

B: In my opinion, you should contact the port side via chief tally to arrange for cargo surveyor to come on board to inspect the damaged containers. The surveyor will complete a survey report. The consignee will finally get the report and manage to get some compensation from the insurance company. After the inspection, the damaged containers can be discharged from your ship. Your captain should give a detail report to your owner letting him know the true situation of the case.

A: OK, that's a clear picture. I'll follow those steps, thank you very much.

Program 6　Basis for Tallying Containers

　　Basis for tallying containers are shipping documents which are selected and applied based on the mode of containers' movement

　　Containers inward to or outward from a port in ocean shipping business must go through the indispensible procedure of tallying before discharging or loading, which involves several documents acting as the base for the tallying of the imported or exported container.

　　The basis for the tallying of imported containers is the paper called Import Cargo Manifest. It shows the containers and the goods packed in the containers lot by lot carried on board in full particulars and their respective destination port.

　　In practice, the shipping company or its agent will provide with the information about the imported containers to the authorities of container terminal, ocean shipping tally and relative departments in stipulated time to ensure the container ship to berth timely and get discharged smoothly. The documents concerning the imported containers involve Import Cargo Manifest, Bay Plan and Dangerous Cargo List, etc.

　　The Import Cargo Manifest, made up by the shipping company or its agent based on relative materials supplied after the completion of loading of containers (goods) aboard, lists the goods by lots about their bill of Lading No., marks, packages, packing, description, weight, volume and their respective loading port, transshipment port, discharging port and destination, and also notes down the containers carried about their series No., seal No., types, quantity, goods and delivery method as well.

As to the loading of the container for export, the Export Stowage Plan is used as the basis for tallying, which also plays a role as an original proof to the containers that have been loaded on board the ship.

A shipping notice issued by the Shipping Company or its agent will be delivered to the Container Terminal Company before the commence of loading. The Export Stowage Plan, compiled by the Container Terminal Distribution Centre based on the notice, is made up from the CLP which has been checked up with the customs cleared D/R.

The Import Cargo Manifest consists of three parts, that is Stowage Plan, bay Plan and Summary.

Notes

1 Containers inward to or outward from a port in ocean shipping business must go through the indispensible procedure of tallying before discharging or loading, which involves several documents acting as the base for the tallying of the imported or exported container.

外贸运输中进口或出口的集装箱在装卸前必须通过理货关口,其凭借理货依据对进出口集装箱进行理货。

2 In practice, the shipping company or its agent will provide with the information about the imported containers to the authorities of container terminal, ocean shipping tally and relative departments in stipulated time to ensure the container ship to berth timely and get discharged smoothly. The documents concerning the imported containers involve Import Cargo Manifest, Bay Plan and Dangerous Cargo List, etc.

通常为确保集装箱船舶能及时靠泊与顺利卸箱,船公司或其代理人须在规定的时间内向集装箱码头外轮理货及相关单位提供进口集装箱有关资料。所提供的货运单证包括:进口舱单、进口船图和危险品清单等。

3 The Import Cargo Manifest, made up by the shipping company or its agent based on relative materials supplied after the completion of loading of containers (goods) aboard, lists the goods by lots about their bill of Lading No., marks, packages, packing, description, weight, volume and their respective loading port, transshipment port, discharging port and destination, and also notes down the containers carried about their series No., seal No., types, quantity, goods and delivery method as well.

船公司或其代理人在装船完毕后依据相关的资料编制进口舱单。进口舱单逐票列明货物的提单号、标志、件数、包装、货名、重量、体积以及装货港、中转港、卸货港和目的地;同时详细记载了所在运的集装箱的箱号、铅封号、类型、数量、箱内货物情况,以及交付方式。

4 When it comes to the loading of the container for export, the Export Stowage Plan is used as the base for tallying, which also plays a role as an original proof to the containers that have been loaded on board the ship.

对于集装箱的出口装船,以出口预备图作为其理货依据,出口预备图也是出口装载集装

箱的原始凭证。

5　A shipping notice issued by the Shipping Company or its agent will be delivered to the Container Terminal Company before the commence of loading. The Export Stowage Plan, compiled by the Container Terminal Distribution Centre based on the notice, is made up from the CLP which has been checked up with the customs cleared D/R.

集装箱码头在集装箱装船前接收船公司或其代理的装船指令，码头配送中心据此并根据集装箱装箱单，与海关已放行的场站收据核对后制作集装箱预配图。

6　Stowage Plan, bay Plan and Summary.

封面图、行位图和汇总清单。

Vocabulary

Inward ['inwəd]　　　　　　　　　　adj. 进口的，向内的
outward ['autwəd]　　　　　　　　　adj. 出口的，向外的
indispensible　　　　　　　　　　　adj. 必不可少的
particular [pə'tikjulə]　　　　　　　n. 详细说明
Dangerous Cargo List　　　　　　　 危险货物清单
Container Terminal Distribution Centre　集装箱码头配送中心

Exercises

1　Answer the following questions according to the text you have read.

（1）Who is the Import Cargo Manifest?

（2）Who is the maker of the Import Cargo Manifest?

（3）What contents are listed in the Import Cargo Manifest?

（4）What is the Export Stowage Plan?

（5）What is the role of Export Stowage Plan?

2　Fill out the blanks with suitable words or terms based on the text.

（1）The Import Cargo Manifest shows the containers and the goods packed in the containers _____ carried on board in full particulars and their respective _____.

（2）The documents concerning the imported containers involve _____, Bay Plan and _____, etc.

（3）As to the loading of the container for export, the _____ is used as the _____ for tallying.

（4）A shipping notice issued by the Shipping Company or _____ will be delivered to the Container Terminal Company before the commence of _____.

（5）The Import Cargo Manifest consists of three parts, that is _____, bay Plan and _____.

3　Put the following Sentences into Chinese.

（1）These shifting and reloading containers should be discharged to shore first.

(2) The slot in hatch No.3 has been some deformed. Please go there and have a look.

(3) How long will it take to repair the slot?

(4) The side of container has been dented. Please give it a repair.

(5) The ship is down by stern now, some containers should be shifted from Bay No.55 to No.01.

4　Put into English.

(1) 我们不能用溢装集装箱来抵消短卸集装箱。

(2) 我们使用集装箱桥吊来装卸集装箱。

(3) 你们是怎样把集装箱转运到船边的？是用跨运车还是叉车？

(4) 你们使用的正面吊能将集装箱堆几个高？

(5) 你们集装箱码头有货运站吗？

Dialogue

A vessel planner is getting on board of vessel – KTM 0520, the following conversation is between a vessel planner(A) and the Chief Mate(B).

A: Hi, I am a stowage planner from QQCT.

B: Hi, I am an officer on duty, what can I do for you?

A: Could you tell me where the Chief Officer is?

B: Oh, he is upstairs in his room.

A: I see, thank you!

A: Good Morning, I am Lee, the stowage planner from QQCT.

B: Good Morning, nice to see you.

A: I got on board to ask you to confirm the loading plan, here is the floppy disk.

B: What is in it?

A: The disk contains: through, local and re-stow cargo, you may check them by your system.

B: Besides, May I mind you to discharge and load lightly, otherwise you are responsible for any damage caused by your stevedores' rough handling.

A: We have operation regulations in our terminal and I am sure our stevedores know the right way to handle containers. By the way, I was told that you do not have enough locks on your vessel, so you have to bring forth more for our stevedores to complete the loading.

B: Ok, I will ask someone to arrange it. Then could you shift this container from 120582 to 160784, as the height of this row affects our view. Also please shift that container from here to that position in consideration of the stack weight.

A: Affect the view? Let me have a look, oh, sorry, I will correct it. However for the stack weight, and I think it's no problem, you know, my office computer also installs a system of Loadstar as yours and it's automatically calculated by the computer.

(continued)

Program 7 Container Damage-checking Technology

In determination of the responsibility of the parties concerned for the container and the goods in case any damage occurs to the both during the handling of containers, proper damage-checking technology means a lot for the tallying of containers.

(1) For the container imported, the Chief Tally, before discharging, will consult with the ship about the dealing with the original damage of the container, the compiling of the damage record and the respective acknowledge and signing, and give specific requirement of the inspection to his tallymen and the terminal operator. When discharging, the tallymen and the persons sent by the terminal will make receipt and delivery by the shipside, and in case any damage is found or the seal broken or lost, the ship will be asked to be present to give a check and clear the responsibility, and the tallymen will reseal and number it on the record. In addition, the Chief Tally will make up the damage record which is to be signed both by the ship and the party being to blame for.

(2) For the container exported, the Chief Tally, before loading, will consult with the ship about the dealing with the damage of the container, make work records and give specific requirement of the inspection to his tallymen and the terminal operator.

When loading, tallymen and the persons send by the terminal will make receipt and delivery. The tallymen inspect the containers on deck, and in case any damage or the seal broken or lost is found, the tallymen will inform the persons sent by the terminal operator to look it over, and make up the damage record and ask for signature. If badly damaged container or seal missing is found, an immediate notice must be sent to the ship for confirming; in this case, loading can not be commenced without the permission of the ship.

(3) For the transshipment container (loading or unloading), if any damage or sealing undone is found the tallymen will look it over together with the terminal, and a damage record will be made up for confirming and signing by the terminal and party concerned. And the responsibility of sealmaking for the container with seal undone rests on the terminal.

Notes

1 In determination of the responsibility of the parties concerned for the container and the goods in case any damage occurs to the both during the handling of containers, proper damage-checking technology means a lot for the tallying of containers.

集装箱在装卸过程中,采用正确的残损检验工艺,来区分相关方对集装箱及货物残损的责任,这对于集装箱的计理具有重要意义。

2 When discharging, the tallymen and the persons sent by the terminal will make receipt and delivery by the shipside, and in case any damage is found or the seal broken or lost, the ship will be asked to be present to give a check and clear the responsibility, and the tallymen will reseal and

number it on the record. In addition, the Chief Tally will make up the damage record which is to be signed both by the ship and the party being to blame for.

集装箱卸船时,理货人员与码头方人员在船边进行交接。发现箱体损坏、铅封断失,及时通知船方验看和确认责任,理货人员重新施加铅封并在残损记录上写明铅封号。理货长编制残损记录取得船方和责任方签认。

3 If badly damaged container or seal missing is found, an immediate notice must be sent to the ship for confirming; in this case, loading can not be commenced without the permission of the ship.

若发现集装箱严重残损或铅封失落,应及时告知船方,船方同意后方可装船。

4 For the transshipment container(loading or unloading), if any damage or sealing undone is found the tallymen will look it over together with the terminal, and a damage record will be made up for confirming and signing by the terminal and party concerned. And the responsibility of seal-making for the container with seal undone rests on the terminal.

对于中转集装箱(装或卸),发现集装箱未施封或箱体残损,理货人员应会同码头方进行验看确认并编制残损记录,取得码头方和有关方的签认。对未施封的集装箱由码头方负责施封。

Vocabulary

appearance [əˈpiərəns]	n.外观,外表
Chief Tally	理货长
consult with	协商,商量
reseal [riˈsiːl]	vt.重封

Exercises

1 Answer the following questions according to the text you have read.

(1) As to the container imported, what should be done for Chief Tally before discharging?

(2) When discharging of containers, what should be done for the tallymen?

(3) As regard to the container exported what should be done for the Chief Tally before loading?

(4) When loading, what should be done for the tallymen?

(5) For the transshipment container, what should be done for the tallymen if any damage or sealing undone is found?

2 Fill out the blanks with suitable words or terms based on the text.

(1) Whether the appearance and the seal of the container is in good condition during the handling of containers means a lot in determination of the _____ for the container and the goods, in case any _____ occurs to the both.

(2) When discharging, if any damage happens the Chief Tally will make up the _____

which is to be signed by both the _____ and the party being to blame for.

(3) For the container exported, the Chief Tally, before loading, will consult with the _____ about the dealing with the damage of the container, make work records and give specific requirement of the inspection to his tallymen and the _____.

(4) When loading, _____ and the persons send by the _____ will make receipt and delivery between them.

(5) The _____ of seal-making for the container with seal undone rests on the _____.

3 Put into Chinese.

(1) One tallyman works at the ship's side, examining the appearance condition and checking the container number and seal number; another works on deck, inspect the container's top and jotting down its actual stowage.

(2) How many FCLs and LFCs are there on board? And was there any of containers damaged and the loading port during the voyage?

(3) How many TEUs are there in your ship? How many containers will be discharged in Shanghai and how many do you plan to load?

(4) The handling efficiency of our port is rather high. The quay crane completes the cycle in time average of about 2.5 minutes per container.

(5) Although the quay crane is under repair, we believe that there will no problem in having your containers shipped in time, because there is only some small trouble with it.

4 Put into English.

(1) 请问对甲板上的集装箱捆扎有何特殊要求?

(2) 我们需要旋锁和连接锁,请船方提供。

(3) 现在正是低潮,必须到高潮时才能开航。

(4) 请计算一下本班的装货水尺和集装箱箱数。

(5) 请检查一下船上的冷冻箱情况。

Dialogue

B: Really? Yeah you are right, the safety weight is no problem. That's wonderful. then it's much easier for both of us to confirm the load plan since everything is clearly defined on this system. By the way, could you provide me the reefer manifest as well as the reefer list?

A: Oh, for the reefer manifest and list, your Reefer service center Yuan Chang will give you according to the agreement. And the terminal is not responsible for providing them.

B: All right, I know, and I will ask Yuangchang to do that. How about the DG reefer? It is stowed in the correct position?

A: Surely, it's preplanned in strict accordance with the ship's requirements and separated by DG class. Also I wonder what's the facing direction of the reefer engine?

B: Let me show you, see, it faces to the ship's aft.

A: Thank you. Also please tell me if this super freezer with the head letter of MSFU can be stowed on Tier 2? Since the reefer plug of the position you require is damaged.

B: Tier 2? Oh yes, you can shift the freezer there, it's no problem.

A: Thank you. I will adjust the stowage plan accordingly. Besides, there are some additional cargo will be added later on, please leave enough position for these containers and adjust the ballast water accordingly.

B: I will keep an eye on it. Could you please give me the final plan as soon as possible?

A: Of course I will do asap, you know our terminal ensures all vessels must be completed within 10 hours.

B: That's good, no wonder it's called a world class terminal. Finally I'd like to remind you the operation process should be carried out exactly according to the stowage plan, which I have confirmed.

A: Certainly, why not? At the same time, I have to remind you that if the operation stops caused by your side, we have to hold you to sign the "Standby"

B: I certainly know

A: Then keep contact, have a nice stay here in our terminal, see you.

B: See you.

Program 8   Container Tallying Procedure and Methods

Proper tallying procedure and methods ensure the effectiveness and efficiency as well as the correctness and accuracy of container tallying.

During tallying, a tallyman will be assigned to each gang for the tallying of container ship, and more tallymen may join in if required in practice.

As far as the container ship for import is concerned, the tallyman effects his duty by the shipside or in the hold (for roll on/roll off ship). The tallyman must have a best knowledge about the requirements and notes in the Hand-over Record made by the Chief Tally, and get an Import Bay Plan in hand, then check the series number of containers, and give number to the slots in the same bay based on the discharging sequence and log off the Bay Plan, inspect the appearance and seal of containers, and in case any unmoral phenomenon is found a record should be made to prove the fact.

On the end of the shift, the tallymen must check up the tallying figures with the consignee on the wharf or his agent and submit the finished container tally sheet together with the bay plan (with container being free) to the Chief Tally.

The process of tallying. (1) The tallyman effects his duty by the shipside facing one side of the container's door. (2) The tallyman checks the series number of the container discharged and inspects the appearance and seal and spots number on the Slots Plan based on the sequence of discharging, and if any wrong series No. is found notes down the true No. in the blank of the Slots Plan. During the process of discharging, in case any damaged container or seal missing is found the tally-

man must give notice to the terminal to stop operation, and reports to the Chief Tally, who will ask the ship to look over. Moreover, seal-making will be done and the Damaged Container Record made up for the ship to sign. (3) On the hand-over of the shift, the containers undischarged in the bay plan should be spotted with signs, and notes of delivery should be made in details on the Shift Hand-over Record, and the date and signature of the last shift must be put down on the record. The tallymen of the next shift will proceed the work based on the work done by the last shift. 4. After the work of a shift or after the discharging of one bay, the tallyman will hand over the container tally sheet and the bay plan (with container being free) to the Chief Tally for his inspection.

Notes

1 As far as the container ship for import is concerned, the tallyman effects his duty by the shipside or in the hold (for roll on/roll off ship). The tallyman must have a best knowledge about the requirements and the notes in the Hand-over Record made by the Chief Tally, and gets an Import Bay Plan in hand, then checks the series number of containers, and the given number to the slots in the same bay based on the discharging sequence, and logs off the Bay Plan, inspects the appearance and seal of containers, and in case any abnormal phenomenon is found, a record should be made to prove the fact.

就进口集装箱船舶而言,理货员在船边、货舱(滚装船)理货。理货员必须熟悉理货长在交接记录单中布置的工作要求和注意事项,索取船舶进口积载图,检查箱号、同一行位按卸箱先后顺序编号,并圈销航位图,检查箱体外表、铅封状况。如发现集装箱异常情况,如实做好记录。

2 On the end of the shift, the tallymen must check up the tallying figures with the consignee on the wharf or his agent and submit the finished container tally sheet together with the bay plan (with container being free) to the Chief Tally.

工班结束后,理货员应与码头收货人或其代理人核准数字,将已编制的理箱单连同已结束行位图一并交理货长。

3 On the hand-over of the shift, the containers unloaded in the bay plan should be spotted with signs, and notes of delivery should be made in details on the Shift Hand-over Record, and the date and signature of the last shift must be put down on the record.

交接班时,本行位图未能卸完的集装箱,应在行位图上做好明显标识并在交班记录上做好详细记录及交接情况,写上工班日期和签名。

Vocabulary

assign [əˈsain]	vt. 分配,指派
effect [iˈfekt]	vt. 实行,引起,完成
Hand-over Record	交接记录单
sequence [ˈsiːkwəns]	n. 序列,顺序

abnormal [æbˈnɔːməl]	adj.反常的,不正常的
phenomenon [fiˈnɔminən]	n.现象,征兆
shift [ʃift]	n.工班
Slots Plan	箱位图
note down	记录
Damaged Container Record	集装箱残损记录

Exercises

1 Answer the following questions according to the text you have read.

(1) As far as the container ship for import is concerned, where does the tallyman effects his duty?

(2) How does the tallyman effect his duty?

(3) On the end of the shift, How do the tallymen do?

(4) How does the process of tallying proceed?

(5) During the process of discharging, in case any damaged container or seal missing is found, what does the tallymen do?

2 Fill out the blanks with suitable words or terms based on the text.

(1) When the container tallying goes, one tallyman will be assigned to _____ handling the container ship, and _____ may join in if required in practice.

(2) As far as the container ship for import is concerned, the tallyman must have a best knowledge about the requirements and the notes in the _____ by the _____.

(3) On the end of the shift, the tallymen must check up the _____ with the consignee on the wharf or his agent and submit the finished container tally sheet together with the _____ to the Chief Tally.

(4) The tallyman checks the series number of the container discharged and inspects the appearance and _____ and spots number on the _____ based on the sequence of discharging,

(5) On the hand-over of the shift, the containers unloaded in the bay plan should be spotted with signs, and _____ should be made in details on the _____.

3 Put into Chinese.

(1) According to the Bay Plan, there is a heavy lift about 60 tons at Bay No.53 on deck. It is over the lifting capacity of our quay crane. We are going to discharge it by the floating crane.

(2) In addition, when you are using the floating crane to unload the heavy lift, please inform the Duty Officer.

(3) If any damaged containers and containers' seal off are found, you must inform the Duty Officer to have an inspection. Otherwise, I'll not sign.

(4) There are 180 containers are to be loaded on Wharf No.8, among them we have 20 heavy ones, 140 reefer containers and 20 dangerous containers for which utmost care must be taken.

(5) Although the quay crane is under repair, we believe that there will no problem in having

your containers shipped in time,because there is only some small trouble with it.

4　Put into English.

(1)我们要先检查一下集装箱的外部状况。

(2)请把这些货物装在平板集装箱内。

(3)卸冷冻集装箱前务必先把插头拔下。

(4)请将集装箱桥吊移到2号泊位。

(5)这个集装箱铅封失落而且顶部有凹陷。

Dialogue

A phone call between ship planner(A) and the planner of Sealand(B)

A:Hi,this is ship planner from QQCT speaking,I want to talk with Mr.Louis,the planner in charge of Sealand Charger.

O/P:Please hold on and I will relay it to him.

B:Hello,this is Louis speaking.What's the matter?

A:I think there is an error for your import EDI.judging from the restow figure you give me.

B:Really? Could you explain more clearly?

A:The restow figure you give me is only 14,however,referring to your stowage plan, we must restow many more containers if the Bay 30 is completly loaded,

B:Then how many containers to be restowed?

A:Altogether 44 restows,according to the EDI sent to us by ship coordinator,when departing from last port.And in which you want to load the whole Bay 30 with Qingdao local cargoes.

B:let me think,ok,that's alright,you can load some restows on Bay 10 above the deck.And the remaining can be loaded on Bay 54 on the deck.

A:The weight of restows is very heavy,so I want to shift some to Bay 54 under deck.

B:It's unnecessary,because Bay 54 is for port of Kobe,and Kobe is the next port of call so it should be no problem.

A:By the way,to tell you that the gate-in figure is a bit different from you expected in the preplan,can you make a little change? If yes please give me a revised one.

B:Ok,could you please give me the new summary?

A:Well,I will send it to you by the E-mail within 10 minutes.What's more,maybe a little additional cargo for this voyage,and you can ignore it.I will make a slight adjustment after you give me the new preplan at that moment.

B:Certainly,I will do that the soonest possible.Would you please give me the EDI after you finished the stowage plan?

A:Of course,by the way I have another request,could you give me the confirmation of restow figures by email?

B:No problem,and thanks for your kind help,I am very sorry for the trouble caused to you.

A:Also thank you very much,bye.

Appendix 1　Sentences for Cargo Tallying

001　请问,你是这船上的船员吗?
　　　Excuse me? are you a seaman on this ship?

002　你以前到过我们港口吗?
　　　Have you been to our port before?

003　你们港每年的吞吐量是多少?
　　　每年 2 亿多吨。
　　　How many tons of cargo can your port handle a year? (Or: What's the cargo throughput of your port a year?)
　　　Over 2 hundred million tons a year.

004　谁在敲门?
　　　是我,理货长。
　　　Who is knocking at the door?
　　　It's me, Chief Checker.

005　我是外轮理货公司的理货长,我姓李。
　　　I'm the Chief Checker from the Ocean Shipping Tally Company. My name is Li.

006　抽支烟?
　　　我不抽烟,谢谢!
　　　Have a cigarette?
　　　No, thanks. I don't smoke.

007　你喝饮料吗?
　　　好的,请来点。
　　　要茶还是咖啡?
　　　请来杯茶。
　　　你的茶加点柠檬还是奶加糖?
　　　什么都不加。
　　　Would you like any drinks?
　　　Yes, please.
　　　Which do you prefer, tea or coffee?
　　　A cup of tea, please.
　　　How do you like your tea, with lemon or with milk and sugar?
　　　Just plain, please.

008　我们公司正常上班的时间是从上午 7:30 到下午 5:30。

港口理货英语

Our company's normal office hours are from 7:30 a.m.to 5:30 p.m.

009 今天下午1:30开工,再见!

We'll start to work at half past one this afternoon.Have a good day.

010 今晚我下班以后就来找你。

I'll come to see you as soon as I'm off duty tonight.

011 我是这个舱的理货员,你是舵工吗?

I'm a tallyman of this hatch.Are you a Quartermaster?

012 我忘了带纸,你能给我几张空白计数单吗?

I forgot to bring some paper with me.Would you mind giving me a few blank tally sheets?

013 今天是几号?

10月5号,农历八月十五,也就是我国的传统节日中秋节。

What's the date today?

October 5th,the 15th day of eighth lunar month,namely the traditional Mid-Autumn Festival of our country.

014 你们中国人在过去的几年建设中确实取得了非常显著的成就。

You Chinese people have really acquired pretty /remarkable/outstanding/ achievements in your construction for the past few years.

015 暂时谈到这儿吧,再见!

再见。

That's all for the time being.See you tomorrow.

See you tomorrow.

016 邮寄员来取信件了,请打开邮件室。

Here comes the postman for the mails,please open the mail room.

017 值班副过来干什么?

What does the Duty Officer come here to do?

018 刚才谁来找我了?

Who came to see me just now?

019 甲板上走路小心点。

Be /careful/alert/watchful/ when walking aboard.

020 我没有要打字的理货单证,谢谢你。

I have no tally papers to be typed.Thank you.

021 卸货速度这么高,我非常惊奇!

The discharging rate is so high that I'm greatly surprised!

022 你们的装货班轮什么时候开航?

When does your cargo liner sail?

023 大副,我得走了,祝你一路平安!

Chief Officer,I must leave now.Whish you a bon voyage!

Appendix 1　Sentences for Cargo Tallying

024　很抱歉我事先未告诉你。
　　　I'm /exceedingly/purely/ sorry for not having told you in advance.

025　我们将尽力去做。
　　　We'll do it by all means.(Or: We'll do our utmost.)

026　大副,请不要激动,平静点,生气不能解决问题。
　　　Chief Officer, please don't excite yourself. Keep calm. Anger can't solve any problems.

027　抱歉,我发脾气了。
　　　I'm sorry to have lost my temper.

028　给你一些下年的年历,我祝你新年快乐!
　　　Here are some calendars for the coming year for you. I wish you a happy New Year!

029　大副,我代表我的经理,并以我个人的名义祝你航程愉快!
　　　Chief, on behalf of my manager and in my own name, I wish you a pleasant voyage!

030　码头上有许多仓库,里面装着各种各样进出口的货物。
　　　On the docks there are many warehouses with various import and export cargoes in them.

031　卡车、拖车、牵引车和铲车在码头上来来往往。
　　　Trucks, trailers, tractors and forklifts are running to and fro on the docks.

032　码头旁靠着几艘外轮。
　　　Several /oceangoing/foreign/ ships are (lying) alongside the wharves.

033　防雨篷在船首楼左边房间。
　　　The rain tents are in the forecastle port cabin.

034　大副在船尾楼入口出现了。你可以向他说明你的意思。
　　　The Chief Officer shows himself in the poop entrance. You may express yourself to him.

035　王先生,我们将承运哪几种货物?
　　　What kind of cargo shall we carry, Mr. Wang?

036　你们将承运很多种货物,如花生、冬瓜、牛肉、鱿鱼和大葱等。
　　　You'll carry a wide variety of cargoes, /such as/e.g./ groundnuts, winter melon, beef, squid and onion, etc.

037　人们通常用袋子包装谷类,用纸盒包装罐头,用木箱装五金。
　　　People usually pack cereals in bags, canned goods in cartons and hardware in wooden cases.

038　昨天你们的驻船代表给我一张船图。根据船图我们将把钢条和油类装在舱底,上面放五金和谷类。
　　　Your agent gave me a cargo plan yesterday. According to the cargo plan, we're going to stow the steel bars and oils at the bottom of the hold with the hardware and the cereals on top of them.

039　装卸工已经上船了,让我们去看看。
　　　The stevedores are already on board. Let's go and have a look.

040 良好的包装在对外贸易中十分重要。
Good packing is very important in /international/foreign/ trade.

041 请等一会,让我问一下大副。
Please wait a minute. Let me ask the Chief Officer.

042 关于淀粉,大副是怎么说的?
What did the Chief Officer say about the starch?

043 我们通常对照进口舱单检查箱子上的运输标志。
We usually check the shipping marks on the cases against those on the import manifests.

044 运输标志通常由4部分组成,那就是合同号、目的港、批号和箱号。
Shipping marks are generally /made up of/involve/consist of/ four components, /i.e./that is/ the contract number, the destination port, the lot number and the case number.

045 在其他箱子上你可以发现不同的警告标志,例如"小心轻放"、"勿摔"、"必须平放"、"勿用手钩"、"此边向上"。
On the other cases you can find different care marks such as "Handle with care", "Don't drop", "Keep flat", "Use no hooks" and "This side up".

046 我不知道这些茄子的目的地。
I don't know the destination of the egg plant.

047 码头主要由码头前沿、仓库和办公室组成。
Docks are generally made up of /wharves/aprons of docks/jetties/piers/quays/terminals/, warehouses and offices.

048 我们的装卸工都很了解警告标志。
Our dockers know the care marks very well.

049 将开六个舱。请做好准备。
There will be 6 hatches in operation. Please keep fit.

050 你们用公制表示重量,是吗?
You use metric system for expressing weight, don' you?

051 我对英制不熟悉,请告诉我关于其换算的一些情况好吗?
I'm not familiar with the British System. Would you please tell me something about the conversion?

052 一英吨等于1.016公吨。但一英磅只有0.454公斤。一英吨等于2240英磅。
One long ton equals 1.016 metric tons. But one pound is only about 0.454 kilo. There are 2240 pounds in a long ton.

053 一英尺等于12英寸。一码等于3英尺。一英里等于1760码。
One foot equals 12 inches. Three feet make a yard. There are 1760 yards in a mile.

054 你们所有舱口都有吊杆是吗?
You have derricks at all the hatches, don't you?

055 我们码头前沿有许多龙门起重机,我们还有一些浮吊用于重件。

Appendix 1　Sentences for Cargo Tallying

We have many gantry /cranes/hoists/ on the wharves. We also have some floating cranes for heavy lifts.

056　大量卡车和拖车正忙着把黄玉米从仓库运到船边。
Plenty of trucks and trailers are busy transferring the yellow maize from warehouses to the ship's side.

057　装卸中最有用的工具是:滑车、钩环和货钩。
The most useful /tools/facilities/ in handing are blocks, shackles and cargo hooks.

058　我们把络绳吊索用于袋子,帆布吊索用于包、钢丝吊索用于钢铁,托盘用于木箱和纸箱,桶钩用于桶装货。
We use rope slings for bags, canvas slings for bales, steel slings for iron, cargo trays for cases and cartons, and drum hooks for cargo in drums.

059　码头工人通常根据货物包装形式选择工具。
The dockers usually choose their tools according to the cargo packing style.

060　我们通常用货盘给散货做关。
We usually use cargo trays to make slings for bulk cargo.

061　另外,工具房里还有斧子、锤子、锯、扳手和撬棒,等等。
Besides, there are also axes, hammers, saws, spanners and crowbars, etc. in the tool house.

062　桶装货你们怎样做关?
How do you make slings for cargo in drums?

063　请告诉水手长打开所有舱并把2、4舱吊杆摆到外档,其余的摆到里档。
Please tell the Bosun to open all the hatches, and swing the derricks of Hatch No.2 and No.4 to the /seaside/overside/ and the rest to the /shoreside/alongside.

064　每个吊杆的安全工作负荷是多少?
What's the /safe working load/S.W.L / of each derrick?

065　双杆联吊的负荷量只是3吨。
The lifting capacity of the derricks in union purchase is only three tons.

066　请在2舱和4舱外档安装好绳梯,因为装卸工要下到驳船上。
Please fix up rope ladders at Hatch No.2 and No.4 overside, because the stevedores will go down to the /lighters/barges.

067　3舱左舷吊杆太低,请把它升高一点。
The port boom at Hatch No.3 is too low. Please top it a little bit.

068　请把舷梯降低一点。
Please lower the gangway a little bit.

069　请把3舱吊杆移到里档,因为我们的浮吊要到外档卸重件。
Please swing the derricks at Hatch No.3 to the shoreside because our floating crane will come alongside to unload the heavy lifts.

070　现在我们要把外档的甜菜渣卸到驳船上。

— 147 —

Now we are going to unload the beet pulp pellet overside into the barges.

071 我会告诉电工对它进行检查。
I'll tell the electricians to have a check at it.

072 我将让水手长把滑车换成新的。
I'll get the Bosun to change the blocks for new ones.

073 一舱左舷的吊货索和保险索用坏了,请把它们换掉。
The cargo runner and the preventer wire of Hatch No.1 port side are worn-out. Please change them.

074 绞车没电了。码头工人不得不待时,直到来电。
There is no power for winches. The longshoremen have to stand by until the power comes.

075 你使电动机超负荷了吗?
Did you overload the electric motor?

076 包装相同的商品的亏舱率平均为10%。
The rate of broken stowage on uniform packaged commodities averages 10 percent.

077 小件耐久货物可用作填隙货物来填充小缝和空位。
Small pieces of durable cargo can be used as filler cargo to fill in the interstice and void space.

078 五舱左舷绞车出了故障,请让轮机员们尽快将它检查一下。
Hatch No.5 port winch is out of order, please have the engineers inspect it as soon as possible.

079 天黑了。请在各舱掌上货灯。
It's getting dark. Please fix up the cargo lights in all the holds.

080 以前只有一艘带五层舱的船来过我港。
There was only one ship with orlop deck called at our port before.

081 另外,船图表明2舱底舱后部要装300吨汉堡的锡板,分成4票,它们是451、452、453、和472号装货单。但根据装货清单,有500吨汉堡锡板,我想船图一定有某些错误。
By the way, in Hatch No.2 lower hold aft part, the plan shows 300 tons of Hamburg tin plates in 4 lots, they're S/O Nos.451,452,453, and 472. But according to the loading list, there are 500 tons of tin plates for Hamburg. I think there must be some mistakes in the plan.

082 其余亚丁石蜡安排在4舱底舱前部,可能船图把它漏掉了。
The rest of the Aden paraffin are arranged in Hatch No.4 lower hold fore part. Maybe it's omitted in the plan.

083 1舱底舱的后部的过境货是去亚历山大的,2舱3层舱前部的是去安特卫普的,3舱深层舱是去鹿特丹的,4舱二层舱两翼是去马赛的,就这些。
The through cargo in Hatch No.1 lower hold aft part is (bound) for Alexandria, No.2

Appendix 1 Sentences for Cargo Tallying

lower tweendeck fore part for Antwerp, No.3 deep tanks for Rotterdam, and No.4 upper tweendeck both wings for Marseilles. That's all.

084 现在让我们核对吧,我想首先检查卸货港序。
Let's check it up now. I'd like to check (up) the rotation of discharging ports first.

085 你想要 1 份 3 舱的计数单复写副本吗?
Would you like a carbon copy of the tally sheets for Hatch No.3?

086 你可以根据装货清单编 1 份积载图。
You can make out the stowage plan according to the loading list.

087 为把甘草精装在阴凉处,请别把它装在 4 舱。
In order to put the licorice extract in cool place, please don't stow it in Hatch No.4.

088 船上有很多阿姆斯特丹的过境货,别把它们卸在岸上。
There are a lot of through cargoes for Amsterdam on ship. Don't discharge them ashore.

089 请在底舱铺双层衬垫在二层舱铺单层,并在必要处铺上席子。
Please put double dunnage in the lower holds and single in the tweendeck and lay mats where necessary.

090 你们最好用方木垫机器箱。
You'd better use square wood to dunnage the machinery cases.

091 请在每层桶上都放一层木板以防移动。
Please put one layer of planks on each tier of drums to prevent them from moving.

092 生铁块不必衬垫,但装完后需在上面盖上席子和木板,我想在上面堆一些蚕豆、利马豆和豌豆。
No dunnage is needed for pig iron. But it should be covered with mats and planks on top after it is loaded. I /want/intend/ to stow some broad bean, lima bean and pea on top.

093 不同港口的货需用网隔开,同一港口的大票货用色带隔开。
The cargo for different ports must be separated with nets and the big lots for the same port must be separated with colored tapes.

094 网和带子藏在船首楼里,你可以向值班副要。如果不够,他会告诉我,然后我将向外轮供应公司再订购一些。
The nets and tapes are stored in the forecastle cabin. You may ask the Duty Officer for them. If not enough, he'll tell me and in my turn I'll order some more from the Ship Chandler.

095 内理代表货主或收货人理货,但他们本身属于装卸公司。
The warehouse keepers tally cargoes in lieu of the cargo-owner or the consignee, but they themselves are attached to the stevedoring company.

096 你可以从值班驾驶员那里取得垫舱和隔票物料。
You can get the materials for dunnaging and separation from the Duty Mate.

097 本次航程上有许多在神户转口的货物,它们必须与神户直达货分开。
There is a lot of cargo with transhipment at Kobe on this voyage. They must be separated

from /the Kobe direct cargo/the cargo direct for Kobe.

098 转口货不必一票一票地分开，但不同目的的港的货物必须清楚的分开，否则，在卸货港会造成很多麻烦。
It's not necessary to separate the transshipment cargo lot by lot. But the cargoes for different destinations must be clearly separated, otherwise it'll /cause/make/ a lot of trouble at the discharging ports.

099 所有选港货都安排在2舱上二层舱。
All the optional cargo is arranged in Hatch No.2 upper tweendeck chamber.

100 另外，每票选港货都必须堆在一处，因为这样我们便可在收货人指定的任何一个港口卸下任何一票。
Furthermore, each lot of the optional cargo must be stowed in one block, because in this way we can discharge any lot at any port appointed by the consignee.

101 新加坡货装完后，我们将开始装香港的转口货。
After the Singapore cargo is loaded, we'll start to load the cargo with transhipment at Hong Kong.

102 你要多注意选港货，因为卸货港是未定的。
You have to pay more attention to the optional cargo. Because the discharging ports are/not fixed/uncertain.

103 请把垫舱物料准备好，否则今晚我们不能开工。
Please get the dunnage materials prepared, otherwise we can't work tonight.

104 卸巴塞罗纳机器箱时请通知值班副到场。
When discharging the Barcelona machinery cases, please tell the Duty Officer to be present.

105 大副，装冻虾仁有特殊要求吗？
Chief Officer, are there any special requirements for loading the reefer shelled shrimps?

106 因舱容可能不够，你们须尽可能把冷藏货装得紧一些。
As the space may not be enough, you have to stow the reefer cargo as close as possible.

107 不要把河蟹堆到舱顶，你们必须留一些空间用于冷却。
Don't stow the hairy crab up to the deckhead. You have to keep some space for cooling.

108 你们要把冻猪肉前后堆放，不要交错。
You should stow the frozen pork pieces fore and aft, not crosswise.

109 至于纸盒，请每5层铺一层小木棒，如果有箍脱落，请把它们重新加箍。
As for the cartons, please put one layer of egg sticks every five tiers high. And if there are any hoops missing, please re-hoop them.

110 现在舱内温度约是零下5摄氏度。
The temperature in the hold now is about five degrees below zero centigrade.

111 2小时后我们就能达到所需温度。
We will have the required temperature in 2 hours.

Appendix 1　Sentences for Cargo Tallying

112　温度升高时,我还要继续冷却。
　　　I'll resume cooling when the temperature is up.

113　让我们等一下保温箱,不用等很长时间。
　　　Let's wait for the isothermal vans. It won't take a long time to wait.

114　让冷冻鸡蛋保持在零下 15 摄氏度即华氏 5 度。
　　　Keep the frozen eggs at the temperature of /15 degrees below zero centigrade/minus 15 degrees centigrade/, namely 5 degrees Fahrenheit.

115　驻船代表直到今早才把预配图交给我。
　　　The Agent didn't give me the /pre-stowage plan/preliminary stowage plan/ until this morning.

116　我得对配载图进行检查,计算重量并调整船吃水。
　　　I have to check up the initial plan, calculate the weight and make some adjustment to the ship's draft.

117　过会我要给你看空箱舱单。
　　　I'll show you a manifest of the empty vans later.

118　所有重集装箱都在前方堆场吗?
　　　Are all the loaded vans on the marshalling yard?

119　码头上我们有两架装卸桥。
　　　We have 2 portainers on the wharf.

120　我们通常用集装箱卡车和底盘车而不是跨运车来把箱子运到船边。
　　　We usually use container trucks and chassis but not straddle carrier to transfer the vans to the ship's side.

121　一个人在船边工作,检查外表状况,核对箱号、封号,另一个人在甲板上工作,检查箱顶,记录箱子的实际积载位置。
　　　One works at the ship's side, examining the apparent condition and checking the container number and seal number. Another works on deck, inspecting the container's top and jotting down its actual stowage.

122　一旦出现问题,我们就联系有关部门解决,否则就做出记录,在其基础上,你可以在场站收据上加批注。
　　　In case there is any problem, we'll /contact/come into contact with/ the parties concerned and ask them to solve it. Otherwise a record will be made out and on its basis you can put annotations on the dock receipt.

123　请在 2 舱舱口位四周留 2 英尺宽的通道走路。
　　　Please leave /a passage two feet wide/a two-foot-wide passage/ around Hatch No. 2 hatchway for walking.

124　现在的问题是能否用你们的重吊杆搬这两台掘土机。
　　　Now the question is whether we can take the 2 excavators with your jumbo boom.

125　虽然现在船体有点偏,但这个舱完货前我会保持船体平衡。

— 151 —

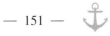

Although the ship slants now, yet we can manage it upright before completion of loading in this hold.

126 我的建议是你们应当用浮吊来搬这两台设备。
My suggestion is that you should use a floating crane to lift the 2 equipments.

127 除掘土机外,还有3台压路机要装。
Besides the excavators there are 3 road rollers to load.

128 它正好在我们重吊杆的负荷以内。
It's just within the lifting capacity of our jumbo.

129 你须提前24小时通知我。
You must give me a 24 hours' notice.

130 组装起这个重吊杆需多长时间?
How long will it take to set up the jumbo?

131 请把掘土机放在4舱甲板,一边一个,并把压路机装在2舱2层舱舱口位。掘土机必须绑紧并楔牢。
Please put the excavators on Hatch No.4 deck, one on each side, and the road rollers in Hatch No.2 tweendeck hatchway. The excavators must be tightly lashed and properly wedged.

132 我会让装卸工照办。
I'll tell the stevedores to do it accordingly.

133 混凝土搅拌机的积载有一些特殊要求。首先,把2层舱交错铺满两层铁棒,一定要使其平整,接着盖上一层厚铁板,这样最后你就可把搅拌机放在上面。
There are some special requirements for the stowage of the concrete mixers. First put 2 tiers of steel bars/crisscross/crosswise/all over the tweendeck, be sure to make them perfectly flat and then cover them with a tier of thick steel plate. In this way you can stow the mixers on top eventually.

134 我会通知装卸领班让工人将这些重机器箱装紧,并注意重量要均匀分布在底箱上。
I'll contact the foreman to tell the stevedores to stow the heavy machinery cases closely and note the even distribution of the weight on the bottom cases.

135 水手们今天上午一直在修发动机。
The sailors have been repairing the engine all morning long.

136 成组货能在你们的装卸进度表上标示出来吗?
Can the unitized cargo be identified in your diagram of loading/discharging progress?

137 我们用看船舶吃水的方法来取得整船散木薯干的载货量。
We/get/obtain/the whole shipment of bulk dry cassava by reading the ship's draft.

138 至于各舱散货的载货量,我们用三种方法来取得,即如果货物从驳船上来,就看驳船的吃水,从货车上来就看车皮容积,从露天堆场上来就计抓斗数。
As to the bulk cargo quantity of each hold, we obtain it in three ways, that is, if the car-

Appendix 1　Sentences for Cargo Tallying

go is from lighters, we read their drafts, if from wagons, we calculate their capacity, and if from open/yards/storage space/, we count grabs.

139　船舶载重标尺是用英吨表示的吗?

Does the ship's deadweight scale show in long ton?

140　加快货物装卸作业需考虑到装卸设备位置的适当安排。

Expediting the cargo operation will take into consideration the suitable/device/laying out/of handling equipments' position.

141　船在港期间每天消耗 10 吨柴油 20 吨淡水。

The consumption of diesel oil per day is 10 tons and fresh water is 20 tons when ship is in port.

142　如果想使煤平整最好申请特殊平舱。

You'd better apply for special trimming if you want to make the coal level.

143　考虑到船舶稳定性,你们最好从左舷侧抽出 10 吨压舱水。

With/regard/respect/reference/to the stability, (Or: For stability sake, or: For stability's sake,) you'd better pump out 10 tons of ballast water from the port side.

144　你向外代申请特殊平舱了吗?

Have you applied to the Ocean Ship Agency for the special trimming?

145　2 舱青豆不平,请告诉工人好好平整一下。

The green pea in Hatch No.2 isn't level. Please tell your stevedores to trim it well.

146　调度室派来了 5 个工班来卸二氧化钛。

The/Stevedore Office/Stevedore Department/has sent five gangs to unload the titanium dioxide.

147　既然酒、烟和食品都是外交物资,它们就决不能与船用冷藏室的危险货物装在一起。

Since the wines, cigarettes and/provisions/food stuffs/are diplomatic goods, they're by no means to be stowed together with the dangerous cargo in the domestic chamber.

148　还有,二层舱对于像雕刻品这样的贵重物品不是一个合适的地方。

Also, the tweendeck is not a/suitable/desirable/proper/place for costly cargo like carvings.

149　把加载货装在与二副房间隔壁的备用舱内。备用舱的钥匙在值班副手里。

Put the additional cargo in the spare cabin next to the Second Officer's room. The Duty Officer keeps the key to the spare cabin.

150　你为这些工艺美术品安排好房间了吗?

Have you arranged any space for the arts and crafts?

151　把你们代理人昨天提到的那些化妆品装在 2 舱二层舱左舷的保险房。看起来空间足够。

Put the cosmetics your agent mentioned yesterday in Hatch No.2 tweendeck port locker. Looks like the space will be enough.

— 153 —

152 理货员与收货人是在舱内进行双边理货交接的,码头掉袋已算在总数内。
Delivery and taking delivery of cargo was exercised between our tallymen and the consignees in the hold. The bags scattered on the wharf had been already included in the grand total.

153 把残损箱子原本放在那里,因为值班副要来检验。
Leave the broken cases as they are because the Duty Officer will inspect them.

154 装外交物资前请通知我,因为我要检查包装。
Please inform me before loading the diplomatic goods, because I'll check the packing.

155 贵重物品太多,以至于备用舱舱容可能不够,请告诉你们的装卸工装得紧密一些。
There is so much valuable cargo that the space of the spare cabin may not be enough. Please tell the stevedores to make a close stowage.

156 请在舱口位四角用袋子搭一条垂直通道或孔道作为通风装置,每隔6层高水平安放一层木风筒。
Please make/a vertical/an erect/tunnel or vent with bags as a ventilator at each corner of the hatch square, and fix one layer of wooden ventilators horizontally every 6 tiers high.

157 怎样安装水平通风筒?
放两行纵向木风筒和两行横向木风筒与垂直通道连接起来。
How to fix horizontal ventilators?
Put 2 lines of wooden ventilators fore and aft and the other 2 lines athwartship, making them joined to the vertical tunnels.

158 告诉工人们在靠舱壁处留出30厘米宽的距离,在中间留一个35厘米宽的交叉通道。
Tell the stevedores just to keep a 30-centimetre space apart from the bulkheads and leave a 35-centimetre crossway in the middle.

159 不用担心,我们的工人对装大米很有经验。
Don't worry. Our stevedores are well experienced in loading rice.

160 还有一件事,船舷外的甲板水排水孔和机舱水排水孔都须盖好,以防水被排到驳船上。
One more thing, all the scuppers and discharge openings overboard must be properly covered so as not to let the water be drained to the lighters.

161 你须再订购100米通风筒,否则我们就不能做好充分的通风。
You have to order 100 metres of ventilators more; otherwise, we can't make adequate ventilation.

162 告诉工人把船肋骨、梯子、舱壁、柱子、地轴用油纸封好。
Tell the stevedores to cover the frames, ladders, bulkheads, stanchions and shaft tunnel with plastic paper properly.

163 所有铁质结构都必须盖好,以防汗湿。

Appendix 1 Sentences for Cargo Tallying

All the steel structures must be well covered in order to prevent sweating.

164 一部分大蒜是从外档驳船来的,其余是从里档卡车来的。
Some garlic is from the lighters overside, the other is from the trucks wharfside.

165 你说得对,我会负责好这事的。
You're right. I'll see to it.

166 我想知道这200瓶水杨酸的具体位置。
I'd like to know the specific location of these 200 bottles of salicylic acid.

167 醋酸(乙酸)有腐蚀性,请把其装在5舱甲板两边,在货物和舱口围板间留一条通道。
The acetic acid is corrosive. Please put them in both sides of No.5 deck, leaving a passage between the hatch coaming and the cargo.

168 你最好事先在那里划一条白线。
You'd better mark a white line there beforehand.

169 硝酸钾是爆炸物品,运输过程中它需要全面细心的保管。
The potassium nitrate is of an explosive nature. It calls for overall and careful custody in the process of carriage.

170 我们要把柳制品堆成两层吗?
Shall we stow the willow/goods/product/in 2 tiers?

171 请掌上两盏安全灯。
Please set up 2 safety lamps.

172 纺织设备可以堆几层高?
How many tiers can the textile equipments be stowed in?

173 漂粉精遇水易爆炸,这已在危险货物清单中标明了。
The bleaching powder will easily explode when it's in contact with water. It's clearly/stated/indicated/on the dangerous cargo list.

174 把靠外的袋子交叉堆放并把垛边码齐,这样袋子在航行中就不会倒塌。
Put the outer bags across each other and keep the outside ones straight so that the bags may not fall during the voyage.

175 把重量轻的货件堆在里面,外面堆放重的,因为我们在下个港口要在上面装其他货物。
Block up the light packages inside and put the heavy ones outside, because we're going to load some other cargo on top at the next port.

176 如果舱容不够,你们可以在舱口位再用一节梁位,但要留出一点小空位。
In case the space is not enough, you can use one more section in the hatchway, but leave a small margin.

177 你们可以用整个底舱装棉布,但在此之前必须拆掉墩子。
You can stow the cotton piece goods all over the lower hold. But you have to take off the platform before that.

178 因山羊皮有一种强烈气味,绿茶会被污染,把它们装在不同地方不更好吗?
As the goat skin gives off a strong smell, the green tea will be badly stained. Wouldn't it be better to put them in different places?

179 在备用舱请由里往外装食品。
Please stow the edible goods/from inside out/from inside and work outwards/in the spare cabin.

180 如果按您要求的数量装货,恐怕前后吃水差要超过50厘米。
If we load cargo in compliance with your figures, I'm afraid that the trim would exceed 50 centimetres.

181 若容积不够,请告诉我余数,我将为剩余的咸鱼安排另一个舱。
If the space is not enough, please tell me the balance. I'll arrange the remaining brined fish in another hatch.

182 把机器箱堆到舱顶很难,就安全性而言,把它们移到4舱怎么样?
It's very difficult to block the machinery cases up to the deckhead. So far as the safety is concerned, how about shifting them to Hatch No.4?

183 就我所知,我们浮吊臂太短,够不到船舱中心,你们船甲板很宽,尤其4舱,所以我建议你们抽进一些压舱水使船向外档倾斜一点。
So far as I know, the arm of our floating crane is too short to reach the middle of the hatch. Your ship has a wide deck, especially at Hatch No.4. So I suggest you pump in some ballast water to make the ship listing a little bit overside.

184 你们把大枣安排在5舱与立特粉一处,然而后者容易吸水,这会使枣受污染,使立特粉硬化。
You've arranged the largo dates in Hatch No.5 together with the lithopone while the latter is liable to absorb moisture. This will make the largo dates tainted and the lithopone hardened.

185 这会节省我们许多隔票费用。
This will save us a lot of separation expenses.

186 不能再往6舱移牛皮纸了,否则将使船翘头太厉害了。
You can't shift any more kraft paper into Hatch No.6, otherwise the ship will be/down by the stern/trim by the stern/ too much.

187 我说的你都听懂了吗?
Are you all clear about what I said?

188 如果1舱舱容有余,你们可以移一些同港口的货物过去。
If there is any space left in Hatch No.1, you may shift some other cargo for the same port there.

189 根据港章,如果船舶超载或前倾是不准离港的,因此,我们只好不时地准确计算吃水以保持前后吃水平衡。
According to the Harbour Regulations, if a vessel is overloaded or/down by the head/

Appendix 1 Sentences for Cargo Tallying

trim by the bow/, she is not permitted to leave the port. Therefore we can't help calculating the draft accurately now and then, so as to keep the ship on an even keel.

190 那里空间几乎满了,我们最多只能装大约 10 吨。
The space there is nearly full up. We can stow only approximately 10 tons at most.

191 调整一下尖舱里的淡水,把淡水从首尖舱抽到尾尖舱,这样我们就不用在积载图上做修改了。
Adjust the fresh water in the peak tank. Pump the fresh water from the fore peak tank into the aft. Then we needn't make any alterations on the cargo plan.

192 本工班结束时,你必须尽早告诉我每舱的余数。
At the close of this shift you have to tell me the balance of each hold as early as possible.

193 现在前后吃水怎么样?
船躬头 2 英尺。
How is the ship's draft now?
The ship is 2 feet down by the bow.

194 若把剩余干辣椒装在 2 舱,前后吃水会有何变化?
How will the draft become if the remaining dried chilies are put in Hatch No.2.

195 到现在为止,一切运行正常。
Up to now, everything has gone well.

196 这是装货单,供你参考。
Here are the Shipping Orders for your/reference/comparison.

197 没有货物漏装,但有 3 票货物取消了,即 83、114 和 212 号装货单。并且有 150 件玩具退关。以上都是由于容积不够。
No cargo short shipped. But 3 lots are cancelled, namely S/O Nos.83, 114, and 212. Also, there are 150 packages of toys shut out. That/is due to/rests with/the insufficiency of cubic capacity.

198 为什么把叶粉收据放在一边?
Why put aside the Mate's Receipt for the leaf meal?

199 他们争论商讨得很激烈,最后他们对这些批注达成了协议。
They argued and discussed heatedly. At last, they came to/an agreement/a compromise/ about the remarks.

200 因舱容不够,109 号装货单 10 箱河虾退关。
10 cases of shrimp of S/O.No.109 are shut out because of the insufficiency of space.

201 原始积载图和驳船载货清单在事务长那儿,过后我会给你。
The original stowage plan and the boat notes are/kept by/in the possession of/the Purser. I'll give you afterwards.

202 请在我们的船离开之前及时归还货损货差清单。
Please return the exception list in due course before our ship's departure.

— 157 —

203 调度室主任想再要一套进口舱单,你有备用的吗?

The chief of the stevedore office would like to have one more set of import manifest. Do you have any spare ones?

204 装货港工人干活很令人满意。

All the work done by the loading port stevedores was quite satisfactory.

205 每个舱的鱼粉全部卸完后要把舱底的油纸卷起来。

Wind up the polythene papers on the bottom after all fish meal is discharged in each hold.

206 如果你疏忽大意漏掉一钩,理货数字就不正确了。

If you miss out one sling inadvertently, the tally figure will be inaccurate.

207 我想再强调一下,记数单上不能删除铁板的重量,否则同尺寸不同重量的铁板就会混淆。

I'd like to emphasize it again. Weights of the steel plates should not be struck out in the tally sheets. Otherwise there will be a confusion of the steel plates of the same measurements but not the same weights.

208 "SMP"是"South Ampton"的缩写,由于空间太挤我把这块内容放在了图下面。

"SMP" is the abbreviation of "South Ampton". My putting the mass in the underside of the plan is attributable to the congestion of the space.

209 我们航行中的天气很坏,波涛怒吼,甚至都掠过了甲板,船摇摆颠簸了两天。

The weather on our voyage was very bad. The heavy seas were roaring and so far as to swept across the deck. The vessel was rolling and pitching for 2 days.

210 风暴对货物没造成多大损害,因为它们装得很好,绑得很牢固。

The storm/resulted in/did/little damage to the cargo because they were well stowed and securely lashed.

211 货件在暴风雨中倒塌,互相挤压。

The packages collapsed and crushed one another during the storm.

212 举例说:操作不慎,包装缺陷,衬垫不当,积载不良都可能造成货物残损。

Damage to cargo may arise from, for example, careless handling, insufficient packing, improper dunnaging and bad stowage.

213 你们可以把轻微残损卷筒纸卸上岸,之后我会在记录上签字。但若发现严重残损,必须通知我。

You can discharge the paper in reel with slight damage ashore. I'll sign the record afterwards. But in the event of finding any with serious damage, you have to keep me informed.

214 务必把原残和工残分清。

Be sure to make a clear distinction between the damage originally existing and that caused by the stevedores here.

215 你们航程中的天气怎么样?

Appendix 1 Sentences for Cargo Tallying

What was the weather like on your voyage?

216　在南中国海,船遇到了特大台风。
The ship met with a disastrous typhoon in the South China Sea.

217　玻璃系列制品残损归因于装货港工人操作不当。
Damage to the glassware etc. is due to stevedores' careless handling at the loading port.

218　这些桶很脏,并且标志极不清楚。大副从驳船装货清单上查了一下这些桶,它们属于 37 号提单。
These drums are very dirty and the marks are rather indistinct. The Chief Officer has traced these drums from the boat notes. They belong to B/L No.37.

219　硫磺和松香容易着火,所以我们将把它们直接卸到货车上。
Sulphur and resin are very easy to catch fire. So we'll discharge them/direct/directly/into trucks.

220　糠醛、汽油和乙炔是易燃物,溴是腐蚀性货物,滴滴涕原粉是一种剧毒货物,你们一定要采取安全措施卸它们。
Furfural, gasoline and acetylene are inflammable cargoes, bromine is of a corrosive nature, and DDT technical powder is a strongly poisonous cargo. You have to take safety measures to discharge them.

221　港章规定绝对禁止在仓库和库场内存放汽油。
According to the Port Regulations, it's absolutely/forbidden/prohibited/to keep the gasoline in the godowns and on the wharf yards.

222　下午我们要卸集装箱,给我有关单证好吗?
We're going to discharge containers this afternoon. Will you please let me have all the relevant papers?

223　卸冷冻集装箱前不要忘记切断电源。
Don't forget to cut off the electricity supply before discharging the reefer container.

224　我会告诉装卸工注意黑陶的易碎性。
I'll tell the stevedores to/attend to/pay attention to/the fragility of black pottery.

225　我正在检查卸货顺序。
I'm checking the discharging/sequence/rotation/procedure.

226　我们装卸桥的效率是每小时 20 个箱。
The efficiency of our portainer is 20 vans per hour.

227　根据行位图,17 号位应有 15 个上海的箱子。
In accordance with the bay plan, there should be 15 Shanghai vans in Bay No.17.

228　我们发现一个箱号为 SCXU693891 的集装箱不在集装箱清单内。
We found a van (with the number) of SCXU693891 beyond the container list.

229　切断供气不是我的职责范围,请与值班副联系。
Cutting off the gas supply is/beyond my power/not my business/out of my duty. Please contact the Duty officer.

230　直到下午很晚电工才开始修起货机。
　　　It's not till late afternoon that the electrician began to repair the winch.

231　很显然有一个箱子在科伦坡港错卸了。
　　　Obviously there was one van mislanded at Colombo.

232　一般说来,我们每一个工组每一班能卸1000吨。
　　　Generally speaking, we can discharge 1000 tons each gang per shift.

233　照此速度,你们能在3天内干完。
　　　At such a speed, you can finish the work within three days.

234　再者,不要撞击舱口围板。
　　　What's more, don't bang against the hatch coaming.

235　能借一下你船的载重标尺用一下吗?
　　　Would you mind lending me the/draft scale/deadweight scale/of your ship?

236　船舶靠泊时,我们在小麦里发现了虫子,并让舵工将船移靠浮筒熏了一下。
　　　We/found/discovered/insects in the wheat when the ship was at the buoys, and let the quartermaster shift the ship to the buoys for fumigation.

237　简言之,大部分木薯粉将卸到驳船,其余卸到仓库。
　　　In short, most of the/cassava/cassawa/powder is to be discharged to lighters and the rest to godowns.

238　货物和船体都没有受到损害。
　　　Neither the cargo nor the vessel is/imperiled/imperilled/impaired.

239　谷物吸扬机到来之前我们就已申请熏舱了。
　　　We had applied for fumigating holds before the grain sucker came.

240　由于舱内管道漏缝大量卫生纸被污染了。
　　　A considerable amount of toilet paper was tainted owing to the leakage of the pipes in the holds.

241　告诉工人一步一步地移动操纵杆。
　　　Please tell the dockers to move the controller handles step by step.

242　如果我们没加什么的话,根据载重标尺你们到现在已装了20000吨了,但实际上我们已向燃料舱加了400吨燃油,所以到此为止实际装的货物量应为20000减400吨。
　　　If we haven't bunkered anything, you have loaded 20000 tons on the basis of the deadweight scale. But in practice we have replenished 400 ton of fuel oil to the bunker, so the amount actually loaded so far should be 20000 less 400 tons.

243　如果有湿损或破损的袋子,把它们放在舱内一旁,先让我检查一下,再卸到岸上。
　　　If there are any wet or torn bags, put them aside in the holds. Let me examine first and then discharge them ashore.

244　化肥袋排列整齐,内货完整。
　　　Fertilizer bags are in good order and the contents are intact.

245 舱单上注明的这些备用袋在什么地方?过会指给我看好吗?
Where are the spare bags as stated in the manifest? Will you please show me later?

246 你们的装卸工先卸了羊角桩底下的袋子,而不是先卸上面的,所以这些袋子被羊角桩刺穿了。
Your stevedores discharged the bags below the cleats first instead of those over. So these bags are pierced by the cleats.

247 我们已经派了一个工组来卸精密仪器。
We've arranged for one gang to unload the precision apparatus.

248 英使馆家具连同展览品一行行一层层整齐地装在2舱2层舱两翼。
The furniture for the British Embassy, together with the exhibition goods, is stowed in Hatch No.2 tweendeck both wings in neat and uniform rows and tiers.

249 重吊杆已经坏了很长时间了,安全起见,你们最好用浮吊。
The jumbo has been out of use for a long time. You'd better use a floating crane for safety's sake.

250 我房间里有2件波兰领事馆的行李。
In my cabin there are 2 pieces of luggage for the Polish Consulate.

251 我们在装货港一件件地检查使馆物资,希望你们也这样检查。
We checked the embassy goods package by package in the loading port. You'd better check them in the same way.

252 我在保险房发现5件坦桑尼亚精密仪器但提单上说有6件。
I found five packages of Tanzania precision apparatus in the locker but the bill of lading/says/indicates/six.

253 机车、农用工具、锅炉、发电机和流动式起重机都是裸装的。
Locomotives, agricultural tools, boilers, generators and mobile cranes are/naked/unpacked.

254 理货长,卸毛毯时我必须在场,请事先通知我。
Chief Tally, I must be on the spot when you are discharging the carpet. Please inform me beforehand.

255 你们可用单杆双索卸5吨以下的重件。
You can use a single derrick with double wires to discharge the heavy lifts below five tons.

256 我的意思是让船仅仅倾侧一点,这便于操作过程中吊杆的摆动。
I mean to keep the ship only a little bit listing. It can/facilitate/convenience/the swing of the boom during operation.

257 我们将派3个工组,即1、3、5舱。
We'll assign three gangs, i.e. Hatch Nos.1, 3 and 5.

258 你认为下午流动式起重机能来吗?
这要看你什么时候申请的。

Do you think the mobile crane will be available this afternoon?
It/depends/is dependent on/when you apply for it.

259 我被通知把我的船开到锚地等候空泊位。
I'm informed to shift my ship to the anchorage and wait for a free berth.

260 你把吊杆降低一点好吗？这样便于前部货物的积载。
Will you lower the boom a little bit? This will facilitate the stowage of fore part cargo.

261 水位随潮汐而变，你预计能在下次退潮前装完吗？
我说不准，因为我不知道潮汐时间。
The/water level/water/varies with the tide. Do you estimate that loading can be accomplished before the coming ebb tide?
I can't tell, for I am unknown of the tide table.

262 停工是由起吊大梁造成的。
The stoppage is/due to/caused by/the heaving up of hatch beams.

263 请把绳梯装备起来。
Please fix up the rope ladders.

264 请提前卸掉捆绑，防雨篷一搭好装卸工就继续工作。
Please take off the lashings beforehand. The stevedores will/go on with/resume/their work as soon as the rain tents are fixed up.

265 这吊货索 3/10 的钢丝断了，为了安全，我建议换掉它。
The cargo runner has three tenths broken wires. I suggest you replace it for safety.

266 这个单吊杆齿轮结合严密。
This single derrick has a married gear.

267 现在下雨，晚上可能转晴。
It's raining now. It will probably clear up this evening.

268 现在他们正在搭梁。
At present they are putting on the beams.

269 "作业时间、杂项作业（额外作业）、其他服务签证记录"是从调度室来的。
"Working Time, Extra Labour and Hiring Record" are from the/stevedore office/dispatcher's office.

270 根据进口舱单，里面的货物是尼龙线。
The contents inside is nylon yarn as per the import manifest.

271 昨晚因为下起了大雨，我们停止了卸聚氯乙烯。
We stopped discharging polyvinyl chloride, because it rained cats and dogs last night.

272 用不同颜色标识的目的地一目了然。
The destinations marked in different colors can be noted at a glance.

273 工人每关做多少袋？
How many bags do the stevedores make per sling?

274 大副不在船上。我将代表他在记录上签字。

Appendix 1　Sentences for Cargo Tallying

Chief Officer isn't on board.I'am going to sign the record on his behalf.(Or: I'm going to represent him to sign the record.)

275　我要就捆绑的事与大副联系。
　　I'll keep in contact with the Chief Officer about the lashing.

276　我们所有出口货物在装船前都是经过严格检验的,如果达不到标准,货物不允许出口。
　　All of our export cargo is thoroughly examined before shipment.If not up to the standard,the cargo is not allowed to export.

277　装货过程中我们会捡出关内残损货,如果有的话。
　　We'll pick out the damaged cargo in the slings during loading,provided there is any.

278　货物不经货主、海关人员、仓库员和理货员这四方面检查是不准装船的。
　　The cargo is not allowed to ship on board without passing 4 parties, namely, the shipper,the customs officer,the warehouse keeper and the tallyman.

279　你认为什么时候交来大副收据让你签字合适？
　　When do you think it convenient to hand in the Mate's Receipts for your signature?

280　我要分批签收据,我将一天签两次,上午一次,下午一次。这样吧,让我们把它定在上午10点左右和下午4点左右。
　　I'll sign the Mate's Receipts in batches.I'll sign twice a day,once in the morning and once in the afternoon.Thus,let's/make/finalize/it round about 10 a.m.and 4 p.m.

281　残损货不经修补或替换不准出口。
　　The damaged cargo is not allowed to export without being repaired or replaced.

282　2舱氟石的特殊平舱达到了我们的要求。
　　The special trimming for the fluorspar in Hatch No.2 is up to our/requirements/demands.

283　注意蜂蜡上的标志,挑出错误和不清楚的。
　　Pay attention to the marks of the bee wax and pick out the wrong or indistinct ones.

284　当然,船在开航前必须通过联合检查。
　　Undoubtedly,the ship has to pass joint/inspection/survey/before sailing.

285　我们通常每条作业线安排一名理货员,其职责是检查数字、分标志、监督积载和检查任何可能的残损。
　　We usually arrange one tallyman for each gang.His/duty/task/is to check figures,sort marks,supervise the stowage and inspect any possible damage.

286　电报配载图没有给出细节。我正在做配载草图呢。
　　The telegraphic plan doesn't give/full/thorough/particulars.I'm making the draft cargo plan now.

287　你能帮我翻译一下吗？
　　调度的意思是,现在大多数重吊杆都在使用,门机很缺,与4舱相比3舱被认为是装卸时间较长的舱(重点舱),该把门机放在靠近3舱的适当位置。

Can you interpret it for me?

The operator/implies/speaks to the effect/that most of the heavy derricks are in use now.There is lack of jumbo booms.Compared with No.4 hatch,Hatch No.3 is known as the/long hatch/key hold.We ought to locate the jumbo boom in position near Hatch No.3.

288 坦率地讲,本航次货物有些复杂。

Frankly speaking,the cargo is somewhat complicated on this voyage.

289 时间就是金钱。请最大限度地利用你们的人力、物力,缩短船舶在港停时,否则我们的船将会滞期很多天。

Time is money. Please make maximum use of your/manpower/labour power/and material resources to shorten ship's time in port.Otherwise our ship will be/delayed/protracted/too many days.(Or:Otherwise the demurrage will be too many days.)

290 除了配载草图,一切都为装货准备好了。

Except for the/tentative/sketch/initial/draft/rough/cargo plan everything is ready for loading.

291 我建议你先制一个临时配载图让我们开工,然后你就有充分的时间做正式的,你看如何?

I suggest you first make a temporary cargo plan for us to start working,and then you will have sufficient time to make out the formal one.What do you think of that?

292 航海通告已收到,船最快能于22日凌晨3时抵达青岛。

Notice to mariners has been received.The best the vessel can do is to arrive in Tsingtao at three on the morning of the 22nd.

293 请再给我一张草图。

Please/give me/let me have/one more copy of the sketch plan.

294 这张船图做得不好。

The cargo plan is not/well/appropriately/done.

295 暂时没事。有问题我会来找你的。

That's all for the time being.If there is any problem,I'll come to you.

296 下一班装货将鼓足干劲。

The loading will go on in full swing next shift.

297 从某种程度上看,所有舱都适合装芦笋。

In some degree,all the hatches are suitable for loading asparagus.

298 我的中文配载图只表明粗略的配载情况,我想对照原始配载图把它检查一下以防止某些可能的错误。

My tentative cargo plan in Chinese simply shows rough stowage.I'd like to check it with the original one to avoid any possible mistakes.

299 出于安全考虑,我改变了主意,把手表和照相器材装在我的房间里,而是没有装在船尾楼里。

Appendix 1 Sentences for Cargo Tallying

Considering the safety, I changed my mind to put the watches and the camera materials in my cabin instead of in the poop cabin.

300 你要原始配载图干什么?

What do you want the original tentative plan for?

301 187号装货单的大闸阀被漏掉了,208号装货单生漆的位置还没定下来。

The valves under S/O No.187 were omitted. The location of the raw lacquer under S/O No.208 hasn't been decided yet.

302 松节油有强烈的气味,萝卜干会被污染。

The turpentine has strong odours; the dried turnips will be tainted.

303 你知道粮食的自然特性,它是易自热物质。我们必须保证它在舱内有充分的空气环流。

You know grain's nature. It's liable to spontaneous heated. We must ensure it adequate air circulation in the hold.

304 A泊在高潮时水深17米,低潮时水深10米。

It's 17 metres deep in high tide and 10 metres in low tide at berth A.

305 我再检查一遍。我犯了一个愚蠢的错误。谢谢你及时提醒我纠正它。

Let me recheck it. I committed a silly mistake. Thank you for reminding me to correct it in time.

306 请写下对文具衬垫和隔票的要求。
好的,我将把它们写在备注栏下。

Please write down the requirements for separation and dunnaging to the stationery.
All right. I'll put them down/under/beneath/the remarks column.

307 不算散装粗石蜡,3舱安排的货物总重量是1500吨。

Excluding the bulk paraffin wax, the total cargo weight arranged in Hatch No.3 is 1500 tons.

308 大副正忙着制积载图,你最好过会再跟他谈。

The Chief Officer is occupied in making the stowage plan. You'd better talk to him later.

309 请完整地拼一下单词"X线胶片"好吗?
大写的"X",连字号,小写的"ray",空格,小写的"film"。另外别忘了在它下面划一条线作为特殊货的标记。

Would you please spell the word "X-ray film" in full?
Capitalized "X", hyphen,/minuscule/miniscule/"ray", blank space and miniscule "film". One thing more, don't forget to underline it as the notation of special cargo.

310 理货间太热了,我们都出了一身汗,请让水手长去拿一个电扇来。

The tally room is very stuffy. We're all of a sweat. Please tell the Bosun to fetch an electric fan for us.

311 有几票异味货物待装,请在配载图上写出来。

There are several lots of smelling cargo to load. Please note them down in the cargo plan.

312 这条输送带是专门用来输送木片的。
This/transmission belt/conveyor/conveyer/is specially used to transmit wood/scraps/chips.

313 请告诉理货员严格按照给定的各个数字装货。
Please tell the tally clerks to load the cargo strictly according to the given respective figures.

314 如果2舱2层舱的名古屋货上部空间有剩余,你最好移一些刺绣品填满它。
If there is any space left on top of the Nagoya cargo in Hatch No.2 tweendeck, you'd better shift some embroidery to fill it up.

315 在3舱2层舱后部,请用2节梁子装横滨的桐油,如果舱容不够,你们可以左右延伸1节梁位。
In Hatch No.3 tweendeck aft part, please use 2 sections to load Yokohama tung oil. If the space is not enough, you can extend 1 section in the both wings.

316 骨粉和薄荷油应紧靠3舱2层舱前壁装。
Bones meal and menthol oil should be stowed against the fore bulkhead of Hatch No.3 tweendeck.

317 用这些袋子的一小部分在船中线处造一堵墙,留其余的用来稳定散装黄豆。
Use a small part of the bags to make a wall in the place of centerline and leave the rest to stabilize the bulk/soyabeans/soyas/soys.

318 两个深舱的高锰酸钾要保持平衡,而且也要进行特殊平舱。
Keep the potassium permanganate in balance between the two deep tanks, and make a special trimming, too.

319 请做出快速决定,因为危险货不允许长时间放在码头上。
Please make a/quick/prompt/rapid/immediate/decision because the hazardous cargo is not allowed to keep long on the wharf side.

320 鉴于牙膏包装的脆弱性,把它装在底部毕竟不是长久之计。你可以把它装在1舱后部,把那里的榨菜移到4舱。
In view of the weakness of the packing of the toothpaste, it's not a permanent plan to stow it in the bottom after all. You can put it in Hatch No.1 aft part and shift the preserved vegetables there to Hatch No.4.

321 我们总是采取必要措施保证我们工人的安全,装危险货物时他们必须穿戴劳动防护用具如面具、手套,安全第一,你知道。
We always take necessary measures to ensure the safety of our stevedores. When loading dangerous cargo they have to wear labour protective appliance, such as masks and gloves. Safety first, you know.

322 水泥和糖决不能装在同一个舱,因为其性质互抵。

Appendix 1　Sentences for Cargo Tallying

Cement and sugar are by no means to be kept together in the same hold, for they are counteractive in nature.

323　现装和现提都是直取作业的形式。
Alongside uninterrupted loading and shipside delivery are both of the forms of direct transshipment.

324　保持铁页在舱内平衡,否则船要倾侧的。
Keep the steel sheets in balance in the hold.Otherwise the ship will be listing.

325　每层桶必须盖上大量板子以便使得重量平均开来。
Each tier of the drums must be covered with plenty of boards in order to obtain even distribution of the weight.

326　我估计亏舱是 3500 立方英尺,即我给了 35% 的亏舱率,所以你们共有 13500 立方英尺,何以会出现舱容不够呢?
I estimate the broken space at 3500 cubic feet, that's to say I put the rate of the/broken space/broken stowage/breakage/at 35 percent.Hence, you have 13500 cubic feet in all.How come the space is not enough?

327　或许你算错了。
Maybe you are/out/wrong/in your calculations.(Or: Perhaps you have made some/mistakes/negligences/in your calculations.)

328　试一试吧,到处都能挤出空间,否则,将不可避免地把一些棉衬衫料子退关了。
Have a try, please.Space is tight everywhere.Otherwise it is unavoidable to shut out some cotton shirting.

329　请告诉装卸指导员对卡拉奇瓷器的一部分进行翻舱,我估计里面仍有一些空间。
Please tell the Foreman to restow part of the Karachi/porcelain ware/enamel ware/earth ware/chinaware/pottery ware.I /suppose/conjecture/there is still some room inside.

330　计划装在四舱底舱的哥本哈根的树胶脂还没来,但计划装在二层舱的奥斯陆的小地毯已到了,那么我们能否把小地毯与树胶脂的位置调换一下?
The Copenhagen gum rosin which is to be loaded in Hatch No.4 lower hold hasn't arrived yet.But the Oslo rig which is to be loaded in the tweendeck has already arrived.So can we change the location for the rig with that for the gum rosin?

331　我们将要装的哥德堡的鸭毛被驳船上来的不来梅的焊条压在了下面。
The Gothenburg duck feathers we're going to load are stowed under Bremen/electrode/solder wire/which is from the lighters.

332　我有急事,请一定帮我叫一下大副,告诉他有 50 箱生啤酒是退关货,不能装上船的。
There is an urgent matter.Be sure to call the Chief for me and tell him there are 50 cases of/draught beer/beer on draught/which is cancellation cargo not to be shipped on board.

— 167 —

333 因起货机出故障4舱装货停止了。
Loading at Hatch No.4 stopped owing to the breakdown of the winch.

334 1舱2层舱的空间是为赫尔辛基港和格拉斯哥港保留的。
The space in Hatch No.1 tweendeck is reserved for Helsinki and Glasgow.

335 船稍微有点前倾,你可以抽一些水或油来调整吃水。
The ship is tipping forward a little bit. You can pump some water or oil to adjust the draft.

336 这些磨损袋都是二手袋,这都在装货单上表明了,至于这些破袋,我将告诉发货人将他们缝好。
The worn-out bags are all second-hand bags as stated in the S/O. As to the torn bags, I'll tell the Shipper to resew them up.

337 如果你发现包装不良,我们将把它们修复或替换。
If you find anything wrong with the packing, we'll have them reconditioned or replaced.

338 4舱4层舱舱口位过境货挡路。
The through cargo in No.4 lower tweendeck hatchway stands in the way.

339 上2层舱舱口位只被占据了一半,你还可利用另一部分的空位来装2层舱的货。
The upper tweendeck hatchway is only half occupied; you can still use the opening of the other part to put the cargo in the tweendeck.

340 如果吊钩碰到梁上就会发生严重事故。
If the sling bumps against the beam,/grave/serious/accident may follow.

341 如果把雅典的纤维板装在5舱的前部,那么怎样安排原定装在那里的缝纫机呢?
If put the Athens fibreboard in Hatch No.5 fore part, then how do you dispose of the sewing machines which were to be stowed there?

342 根据配载图,我们应先装达累斯萨拉姆的浴巾,但现在八幡的青岛贝雕已错装到了那里。你能在配载图上改动一下吗?(或:你能重新把它们安排一下吗?)
According to the tentative cargo plan, we should first load the Dar es Salaam bath towel. But now the Qingdao shell carving for/Yawata/Yahata/has been misloaded there. Can you make a change in the tentative plan? (Or: Can you rearrange them?)

343 请把3舱舱口位的无焊缝钢管暂时卸下一部分,以便工人们利用空位来装底舱。
Please unload a part of the weldless steel tubes in Hatch No.3 hatchway for the present so as to the stevedores can use the opening to fill in the lower hold.

344 这些破袋是工人挑出来的,我们会通知发货人把他们换成新的。
These torn bags are picked out by the dockers. We will inform the Shipper to replace them by new ones.

345 装货是什么时间完成的?我要把它记入航海日志。
装货是在00:30分完成的。
When was the loading/completed/over/accomplished/ended?
The loading was completed at 00:30 hours.

Appendix 1　Sentences for Cargo Tallying

346　这是货物的实际积载图,请签字。
　　　This is the stowage plan for the cargo actually loaded.Please sign it.

347　发货人跟大副正在调度室谈论蓖麻籽袋子破损的事。
　　　The Shipper and the Chief Officer are discussing the torn bags of castor seeds at the Dispatch Office.

348　葡萄酒限定只能从甲板堆到离舱顶12英尺以内。
　　　Port wine can only be stowed restriction-wise from the deck to within 12 inches of the overhead.

349　这个箱子是错港货。贴目的港标志的地方被磨损了。
　　　The case is overcarried cargo.The/division/segment/portion/where the port mark is posted is scraped.

350　请详细告诉我关于货物状况的一些情况好吗?
　　　Would you please tell me something about the cargo condition in detail?

351　这艘船装配了麦氏舱盖,换句话说,装配了自动舱盖。
　　　The ship is/equipped/furnished/with MacGregor,in other words,with automatic hatch covers.

352　在安特卫普,所有铜条都是用载货卡车运送的。
　　　In Anterwerp,all the copper bars were brought alongside by lorries.

353　檀香木之间没有隔票,由于它们长度不同,所以你可以轻易把它们分开。
　　　There isn't any separation between the sandalwood.You can distinguish them easily as they are all in different length.

354　无缝钢管和不锈钢条不同票被涂成不同颜色。
　　　The seamless steel tubes and the stainless steel bars are painted in different colours by lots.

355　虽然科学仪器包装一样,但在标志上各票是不同的。
　　　Although the packing of the scientific instrument is of the same,yet the lots are different in marks.

356　你可以向大副询问关于分歧和批注的事。
　　　You can inquire of the Chief Officer about the/discrepancies/disputes/and remarks.

357　如果合成纤维混票,我会为你签字证明。
　　　If the different lots of synthetic fibre are mixed up,I'll sign for you to certify it.

358　为了安全,还是由你们的人来开油舱盖好。
　　　For safety's sake,it's preferable for your men to take off the oil tank lids.

359　装卸工只卸中间的袋子,留着两边的不动,这样卸货是不安全的。
　　　The stevedores are discharging the bales only in the middle,leaving those in both wings untouched.It's not safe to unload in this way.

360　他们一卸完中间的整票纸浆,就会从两边卸的。
　　　As soon as they finish the whole lot of pulp in the middle,they'll discharge them from

both wings.

361 装卸工从高处向舱里抛袋子,这使得大量袋子松口。
The stevedores/tossed/threw/the bags from high place into the hold. That brought on a lot of bags with seams slack.

362 昨天我向装卸工指出拽吊索不要太猛,但他们不听,今天他们拽得更厉害了。
Yesterday I pointed it out to the stevedores that they/dragged/towed/pulled along/the slings too roughly. But they didn't listen to me. Today they drag the slings even more violently.

363 装卸工听不懂你的话,情有可原。
The stevedores are justifiable for they are unable to catch what you say.

364 现在,一方面请你立即打开电源,另一方面我将告诉装卸工注意他们的操作。
Now, on the one hand, please turn on the power (supply) at once, on the other hand, I'll tell the stevedores to pay attention to their handling.

365 装卸队长已经看过了舱边的磨损。
The Chief Foreman has looked over the chafing on the edge of the hatch coaming.

366 当货物从舱两头吊起时,吊货索偶然地摩擦舱边是难免的。
When the cargo is/taken/hoisted/out from the 2 ends of the holds, it's unavoidable that the cargo runner will by accident rub against the edge of the hatch coaming.

367 从现在起请不要随意断电,你知道,中断会降低卸货速度,这对船方和港方都不利。
Please don't cut off the power supply/at will/willfully/arbitrarily/from now on. As you know, the interruption will surely slow down the speed of discharging. It's unfavorable to both the ship and the port.

368 请告诉工人从现在起平稳操作。
Please tell the dockers to handle smoothly/hereafter/thereafter.

369 如果理货员待时由船方引起,将由分公司做出记录并及时让船方签字。
If tallymen's stand-by is caused by the vessel, a record shall be made out by the Branch Company and be duly signed by the vessel.

370 没必要把工人从1舱转到3舱,因为你们的电工说只需约半个小时就能修好绞车。
There is no need of shifting the stevedores to Hatch No.3 from Hatch No.1. Because your electrician said it would take only half an hour to finish the repairing of the winch.

371 1舱绞车正在修理当中。
Hatch No.1 winch is under repair.

372 请快点修理。越快越好。
Please speed up the repairing. The sooner the better.

373 我公司业务章程规定,理货长主管整个船的理货工作,而理货员主管各自的舱口。
It's stipulated in the Business Regulations of our Company that the Chief Tally is in

Appendix 1　Sentences for Cargo Tallying

charge of the tallying work of the whole vessel, while the tallymen take charge of their respective hatches.

374　把所有的破袋集中起来,最后一同出舱,这有助于数字清楚。
Make a/concentration/gathering/of all the torn bags and do the outgoings/totally/together/at last.This will help to the clarity of the figures.

375　从星期一以来 2 舱的小牛肉已卸了 5 个班,现在剩下不多了。
Since Monday,Hatch No.2 veal has been discharged for five shifts.Now there is little left.

376　根据租船条款,中租对衬垫费负责。油纸在巴生港太贵了,所以为了中租的利益,我只买了 10 卷。
According to the terms of the Charter-party,/Zhongzu/the China National Chartering Corporation/is responsible for the cost of the dunnage.Polythene paper is too expensive in Port Kelang.Therefore I bought only 10 rolls in the interests of Zhongzu.

377　所有橡胶应按等级分隔而不是按标志。
All the rubber is to be separated only by grades/regardless of/dispense with/the marks.

378　在舱里对滑石粉进行分标志将花相当多的时间,最好的办法是在岸上进行分标志。
It'll take considerable time to sort out the marks of talc powder in the holds.The best way is to sort them out ashore.

379　铝锭原先是打成捆的,为了装更多货我们给它散了捆。我们得充分考虑租船人的利益。
The aluminum ingots are originally packed in bundles.We off-bundled them only for taking more cargo.We should take the charterer's benefit into full consideration.(Or: We should be fully considerate of the charterer's benefit.)

380　同票的每捆数量都是一定的。
The quantity of each bundle is fixed for the same lot.

381　供货商发电报给买方代理人说由于"大和丸"轮的船机故障船不能于原定日期到达。
The supplier cabled his buyer's agent that the S.S."DAIWA MARU" would not arrive on the original date for the engine failure.

382　你认识的那位理货长已调到外轮代理公司了。
The Chief Checker whom you are acquainted with has been transferred to PENAVICO.

383　多少件是一捆?
How many pieces make a bundle?

384　2 舱 3 号和 5 号提单的乙烯醇缩树脂混装了,请你去验看一下。
Hatch No.2 polyvinyl acetal resin under Bill of Lading No.3 and 5 are mixed up.Please go to have a look at them.

385　麻烦的是只有铝捆上有漆,铝块上没有漆。所以我们很难取得不同票的准确

— 171 —

数字。
The trouble is the paints are only on the bundles of aluminum ingots but not on each piece. So we can hardly get the accurate figures for different lots.

386 根据港章,如果货物标志不清就不能出口。
In terms of the Port Regulations, if the cargo marks are illegible, the cargo can't be allowed to export.

387 我不知道太子港发生了什么事,我只是说明了船上货物现在的状态。
I'm not fully aware of what happened at the Port-Au-Prince. I merely mean the present state of the cargo on board.

388 装卸过程中可能出现工残,这是常识。
Stevedores' damage may arise in the progress of loading and discharging. That's common sense.

389 五舱有一些带干水渍的胡椒袋,暂时把它们放在那儿。
There are some bags of pepper with dry water stains in Hatch No.5. Please put them aside for the time being.

390 这个钥匙打不开这个锁。
The key doesn't fit the lock.

391 铬块短捆溢支。
The chrome ingots are short-landed in bundles and over-landed in pieces.

392 你的句子冗长且意义含糊。
Your sentence is too lengthy with ambiguity

393 此次航程上共有3个港口,始发港是奥克兰,中途港是三宝垅,终点港是蛇口。
In all there are three ports on this voyage. The first port of departure is Auckland. The port of call is Semarong and the terminal port is Shekou.

394 所谓个别装卸工故意破坏纸箱,这纯属捏造。
It's purely a fiction that individual dockers intentionally injure the cartons.

395 我承认当时我在场,但我告诉装卸工把它们换成新的,并且在我下班之前他们就已经换掉了这些破袋。
I acknowledge that I was on the spot then. But I told the stevedores to replace them by new ones, and before I was off duty they had replaced the torn bags already.

396 如果这样我将不加批注签证。
If so, I'll sign the papers without putting any remarks.

397 看,这一关仅有19袋,为什么这关少了1袋,请你问一下信号员好吗?
Look, this sling contains only 19 bags. Why is this sling short of one bag? Can you ask the signalman about it?

398 在吊钩上升过程中,1个袋子掉了,我们会在下一关补上。
One bag falls while the sling is going up. We'll make up for it in the next sling.

399 眼见为实,这事你弄确定了吗?

Appendix 1　Sentences for Cargo Tallying

Seeing is believing.Have you made it certain?

400　我们只理件数,而不管单件的重量,所以你最好把批注改为"对重量不负责任"?

We only tally the packages but ignore the weight of each package. So you'd better change the remark to "not responsible for the weight".

401　所有关都是这种形式。

That's the form of all the slings.

402　5 袋椰仁干泡了,因为它们堆在船舱附近。

5 bags of copra are soaked because they were stacked near the bilge.

403　我们下班了,让我们对数吧。

We're off shift now.Let's check up the figures.

404　内货从钩里正往下撒落,里面肯定有破袋。

The contents are dropping from the sling.There must be some torn bags inside.

405　2 个袋子皮破且内货外漏,3 袋口松。请记下来。

2 bags cover torn and contents exposed, and 3 bags seams slack.Please write it down.

406　工人吃饭时间是什么?

从 11:00 到 11:40。

What's the stevedores' meal time?

From eleven hours to eleven forty hours.

407　这个班什么时候结束?

下午 3 点。

When will this shift end?

At 3 p.m.

408　他们分 3 班昼夜轮流工作,白班从 7:00 到 15:00,中班从 15:00 到 23:00,夜班从 23:00 到 7:00。

They work round the clock in rotation in 3 shifts.The day shift works from 7:00 to 15:00,the swing shift from 15:00 to 23:00,and the night shift from 23:00 to 7:00.

409　务必记下每一关,否则你的总数将与我的总数对不起来。

Be sure to record every sling. Otherwise your/sum/total amount/won't be equal to mine.

410　中班何时开始何时结束?

What times does the swing shift begin and end?

411　据史密斯先生称,王先生是个有能力的理货员。

According to Mr.Smith,Mr.Wang is a competent tallyman.

412　现在我下班了,后天我上白班。

I'm off shift now.The day after tomorrow I'll be on the day shift.

413　工人上午 7 点,下午 3 点,晚上 11 点换班。

The stevedores change their shifts at 7 in the morning, 3 in the afternoon and 11 at night.

414 我要离开一会,别忘了记关。
I'll be away for a while. Don't forget to record every sling.

415 昨晚厨房和船员舱里失窃了。我们想把此事弄清楚,请向港务当局转达我们的意见。
There happened pilferages in the galley and the crew's quarters last night. We want to make it clear. Please/convey/pass on/our idea to the port authority.

416 记录事实是我们的责任,请在记录上签字来证明事实。
It's our liability to record the fact. Please sign the record to certify the fact.

417 以下货物被DDT原粉灰尘污染。
The underneath cargo is/stained/contaminated/with the DDT dust.

418 2舱有几袋角蹄粉由于包装不固而破损了。
Some bags of horn and hoof grain in Hatch No.2 are torn owing to weak packing.

419 首先,我想提醒你别在数字上落了这些破空袋。
First of all, I'd like to remind you not to/miss out/leave out/the torn empty bags in your figure.

420 我们会把它们当成原袋的。
We'll consider them original bags.

421 频繁旋转会引起机器故障。
Frequent rotation of the machine will cause malfunction.

422 考虑到轻微湿损的袋子没包括在这个数字内,我不能缩减这个数字了。
In so far as the slightly wet bags are not included in the figure, I can't cut down the figure.

423 依我看来,我们只能把这个留待明天让商检解决了。(或:我们只有求助于商检解决了。)
In my opinion, we can't help leaving the issue to be decided by the cargo surveyor tomorrow. (Or: We have to resort to the cargo surveyor to solve it.)

424 残损由操作不慎引起。
The damage was caused due to careless handling.

425 我不以为然。如果你们事先在羊角桩上铺上足够的板子,这些袋子就不至于被刺穿了。你怎么能怪装卸工呢?
I don't think so. If you had put enough battens on the cleats beforehand, the bags might not have been pierced. How can you blame the dockers?

426 这些破空袋你认为是怎么回事?
What do you consider the torn empty bags?

427 请加批注"以商检报告为准",取消原来的批注"有争议"。
Please put the remark "Subject to cargo surveyor's report" and strike off the original remark "In dispute".

Appendix 1　Sentences for Cargo Tallying

428　涂层擦破且尾部排气管弯曲。
　　The coating of paint is scratched and the exhaust tail pipe/bent/curved.

429　24 号提单少一箱零件。
　　B/L No.24 is short of one box of spare parts.

430　两只盒子被染料污染,3 只箱子脱箍,1 只箱子重钉且内货不明。这票货残损就这么多。
　　2 boxes tainted by/dyes/pigment/coloring matter/dyestuff, 3 cases with hoops missing, and 1 case renailed with contents unknown. That's all for the damaged cargo in this lot.

431　一些板子补过并弯翘了,几根底梁断了。
　　Some planks are patched and warped. Several bottom skids are broken.

432　装卸工在卸货过程中确实损坏了一些袋子,但我已单独为它们作了一个记录。
　　The dockers did have acted to the detriment of some bags during discharging. But I have made a separate record for them.

433　我发觉你们的理货员在理货时聊天,我们怎能信任你们的理货数字?
　　你说的有点夸张。他们的谈话只不过围绕与理货工作有关的事。
　　I become aware of your tallymen's chatting during tallying. How can we trust your tally figures?
　　Your words is somewhat/rhetorical/high-flown/exaggerated. Their conversations merely encompass the things relating to tallying work.

434　谁都难说里面的货物是否完好。因为我们看不见内部。在这一点上,我们理货员只根据外表判断货物。
　　You never can tell whether the contents are in good state, because we can't see the interior. In this regard we tallyman only judge cargo by appearances.

435　有两箱仪器内货格格响。
　　There are 2 cases of apparatus with contents rattling.

436　这 15 桶甲醇除盖子松外,还鼓胀了,你们不妨重修一下。
　　The 15 drums of methyl alcohol, in addition to loose lids, are bulging. You might as well recooper them.

437　这是所有经值班副签字的记录。如果有疑问,你可以浏览手中所有这些记录。这样一切就清楚了。
　　It's the summing-up of all the records signed by the duty officers. If there is any doubt about it, you can go through the records in your hands. And everything will be clear.

438　我同情你,但公事公办,这些残损记录是建立在事实基础上的。
　　You have my sympathies. But business is business. The damage record is/based/founded/established/on the actual facts.

439　恰恰相反,上面所提货物残损是本来就存在的。
　　Just conversely, the above-mentioned damage was originally existed.

440　我反对这种批注。既然你们的值班副检查了所有破袋并认为它们是原残,你怎能

— 175 —

让装卸工负责呢?

I reject such remarks. As your duty officers examined all the torn bags and recognized them original damage, how can you hold the stevedores responsible?

441 你根据什么判断货物状况?

By what do you judge cargo condition?

442 在门司港,轿车都是由熟练司机开进中甲板和下甲板的,不可能发生碰撞。

In the port of Moji, the sedans are all driven into the trailer deck and the lower hold by experienced drivers. There couldn't have been/collision/impaction.

443 20箱人造纤维溢卸,50袋树脂乙烯短卸。这是我们理出的实际数字。我们已检查过好几遍了。

Twenty cartons of/rayon yarn/artificial fibre/are over-landed and fifty bags of polyvinyl resin short-landed. This is the actual figure that we've tallied.

444 我不知道在装货港是怎样理货的,但在这里有双方理货,即理货员代表船方,驳船工人或仓库管理员代表收货人。至于大票的袋子,工人通常做关定型定量。他们既不受贿也不骗人,因此我相信我们的最终数字是正确的。

I don't know how the cargo is tallied at the loading port. But here the cargo is tallied by two sides, that is, the tallyman on behalf of the ship and the lighter man or the warehouse keeper on behalf of the receiver. As regards the bagged cargo in big lots, the stevedores always make slings in fixed form and fixed quantity. They neither take bribes nor play anybody false. So I'm certain our ultimate figure is correct.

445 你的批注根据不足,我听起来好像你怀疑我们的理货数字。

Your remarks are not well grounded. It seems to me that you doubt our tally figure.

446 这正是问题所在。很明显有一钩被你们的理货员漏掉了。

That's just the point. It's obvious that one sling was missed out by your tallyman.

447 这50箱酒精短卸不是出自同一个舱,它出自2个舱,即16箱出自1舱34箱出自2舱。

The shortage of 50 cartons of alcohol doesn't come out of one hatch. It comes out of 2 hatches, that are 16 cartons of Hatch No.1 and 34 cartons of Hatch No.2.

448 你积载图上的总数与舱单上的不一致。

The total amount that appears on your cargo plan disagrees with that on the manifest.

449 事实胜于雄辩。我们已经一遍一遍地查过了货物,既然没错,你就没有理由否认这个数字。

Facts speak louder than words. We've checked the cargo over and over again. Since there's no error, you have no reason to deny the figure.

450 用"货物自然减量"这种批注来描述磷灰土是不合适的。

To use the remark "Normal loss of quantity" describing the phosphate is out of place.

451 我们复核了计数单并复查了货垛,结果都是301件。

We've reviewed our tally sheets and reexamined the/stack/pile, the consequences are

Appendix 1　Sentences for Cargo Tallying

all 301 pieces.

452　黄麻短卸是从哪个舱出来的?
Which hatch does the shortage of the jute come out of?

453　装完货后大副无缘无故地拒签收货单。
The Chief Officer refused to sign the Mate's Receipts after loading for no particular reason.

454　我不知道这件事该怎么办。
I wonder how that is to be done.

455　这是肉眼明显可见的旧损伤,你怎么能在货物异议书上批注"原收原交"?
It's a/visual/visible/former defect. How can you remark /"Delivered as loaded"/ "Discharged as loaded"/on the cargo exception form?

456　许多袋子都有一定程度的破损且内货严重外漏。
A number of bags are worn out to a certain extend with contents leaking badly.

457　船方须支付移货和翻舱的理货费用。
The ship has to pay the tallying fee for shifting and reloading of cargoes.

458　两个箱子用旧板重钉过且裂缝了。
2 cases are renailed up with old planks and split.

459　许多装暖瓶的箱子被磨损且箍带部分生锈。
A number of cartons of vacuum flasks are chafed with their bands partly rusty.

460　不要紧,我敢肯定那不影响内货。
Never mind. I bet that won't affect the contents.

461　所有螺钉全上锈了。
All the screws are wholly rusty.

462　既然不同票苎麻混装了,船方就得支付分标志费。
Since the ramie of different lots has been mixed up, the ship has to pay for sorting marks.

463　操作过程中如不适当注意,就会出现货物残损。
Damage to cargo may/result/arise/if due observation isn't paid to handling.

464　有些靠近锅炉房的箱子里面的粘胶冒出。
In some instances of the cases adjacent to the boiler room the inside/sticky/glutinous/ glue oozed out.

465　你没签这两张。
You've/failed/neglected/to sign these 2 pieces.

466　我认为加批注毫无必要。
I deem it/unnecessary/not requisite/unessential/dispensable/to put remarks.

467　你对进口灯泡加了批注,可现在你又不同意我对出口丝绸制品加批注,这合理吗?
You have put some remarks regarding the inward bulb, whereas now you don't agree to my putting any remarks concerning the outwards silk fabrics. Is it/reasonable/legiti-

mate?

468 关于进口货,我确实加了一些批注,因为所有的残损痕迹明显是旧的,但至于装到船上的出口货物,都很好,你所提到的破袋实际上已在发现后换掉了。你们二副没向你报告调换的事,这不是我的错,你知道,我们中国理货员尊重事实。
With respect to the inward cargo, I did put some remarks because all the traces of damage are apparently old ones. But as to the outward cargo loaded on board, it's all in good condition. The torn bags you mentioned were actually replaced right after they were discovered. Your Second Mate didn't report it to you about the replacement. That's not my fault. You know that we Chinese tallymen respect facts.

469 除了"大量"一词,发货人同意你的批注,他希望你写下具体数字。
Except for the words "a lot of", the Shipper agrees to your remarks. He hopes you'll put down a/definite/concrete/figure.

470 依我的观点,钢材轻微弯曲是自然现象,根本不影响货物质量。
In my opinion, it's a natural phenomenon that steel bars get partly bent. That won't affect the quantity of the cargo at all.

471 减去10捆怎么样?
How about deducting 10 bundles?

472 为了保护船东的利益,我拒绝修改我加的批注,但你可以加反批注嘛。批注与反批注是允许同时存在的。
For the purpose of covering the owner's interests, I refuse to revise my remarks. But you may put oppositional remarks. Remarks versus opposition to remarks are allowed to exist simultaneously.

473 我要同发货人及时协商。
I'll/study/confer/with the Shipper in time.

474 等到发货人来了再说,我们现在没有必要争执。
Leave it till the Shipper comes. It's not necessary for us to argue about it.

475 我看见你们的绞车手跳挡操作起货机。他要对事故负责。
I saw your winchman not operating the winch gear by gear. He is liable for the accident.

476 去年我们对绞车大修过一次。
We had the winch overhauled last year.

477 看起来他是个生手,且对工作无经验。
It seems he's a green hand and is inexperienced in his job.

478 我们所有绞车手都训练有素,能熟练操作起货机。
All our winchman are well trained and/skilled/skilful/proficient/practiced/in handling winches.

479 理货员待时不是由于绞车手操作不熟,而是因为绞车坏了。
The tallymen's stand-by was not due to the unskilled handling of the winchman but to the breakdown of the winch.

Appendix 1　Sentences for Cargo Tallying

480　问题在于你们的起货机太旧了,且缺少日常保养,因此当起货机日夜不停地使用时就易损坏。
The question is your winch is too old and lack of routine maintenance.Therefore,it's liable to/get worn-out/be out of order/when working night and day without a break.

481　小事一桩,不必争执。
This is a/trifle/trivial thing.It's not/worth/worthy of/worthwhile/arguing.

482　我不能没有调查就对此事仓促地做出结论。
I can't bring this matter/a speedy/an urgent/conclusion without investigation.

483　我们也不愿浪费时间,我们也想让你船尽早离开。
We aren't willing to waste any time either.We also want to have a quick dispatch of your ship.

484　我的待时时间是2小时,你的是2小时20分钟,你去掉20分钟的免计时间了吗?分歧不大,让我在记录上修改一下。
My stand-by time is 2 hours.But yours is 2 hours 20 minutes.Have you/eliminated/precluded/20 minutes' free time?
The discrepancy isn't too much.Let me/modify/correct/it in my record.

485　你们到我们港口多次了,我们之间已建立起良好的合作关系。
You have been to our port many times. Good cooperation has been/set up/built/between us.

486　由于缺少护舱板,三舱有许多亚麻织品撕破了。
Some linen fabrics were torn in Hatch No.3 owing to the lack of cargo batten.

487　无论你怎么说,我都应根据事实编制记录。
Whatever you say,I should make out a record in accordance with the facts.

488　大副,这是二舱毛织品混装的现场记录,请签字。
Chief Officer,here's the On-the-spot Record for the mixed-up stowage of the woolen fabrics in Hatch No.2.Please sign it.

489　理货长是公证人,既然理货长已签字,就不再有必要让我签字了。
Chief Tally is a/go-between/notary.Since the Chief Tally has signed it,it's no longer necessary for me to sign.

490　上一航次我由于承认了货物短缺而受到船东的严厉批评。
I was/sternly/severely/criticized by the ship-owner on the last voyage for my acknowledging the shortage.

491　我只好编制一份清单表明短捆溢支了。
I can but make a list showing the short-landing of bundles and over-landing of loose pieces.

492　实在没办法,就按你说的办吧。
It can't be helped.Do as what you say.

493　大副不顾我的反对坚持要加批注。

The Chief Officer insisted on putting remarks/regardless of/without regard to/my objection.

494 货物混装给理货员带来极多麻烦。分标志费应由船方负担。

Mixed-up stowage of cargo caused our tallymen excessive amounts of trouble.The sorting charges shall be/born/borne/undertaken/assumed/by the ship.

495 很明显,我们不会把工残归到你们账上。

It's evident that we won't charge the stevedores' damage to your account.

496 至于污染的指甲油,是你们的过失,不是我的过失。

As to the stained nail-polish,the fault lies with you,not with me.

497 你用什么来证明你的观点?

What evidence can you present to/justify/confirm/verify/prove/testify/witness/your views?

498 15个液氮集装箱板子破了,船方值班人员已检查过了。若有疑问,请向他们询问。

There were 15 liquid nitrogen containers with planks broken.They were examined by the ship's personnel on duty.If you have any doubt,you can ask them about it.

499 你们的工人粗率地拽吊索,结果铁板上的衬垫被移开了。这就是铁板被从破袋出来的纯碱污染的原因。

Your dockers towed the slings roughly./In consequence/Upon this/the dunnage was removed from the steel plates.That's why some plates are stained by the soda from torn bags.

500 你所说的根本没有说服力,你可以看见被污染的板上的锈不是一薄层,很明显这样厚的一层锈只能在很长时间内形成,对我方而言,工人卸货过程中一发现板上的尿素就扫去了。

What you say isn't convincing at all.You see the rust on the stained plate isn't a thin layer.It's obvious that such a thick covering of rust can only be formed in a long time. For our part,the dockers swept the urea as soon as they found it on the plates during discharging.

501 让我们共同把这案子交商检处理。

Let's mutually submit the case to the cargo surveyor.

502 你看下面的货物还没动呢。你可以很容易地看出所有破箱上面的旧痕迹。

Look,so far the cargo down below hasn't been touched yet.You can easily find the old traces on all the broken cases.

503 看来唯一的办法就是签字了。

It seems that the only way out is to sign.

504 如果你乐意,就在纸上记下它作参考。

If you like,you may jot it down on a piece of paper for reference.

505 托盘内的橡胶或多或少潮湿并发霉,有一些甚至粘在了一块。

The rubber bales inside the pallets are more or less damp and mouldy,some have even

Appendix 1 Sentences for Cargo Tallying

stuck together.

506 液氮集装箱的破箱数量是 15,其中 7 箱是工残。
The figure of the broken cases of liquid nitrogen container is 15, of which 7 are stevedores' damage.

507 2 舱有 5 箱氨水罐脱钉。
There are 5 aqua ammonia containers off-nailed in Hatch No.2.

508 5 舱带干水渍的黄鼬皮发出难闻的气味。
The weasel skin with dry water stains in Hatch No.5 gives off a horrible smell.

509 1 舱甲板 3 辆卡车上的窗格玻璃打碎了,挡泥板凹了,天线折了。
There are three trucks on No.1 deck with window panes broken, mud guards dented and antennas bent.

510 还有就是,15 辆卡车的底盘锈渍,尤其在船桅房附近的。
Moreover, the chassis of 15 trucks are rust-stained, particularly those near the mast house.

511 请在装货单上加"甲板货由发货人负责"的批注。
Please put down the remarks "Deck cargo at shipper's risk" in the Shipping Order.

512 记录现在托运人那里,将由他提交到保险公司。
Now the record is/at the dispose of/in the possession of/the consignor. It is to be submitted to the Insurance Company by him.

513 3 舱卡车的大多数车厢边挡板和后挡板都没有装配上,它们在舱里到处都是。
In Hatch No.3, the majority of the side and rear walls of the trucks are not/fitted on/rigged up. They spread over in the hold.

514 24 号轿车的后照镜、风屏刮水器、千斤顶、香烟打火机、半导体收音机、备用轮胎和蓄电池丢失。
The rear view mirrors, the windshield wipers, the jack, the cigarette lighter, the transistor set, the spare tire and the storage batteries of Sedan No.24 are missing.

515 把轮胎的气放掉,然后重新充上气。
Deflate the/tire/tyre/and then inflate it afresh.

516 2 舱轿车丢失了什么?
What are missing on the sedans in Hatch No.2?

517 船的剧烈颠簸损坏了车上的一些附件。
The heavy tossing of the vessel damaged some accessories of the cars.

518 2 舱左舷甲板的两辆卡车因绑得不好而碰撞了。
The 2 trucks on No.2 port deck collided because of bad/lashing/binding.

519 除非轿车内胎漏气,否则就不必做记录。
It's not necessary to make out a record unless the inner tube of the sedan is leaking gas.

520 卡车轮胎瘪了,内胎可能被刺穿。

— 181 —

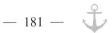

The tires of the trucks are flat. The inner tubes might be punctured.

521 将用双线作业,需调整装舱顺序。

There will be 2 loaders at work. It needs to adjust loading sequence.

522 请分别给我数字。

少75捆,溢3825支。

Please give me the figures/separately/respectively.

75 bundles are short and 3825 pieces over.

523 在装货港长崎工人解开了几十捆,为的是用这些散件填充亏舱。

The stevedores at the loading port of Nagasaki untied several score of bundles in order to fill the broken spaces with the loose pieces.

524 每捆的件数在舱单上未注明。

问题就在于此。

The number of pieces of each bundle is not/stated/shown/on the manifest.

That's just the point.

525 德银每10块打成一捆,请把散件折算成捆。

German silver/Nickel silver/is packed in bundle of ten. Please work out the number of bundles from the loose pieces.

526 船方是货物承运人,加这种批注似乎不合理,同时我想收货人也不会接受的。

As the ship is the carrier of the cargo, it seems unreasonable to put such remarks. Meanwhile I don't think the Consignee will accept it.

527 站在我的立场来说,我不得不保护我的船东的利益,否则我将因此受责难。

On my part, I have to cover my owner's interests; otherwise, I'm to be blamed for it.

528 大副,你已来过几次了,你应该对我们国家有一个很好的了解。我们在业务中从不欺骗。我相信收货人会据实处理这个问题的,如果数字正确,他肯定不会向船东索赔的。请放心好了。

Chief Officer, you have been here many times. You ought to have a better understanding of our country. We never cheat in business. I'm sure the Consignee will deal with this matter according to the fact. If the figure is correct, he will definitely not lodge any claims against the shipowner. Please take it easy.

529 坦率地讲,我对数字感到怀疑。

Frankly speaking, I feel/doubtful/suspectable/about the figure.

530 我也知道这不是一个小数字,所以我们反复检查了几遍。

I also know it's not a small figure. So we have checked it repeatedly.

531 我敢说,你这是偏见。我们理货员是对船方负责的,我们在工作中总是坚持实事求是的态度。所以单证上的东西反映了客观事实。你尽管相信好了。

You have prejudice, I dare to say. We tallymen hold ourselves responsible to the vessel. We always take a practical attitude towards our work. So what appears in the list reflects objective. You may rely upon it.

Appendix 1　Sentences for Cargo Tallying

532　我们都是专业理货人员。我们的队伍受过专门的培训。我们都遵守理货的原则,维护委托方的合法权益。
We are all/personnel/staffs/in the specific field of tallying. Our contingent is specially trained. We all observe the principles of tallying and safeguard the/client's/entrusted party's/legitimate rights and interests.

533　事实是,我们每条作业线有两名理货员,并且作业过程中他们一直在现场,他们工作热心吃苦。
As a matter of fact, we have 2 tallymen for each gang, and they are on the spot all the time during handling. They work earnestly and hard.

534　任何人都难免犯错误,我们虽然不能说自己永远正确,从不犯错,但我们应尽量使错误减到最少,一旦出现错误,我们就改正它。
It's hard for any person to avoid mistakes. Although we can't say we're always correct and never/make/blunder/errors, yet we should minimize our mistakes as few as possible. Once a mistake is occurred, we should correct it.

535　恐怕你们的理货员在计数单上漏记了3钩,因为18捆正好等于3钩。
你猜错了,现在所说的短缺不是出于1个舱而是3个舱,即2舱7捆,3舱2捆,4舱9捆。
I'm afraid your tallyman may miss 3 slings on the tally sheet by chance, because 18 bales/equal to/amount to/are equivalent to/three slings.
No, you haven't guessed it. The shortage in question doesn't come out of 1 hatch but 3, that is, 7 bales from Hatch No.2, 2 from No.3 and 9 from No.4.

536　你用地脚货抵消短卸不行吗?
Can't you set off the sweepings against the shortage? (Or: Can't you offset the shortage by the sweepings?)

537　根据租船公约,承运人责任到货物卸离船舶时止。
According to the Charter-party terms, the responsibility of the carrier shall/cease/be relieved/when the cargoes are discharged from the ship.

538　若仍觉问题棘手,我想你可以加批注"系日照理货数字"。
If you still think it's/an awkward/a troublesome/matter, suppose you can put the remark "According to Rizhao tally".

539　他们使用了先进技术,理货完全机械化,所有货物都是由计算机来理数的。它很少出错,有很多优点,在现代海运业中,它确实是一种先进方法。
They used an advanced technique. Tallying was completely mechanized. All the cargo was counted by automatic calculators. It seldom makes mistakes. It has many advantages. It's indeed an advanced method in modern shipping business.

540　我们赞同机械化理数,将来或早或晚我们也要采用这种方法。但据我所知,以前我曾接触过几艘停靠我港的远洋船。它们运载的货物在装货港也是由计算机理数的。令我不解的是,它们的理货数字结果并不是100%正确。货物卸下后时而

发现或是短卸或是溢卸。这就说明在特定的港口机械理货并不是绝对可靠的。以我的观点,理货数字的正确性主要由理货员对工作的高度责任感决定。即使最新式的机器也会偶尔出错。所以我向你保证我的数字是正确的。

We are/in favor of/in support of/the mechanical tallying. We'll adopt this method likewise in the long run in the future. However, to my knowledge, I have come into contact with several oceangoing freighters calling at our port before. The cargoes they carried are also counted by automatic calculators at the loading ports. It puzzles me that their figures didn't turn out 100% correct. The cargo was now and then found short or over after discharging. This reflects that calculators aren't absolutely reliable at certain ports. From my point of view the accuracy of the tally figure/is decided mainly by/depends fundamentally on/rests basically upon/tallymen's high sense of duty to their work. Even up-to-date machines might occasionally go wrong. So I assure you our figure is correct.

541 你工作出色不会被解雇的。
You work nicely. You won't get the sack.

542 你能否把短卸数字减去一半?
Can you cut down the value of the short-landed cargo in half?

543 我们对理货工作的态度是实事求是,用地脚货来补足短卸是不允许的。
Our attitude towards the tallying work is to seek truth from facts. Using sweepings to make up for the shortage is not allowable.

544 从各舱卸下的货物数字与船图上的不一致。
The figures of cargo discharged from the segregated hatches/don't correspond to/differ from/don't agree with/those on the cargo plan.

545 通过抽查,我发现你们工人时而把残损货装上船。
Through spot check I found your stevedores misloaded the damaged cargo on board/occasionally/at times/now and then.

546 不要把事情看得太严重了,货物短少或溢出在理货工作中是常见的事。
Don't take things too seriously. Overage and shortage is common in tally work.

547 如果你不顾事实拒绝在货物单证上签字,你就不能结关开航。
If you disregard the fact and refuse to sign on the cargo papers, you can't complete the clearance on ship's departure.

548 请你平静下来对这个问题作慎重考虑,否则你将承担由此造成的所有后果。
Calm down yourself and give the matter your careful consideration, otherwise you'll have to bear all the consequences arising therefrom.

549 请让我举一个例子供你进一步参考。例如:我们发现计数单与装货单上的数字之间有出入,尤其计数单上有一些涂改之处。
Allow me to put forward an evidence for your further consideration. For instance, we find some discrepancies between the figures on the tally sheets and those on the Shipping Orders, particularly there are some obliteration on the tally sheets.

550 内理根据记有数量的理货小票检查关内数量。
The warehouse keeper checks up the quantity in the slings according to the numbered tally tickets.

551 "船方对非属实不承担责任"指我毫无疑问地接受摆在我面前的事实,但如果事实不正确,我就不接受任何责任。
"Ship not responsible without prejudice" means I accept the facts presented before me without question but I won't accept any responsibility if the facts aren't correct.

552 在此期间,我将让我的代理人给槟榔屿港发一个查询单以作进一步调查。
In the meantime, I'll ask my Agent to send a tracer to Penang to make further investigation.

553 11箱3级薄荷脑短卸,1级薄荷脑既无短卸也无溢卸。
Eleven cases of Grade No.3 menthol are short delivered. There is neither shortage nor overage of Grade No.1 menthol.

554 让我简明扼要的介绍一下三结合理货方法。它是我们的一种先进的工作方法之一,其含义是:为保证理货的准确性,三方联合检查货物,这三方除了外理还有内理和装卸工人。
Let me/introduce/bring out/describe/the three-in-one tallying method to the point briefly. It's one of our advanced working methods. It means three parties check cargo together in order to/ensure/guarantee/an accurate tally. The three parties,/besides/other than/the tallyman, refer to the warehouse keeper and the dockers.

555 被迫签字不是常有的事。
Signing under/compulsion/protest/is not of frequent occurrence.

556 我的船已完成了出港许可手续,很可能下午就离开。
My ship has completed port clearance and will very likely leave this afternoon.

557 你说的"积载因数"这个术语是什么意思?
What do you mean by the term of Stowage Factor?

558 有可能你们在过驳卸货时把数字弄错了。
Probably you get the figure wrong when transhipping cargo to the lighters.

559 如果你把短卸数字缩小50%,即从总数中扣除12件,我就签字。
If you reduce the figure of shortage by 50%, that's to say, deduct twelve pieces from the total, I'll sign.

560 对不起,这不是交易,我们从不说假话,我们一贯尊重事实,并根据原则办事。
I'm sorry there is no bargain. We never tell lies. We always respect facts and do business on principles.

561 与托运的货物有利害关系的方面是:托运人、承运人和收货人,理货公司只是代表船方工作,本身根本不是权益方。
The interested parties of a consignment are the Consignor, the Carrier and the Consignee. The tally company simply works on behalf of the vessel and is not by nature

an interested party at all.

562 根据业务章程,如果重理数字与原理数字一致,重理费应由船方支付,重理后的重理记录最后将发到船东那里。如果重理数字与原理数字不一致,重理费由我们理货公司承担。

According to the Business Regulations, the retallying charges shall be for the account of the vessel if the retallied figure is in/conformity/accordance/with the original one. A retally note shall be issued as final to the shipowner after retallying. If the retallied figure doesn't correspond to the original one, our tally company will undertake the cost of retallying.

563 如果你拿不定主意,不妨请示你们船长的意见。

If you can't make up your mind, you might as well ask your Captain for his instruction.

564 星期天理 1000 吨货为何要向我们收取附加费?

Why/charge us extra fee/charge us additionally/for tallying 1,000 tons of cargo on Sunday? (Or: Why surcharge us for tallying 1000 tons of cargo on Sunday?)

565 根据我公司理货收费规章,如果在星期天或法定节假日及困难作业下理货将因此收取附加费。

According to the Regulations for Collecting Tallying Fees by our Company, in case any tally is done on Sunday or legal holiday and difficult operations, additional charges shall be collected accordingly.

566 我们按理货收费率的 100% 收取附加费。

We charge extra fee at 100% of the rates of tallying fees.

567 理货费收规则从 1980 年 6 月 1 日起实施。

The Regulations for Collecting Tallying Fees/are effective/come into force/from June 1st, 1980.

568 你们的船期表规定船舶 16:30 离开,请为联合检查做好准备。

Your ship is scheduled to leave at 16:30. Please get everything ready for the joint/inspection/survey.

569 以相同费率收费的货物,不够 1 吨将视作 1 吨。

For cargoes chargeable at the same rate, part of one ton shall be taken as one ton.

570 在这种情况下,我通常加批注"甲板货由发货人负责"。

Under such circumstances, I usually put the remarks "Deck cargo at shipper's risk".

571 "有争议"这种批注任何情况下对收货人来说都是不可接受的。

The remarks "In dispute" are under no circumstances/accessible/acceptable/to the Consignee.

572 集装箱在装箱前已彻底清洗,并且里面先前所有物品都已移走。

The container has been/thoroughly/entirely/cleaned prior to vanning and all evidence of previous contents has been removed.

573 木头、钉子和其他外来杂物都嵌在了甘草之中。

Wood, nails and other foreign materials were imbedded in the licorice.

574 货物装卸期间,理货人员应与船上值班驾驶人员和船员保持联系,以便及时商议与解决有关理货工作的问题。
During cargo handling, the tallymen must keep in/contact/association/with ship's officers or crew members on duty so as to discuss and solve problems relating to cargo tallying.

575 配载图应给每个货舱配以一定数量的货物,使任何一个货舱都不至于需要一种不相称的卸货工作舱时量。
The tentative plan should provide for an amount of cargo in each hold so that no one hold will require an unproportional number of gang hours of work to discharge the cargo.

576 "倒装"并非指货物上面一定有别的货物直接装在它上面,而仅仅是指那货物以这样或那样的方式阻碍着卸货的进行。
"Over stowed" doesn't mean that the cargo necessarily has other cargo stowed directly over it, but simply that cargo is blocking the discharging in one way or another.

577 参照你们12月26日来电,我公司为你在"塔斯门"轮保留杂货总舱容30000包装尺,特此通知,请确认能否装满。
With reference to your cable of December 26, we wish to inform you that we retain/reserve/you on the M.V "Tasman" a total of thirty thousand bale feet of space for general cargo. Please confirm that you are able to utilize the space fully.

578 集装箱理货、理箱规则从1976年7月1日起施行。
Rules for Tallying Containerized Cargoes and Containers take effect as from July 1st, 1976.

579 我们办事公正,这是普遍公认的。
It's/universally/widely/acknowledged that we act on the square.

580 在处理对外事务时,我们坚决贯彻党的政策。
When dealing with foreign affairs we resolutely carry out the Party's/guidelines/policies.

581 我们按每吨0.30元人民币的费率收取重理费。
We collect the retallying expenses at the rate of 0.30 ¥ RMB for per ton.

582 如果船东未授权你这样做,你不妨打电话请示他。
If the shipowner doesn't authorize you to do so, you might as well telephone him for his instructions.

583 这已成为国际惯例。
It has formed an international habit.

584 从这到海员俱乐部有多远?
五站远。
How far is it/What's the distance/from here to the Seaman's Club?

Five stops away.(Or：There are five stops.)

585　我想用一下你的高频电话同公司联系一下。
I'd like to use your VHF (Very High Frequency) telephone to contact our company.

586　洗手间在哪儿？
在尽头左边。
Where is the/W.C/water closet/toilet?
At the left of the end.

587　昨天我把公文包和对讲机忘在理货房间里了。你有没有帮我保存好？
I forgot my briefcase and/walkie-talkie/intercom/in the tally room yesterday.Do you keep them for me?

588　请跟我来,我给出租汽车公司打个电话,让出租车带你去代理公司。
Come along,please.I'll telephone to the Taxi Service to let the taxi take you to the A-gency.

589　没有边防站的同意,任何船员不准整夜留在岸上。
No crew member is allowed to stay ashore/over night/all night long/without the permission of the Frontier Station.

590　中国外理总公司在我国沿海各港口都有分公司。
The China Ocean Shipping Tally Company Head Office has branches in all coast ports of our country.

591　泡沫灭火机和酸碱灭火机的作用不同,前者用于扑灭不溶于水的易燃液体引起的火灾后者用于扑灭竹、木、棉等普通可燃物引起的初起火灾。
The functions of foam fire extinguisher and the soda-acid fire extinguisher are different. The former is used to/put out/extinguish/stamp out/fire disaster caused by combustible liquid that can't dissolve in water.The latter is used to put out conflagration of initial stage caused by common combustive matter,such as,bamboo,wood and cotton,etc.

592　青岛盛产各种鱼类和海珍品。
Qingdao is teemed with varieties of fishes and rare seafood.

593　吃亏的和解强似胜利的诉讼。
A bad compromise is better than a good lawsuit.

594　有理走遍天下。
If one's in the right,one can go anywhere.

595　有规则就有例外。
There is no ruler without an exception.

596　亡羊补牢,为时未晚。
Better late than never.

597　言必信,行必果。你不能言而无信。
One should be as good as one's word.You can't go back on your word.

598　三思而后行。

— 188 —

Score twice before you cut once.(Or: Look before you leap.)

599 外语是人生斗争的一种武器。——卡尔·马克思

A foreign language is a weapon in the struggle of life.—Karl Marx

600 少壮不努力,老大徒伤悲。

Laziness in youth spells regret in old age.

Appendix 2 Sentences for Stevedoring

一 前期准备阶段

1 大副在哪里?
   Can I see the chief officer?

2 大副,我需要你的配载计划/卸货(装货)计划/船舶资料。
   CO,I need your stowage plan/discharging(loading) plan/ship document.

3 请尽快开舱。我们要为卸货做准备。
   Please open/unlock hatches.We need to prepare for loading/discharging.

4 为安全起见,请贵船将安全网拴牢。
   For safety's sake,please fasten the safety net.

5 请安排船员到42贝给冷藏箱拔电。
   Please send someone to unplug the reefer container at bay No.42.

6 请问该船的港序是什么?
   What's your discharging rotation?

7 请问你对装卸有什么特殊要求吗?
   Do you have any special requirement for discharging?

8 我想借用拆固扳手。
   Can I borrow/ use your unlashing spanner?

9 请问卷钢放哪个舱? 放几个高? (钢板:steel plate/sheet;带钢:band/strip steel;型钢:bar steel;工字钢: girder steel;钢锭:steel ingot)
   Where to stow roll-steel? How many tiers high?

10 今天硫磺卸货开5条作业线,你准备卸几舱?
   We plan to have five operation lines for sulphur discharging today.How many hatches do you have for discharging?

11 大副,我有几份文件需要你的签字。
   C/O,I need your signature for several documents.

12 商检验舱后,请你提前准备货泵和管线。
   After inspection,please get ready the cargo pump and pipe line.

13 货检人员对我说并不是所有的货舱都合格。
   The cargo surveyors told me that all the holds were not passed.

14 我需要对接输油臂。(口径尺寸、数量)
   I want to connect the loading arms.(size,quantity.)

Appendix 2　Sentences for Stevedoring

15　作业期间,禁止使用船吊。
　　No use of crane during operation.

16　我会随时看水吃,调整卸货舱别。
　　I'll see to the draft myself and adjust hatches.

17　请问46贝冷藏箱电机朝前还是朝后?
　　What is the motor direction of the reefer container at bay No.46?

18　我们用什么材料垫舱?
　　What can we use for the dunnage?

19　每张提单的货必须用席子隔开吗?
　　Must every Bill of Lading be kept apart with mats?

20　把这些货一直堆到舱顶吗?
　　Do you expect us to stow the cargo up to the top?

二　作业过程

1　现在天气恶劣。注意调整缆绳/放松缆绳/收紧缆绳。
　　Due to the bad weather, please adjust/slack down/make fast the mooring line
　　头缆:head line;(前/后) 横缆:(fore/ aft) breast line;(前/后) 倒缆:(fore/ aft) spring line;尾缆:stern line;缆桩:bitt

2　你的船已经离开码头2米。
　　Your vessel has shifted away from the wharf 2 meters.

3　按照现在的装卸速度,估计什么时候完货?
　　At such a loading/discharging rate, when do you expect the discharging/ loading can be finished?

4　今天预报有大风。请问需要增加缆绳吗?
　　The weather forecast reported strong wind today. Do we need to use more lines?

5　请告诉我们到目前为止船上共压入多少压载水?
　　Please tell us how much ballast water has been pumped in.

6　能否帮忙用压载水校正船舶偏杆?
　　Can you help us adjust the list with ballast water?

7　计划今天下午16:00移泊。由76泊位移至65泊位。
　　Berth shifting is planned at 16:00 this afternoon, from berth No.76 to No.65.

8　开始速度不要太快,控制在_____ m³/h。
　　There is no need to speed up at the beginning. Please keep the loading/ discharging rate at _____ m³/h.

9　货油凝固点是多少?出口阀压力是多少?
　　What is the solidifying point of your cargo and outlet valve pressure?

10　请检查一下船体强度,我们计划在移泊前必须清完1舱。
　　Please check the hull strength. We plan to finish the clean-up of hatch No.1 before berth

— 191 —

shifting.

11 请将第二个船机转到海侧/陆侧。
Please move the second crane to the sea side/ wharf side.

12 由于雾大,开航时间将推迟到明天早上2点钟。
Due to the heavy fog, the departure time will be put off to 2:00 tomorrow morning.

13 请问你对装卸有什么特殊要求吗?
Do you have any special requirement for loading/discharging?

14 在30贝300284位处有一个扭锁打不开。请找船员处理一下。
A twist lock at 300284 of bay No.30 can not be unlocked. Please send someone to deal with it.

15 现在船体已偏向海侧。请及时向陆侧打压舱水。
The hull has listed to the sea side. Please pump in ballast water to the wharf side.

16 船体前部已经离岸壁30厘米。请紧紧头缆。
The fore part of the hull has shifted away from the wharf 30cm. Please heave the head line.

17 我可以现在拆输油臂吗?我要用惰气扫线。
Can I disconnect the loading arm now? I want to use inert gas to clean up.

18 你还需多长时间恢复卸货?外面气温很低。
When can we resume discharging? It's very cold outside.

19 停止卸货时间不能太长,防止输油臂凝管。
If we stop discharging for too long, the loading arms can be blocked.

20 您的承运人的货物含水量太高。请问能否通过污水井排出一部分。
The goods of your carrier contains too much water. Can we discharge some water through bilge wells?

21 8舱后梯子有船损。我们认为是原损。请检查一下。
We think the damage to the aft ladder of hatch No.8 is original damage. Please check.

22 16贝一个卸货危险品少了2个危险品标签。请给我2张。我们帮你们贴上。
2 labels on the dangerous goods at bay No.16 are missing. Find me 2 labels, and I'll stick them on.

23 30贝海侧后部舱里有一个导槽已断裂。请过去看一下。
A cell guide in the aft hold near the sea side at bay No.30 is broken. Please take a look.

24 这个导槽断裂处早已生锈,证明是原损。
The broken point of the cell guide is rusty. It proves to be an original damage.

25 到今天早晨6:00,根据水吃,我们共卸了8万吨。
According to the draft, we have discharged 80000 tons up to 6:00 this morning.

26 我们可以用木板把它同其他货物进行隔票。
We can use planks to separate it from the other cargo.

27 备好消防器材以防着火。

Appendix 2　Sentences for Stevedoring

Get the fire-fighting apparatus ready in case of fire.

28　对危险性货物我们遵循的原则是"装船在后,卸货在先"。
We follow the principle for handling dangerous goods "Last loaded and first discharged".

29　如果没有太多集装箱要写卸的话,我们通常靠在杂货泊位用船的重吊杆来卸。
We usually get alongside the berth for general cargo to discharge the containers with the ship's heavy crane if there aren't too many containers to be handled.

30　今天有空的岸吊太小,无法用来卸你轮的重货。
The shore crane available today is too small to discharge the heavy lifts on your ship.

三　收尾阶段

1　我需要你的时间表。
I need your schedule.

2　淡水加完了。请根据水表数签字盖章。
Fresh water has been done.Please sign.

3　(大副通知我方某冷箱不工作。)我已通知有关人员上船修理此箱。请配合他们的修箱工作。
I have told some technicians to repair the reefer.Please give them some help for the repair work.

4　(船方因某冷箱温度与舱单设置温度不符拒收此箱。)货主10分钟内上船,送保函,请接收此箱。
The cargo owner will get onboard in 10 minutes with the Letter of Indemnity.Please accept this container.

5　为了能顺利开船,请及时检查冷藏箱的温度是否达到舱单中设置的温度。
In order to get underway in time,please check if the reefer temperature meets the requirements by container manifest.

6　请备好车。引水将于16:00从海侧上船。请将舷梯放于水面上3米处。
Please stand by engine. The pilot will embark from seaside at 16:00. Please rig the gangway 3 meters above water.

7　这是我方人员疏忽所致。
It is due to my men's negligence.

8　我要让他们重新堆放,保证使你满意。
I'll have them restow the cases to your satisfaction.

9　货物短缺会不会是由于盗窃而造成的?
Could the shortage of cargo be due to pilferage?

10　大副,与你合作很愉快。
Nice to have worked with you,Chief.

Appendix 3　Tally Papers and Ocean Shipping Documentations

1　APPLICATION FOR TALLY 理货委托书
2　TALLY SHEET 计数单
3　ON-THE-SPOT RECORD 现场记录
4　DAILY REPORT 日报单
5　STAND-BY TIME RECORD 待时记录
6　OVERLANDED/SHORTLANDED CARGO LIST 货物溢短单
7　DAMAGED CARGO LIST 货物残损单
8　DISCHARGING REPORT IN SEPARATE PORTS 分港卸货单
9　CARGO HATCH LIST 货物分舱单
10　STOWAGE PLAN 货物积载图
11　RECHECKING LIST 复查单
12　CORRECTION LIST 更正单
13　LIST OF MARKS-ASSORTING 分标志单
14　TALLY CERTIFICATE 理货证明书
15　STATEMENT OF TALLY ACCOUNT 理货账单
16　CARGO TRACER 货物查询单
17　TALLY SHEET FOR CONTAINERS 集装箱理箱单
18　TALLY SHEET FOR CONTAINERIZED CARGO 集装箱理货单
19　OUTTURN LIST FOR CONTAINERS = LIST OF OVERLANDED/SHORTLANDED AND DAMAGED CONTAINERS 集装箱溢短/残损单
20　OUTTURN LIST FOR CONTAINER CARGO = LIST OF OVERLANDED/SHORT-LANDED AND DAMAGED CONTAINER CARGO 集装　箱货物溢短残损单
21　VANNING/DEVANNING TALLY SHEET 装拆箱理货单
22　RECORD OF CONTAINER SEALING/SEAL-EXAMING 集装箱施封/验封记录
23　NOTE OF PAYMENT 付款单
24　NOTICE OF PAYMENT 认赔通知单
25　LIST OF LOADING/UNLOADING LASH LIGHTERS 载驳船装卸船清单
26　LIST OF CARGO MEASUREMENT 货物丈量单
27　RETALLY NOTE 重理单
28　LASH VESSEL STOWAGE PLAN 载驳船积载图
29　BOAT NOTE 趸(驳)船装货清单
30　CONTAINER LOAD PLAN (C.L.P)= UNIT PACKING LIST (U.P.L)集装箱装箱单

Appendix 3　Tally Papers and Ocean Shipping Documentations

31　CONTAINER CARGO MANIFEST 集装箱货物舱单
32　CONTAINER EQUIPMENT INTERCHANGE RECEIPT 集装箱设备交接单
33　EXPORT/OUTWARD MANIFEST 出口载货清单
34　IMPORT/INWARD MANIFEST 进口载货清单
35　LOADING LIST ＝CARGO LIST 装货清单
36　SHIPPING ORDER (S/O)装货单
37　MATE'S RECEIPT (M/R)大副收据
38　HEAVY CARGO LIST 重件清单
39　DANGEROUS CARGO LIST 危险货物清单
40　SPECIAL CARGO LIST 特种货物清单
41　BOOKING NOTE (B/N)托运单
42　DELIVERY ORDER (D/O)交货单(提货单)
43　DOCK RECEIPT (D/R)场站收据
44　ADVICE OF SHIPMENT 装运通知
45　CONTRACT OF TALLY 理货合同
46　CHARTER PARTY (C/P)租船合同
47　SHIFTING ORDER 船舶移泊通知书
48　PARCEL RECEIPT 小包收据
49　SAILING ORDER 船舶开航通知书
50　ARIVAL NOTICE 到船通知
51　CARGO DELIVERY NOTICE 提货通知
52　NOTICE OF READINESS 装货准备就绪通知书
53　AVERAGE STATEMENT 海损理算书
54　SHIPPING NOTE 装货通知单
55　LETTER OF INDEMNITY 赔偿保证书
56　DIAGRAM OF LOADING/DISCHARGING PROGRESS 装卸进度表
57　SEA PROTEST (OR: NOTE OF PROTEST)海事报告
58　DISCHARGING REPORT 卸货报告,进口船舶情况记录
59　LOADING REPORT 装货报告,出口船舶情况记录
60　CERTIFICATE OF ORIGIN 货物产地证明书
61　EXPORT LICENSE(＝LICENCE)出口许可证
62　LETTER OF SUBROGATION 权益转让书
63　NOTICE TO MARINER 航海通告
64　SHIPPING SOLICIT OPINION FOR STEVEDORING 装卸公司船方意见征求书

Appendix 4 Main Parts of a Ship

hatch	舱口
hatchway	货舱出入口
hatch coaming	舱口围板
hatch cover	舱盖
hatch board	舱板
hold	货舱
lower hold	底舱
deck	甲板
main deck	主甲板
free board deck	干甲板
tweendeck	二层舱
upper tweendeck	上二层舱
lower tweendeck	下二层舱
orlop	下二层舱
bridge	驾驶室
funnel	烟囱
mast	船桅杆
kingmast	主桅杆
rudder	舵
propeller	推进器
gangway	舷梯
rope ladder	绳梯
stern	船尾
bow	船首
starboard side	右舷
port side	左舷
fore part	前部
aft part	后部
both wings	两翼(侧)
chamber	小舱室(房间)
locker	保险房
cabin	房间
poop cabin	尾楼

Appendix 4 Main Parts of a Ship

forecastle	艏楼
center castle	中楼
chart room	海图室
store room	储藏室
tally room	理货间
engine room	机舱
mail room	邮件舱
luggage room	行李房
mess room	餐室
saloon	大厅
dining room	餐室
smoking room	吸烟室
pantry	厨房
rail	栏杆
bulkhead	隔舱壁
shaft tunnel	地轴弄
ladder hole	梯子口
tank	舱（柜）
deep tank	深舱
ballast water rank	压载水舱
bunker oil tank	燃油舱
reserve bunker	备用燃料舱
fuel tank	燃油柜
fresh water tank	淡水柜
anti-rolling tank	减摇水柜
peak tank	尖舱
fore peak	首尖舱
aft peak	尾尖舱
radio room	无线电报房
tonnage well	吨井舱
alley way (corridor)	通道
casing side	穿堂
through hatch	通舱
chain locker	锚链舱
bilge	污水舱
scupper	排水口
mast house	尾下房
refrigerator room	冷藏机房

— 197 —

参 考 文 献

[1] 中国外轮理货总公司.外轮理货手册[M].北京:人民交通出版社,1985.
[2] 孙肇裕.外轮理货业务[M].北京:中国物资出版社,2004.
[3] 宗蓓华.港口装卸工艺[M].北京:人民交通出版社,2003.
[4] 孙利望,等.海事基础英语[M].大连:大连海事大学出版社,2005.